SUPPORTING
THE LEARNING TEACHER
A Source Book for Teacher Centers

SUPPORTING
THE LEARNING TEACHER
A Source Book for Teacher Centers

Edited by
Marilyn Hapgood

Introduction by
Vincent Rogers

AGATHON PRESS, NEW YORK

ACKNOWLEDGMENTS

I went to England twice in the spring and summer of 1972 to gather data for this study, for a period of seven weeks. I also went to Holland for a week to see teacher centers there on the second trip. I am grateful to new and old friends in those countries for their help. In this country, I should like to thank particularly Dr. Stephen K. Bailey of the American Council on Education whose help was invaluable and the New England Programs in Teacher Education and the Noyes Foundation for their partial support for the study. Most importantly, I should like to thank the authors and their publishers for their generosity in contributing to this book:

"Teachers' Centers: A British First," by Stephen K. Bailey, by permission of *Phi Delta Kappan* and the author.

"The Reform of Education and Teacher Education: A Complex Task," by Roy A. Edelfelt, by permission of *Journal of Teacher Education.*

"Research and the Teaching Body," reprinted from *Science of Education and the Psychology of the Child*, by Jean Piaget, by permission of the author and Grossman Publishers, Inc., translation © 1970 by Grossman Publishers, Inc.

"An Inspired Adviser, Robin Tanner," reprinted from *Adventures in Education*, © 1969 by Willem van der Eyken and Barry Turner, by permission of Penguin Books Ltd.

"Woolley Hall and In-Service Training in the West Riding," by Sir Alec Clegg, reprinted from *Revolution in the British Primary Schools*, © 1971, National Association of Elementary School Principals, all rights reserved, and from mimeographed bulletins, by permission of NAESP and the author.

Library of Congress Cataloging in Publication Data

Main entry under title: Supporting the Learning Teacher

Includes bibliographical references.
1. Teacher centers — Addresses, essays, lectures.
I. Hapgood, Marilyn, ed.
LB1745.S95   370'.72   73–82073
ISBN 0-87586-044-3

(continued)

ACKNOWLEDGMENTS (continued)

"Teacher Centres: A Primary School View," by Colin Richards, by permission of *Trends in Education*, Department of Education and Science (HMSO).

"Developing Teacher Centres," by J.G. Owen, by permission of *Trends in Education*, Department of Education and Science (HMSO).

"The Philadelphia Teacher Center," by permission of Mrs. Lore Rasmussen, Director, Learning Centers Project.

"A View from the Shop," by permission of Dr. Donald Rasmussen, Director, Philadelphia Teacher Center, School District of Philadelphia.

"The Teachers' Active Learning Center: An American Adaptation of British Teacher Centers," by permission of Amity P. Buxton, Florence Bradford, Sujenna Kofsky, Amada Escosteguy Brown, Marilyn Burns, Kazuhir Tsuruta, © 1972 San Francisco Teachers' Active Learning Center.

"Resources, Teachers, and Designers," by Jack Walton, by permission of *Forum for Discussion of New Trends in Education* and the author.

"A View of Resource Centers," by Ron Mitson, by permission of *Ideas* and the author.

"Teacher Centres — Some Suggestions for a Strategy," by D.N. Hubbard and J. Salt, by permission of *Forum for the Discussion of New Trends in Education* and the authors.

"A Center in Maryland," by Leon Boucher, by permission of *Trends in Education*, Department of Education and Science (HMSO).

"Toward a Partnership in Teacher Education," by permission of Maryland State Department of Education, James A. Sensenbaugh, Supt.

"Teachers, Trainers, and Development Centres," by Alex Evans and Cynthia France, courtesy of *Dialogue*, Schools Council Newsletter, Nos. 6 and 7.

"Passages from the James Report," from *Teacher Education and Training*, by permission of Her Britannic Majesty's Stationery Office.

"The Whys and Hows of Teacher Centers," by William Fibkins, by permission of *Phi Delta Kappan* and the author.

"A U.S. Plan for Education Renewal," by Sidney P. Marland, Jr., © 1972 by The New York Times Company, reprinted by permission.

"Teacher Power and Local-to-Local Delivery," by Allen Schmeider, by permission of *Journal of Teacher Education*.

"An Interview with Don Davies," from *Audiovisual Instruction*, January 1973, Vol. 18, No. 1, pp. 11–15, reprinted by permission.

"Teacher Centers: Can They Work Here?" reprinted by permission of the author and *Phi Delta Kappan*, January 1973.

"A Teacher Looks at Teaching Centers and Educational Reform," by J. Michael Crosby, by permission of *Journal of Teacher Education*.

Contents

Contributors

Ronald Arnold is Her Majesty's Inspector of Schools, Eastern Region.

Stephen K. Bailey is Vice President, American Council on Education.

Leon Boucher is head of the Education Department, Chester College, Cheshire.

Amity P. Buxton is Director, Teachers' Active Learning Center, San Francisco.

Sir Alec Clegg has recently retired as Chief Education Officer, West Riding of Yorkshire.

J. Michael Crosby is a social studies teacher, Wilde Lake High School, Columbia, Maryland.

Don Davies is now Professor of Education and Director, Institute for Responsive Education, Boston University.

Roy A. Edelfelt is a member of the staff of the Division of Instruction and Professional Development, National Education Association.

Mary Ellison is Primary Schools Adviser, Shropshire.

Alex Evans has recently retired as General Secretary of the Association of Teachers in Colleges and Departments of Education.

William Fibkins is coordinator of the Bay Shore – Stony Brook University Teachers' Center, Bay Shore (New York) public schools.

Audrey Griggs is a Field Officer, the Schools Council.

John Harkins is Headmaster, Lower School, Germantown Friends School, Philadelphia.

D.N. Hubbard is Lecturer, Primary Education, University of Sheffield.

Sidney P. Marland, Jr. is a former U.S. Commissioner of Education and Assistant Secretary for Education, now President, College Entrance Examination Board.

Ron Mitson is Headmaster, Codsall Comprehensive School.

J.G. Owen is a former joint secretary of the Schools Council, now Deputy Chief Education Officer, Devon.

Jean Piaget is a world-renowned psychologist and philosopher who lives and works in Switzerland.

Paul S. Pilcher is an Ed.D.candidate at the University of Massachusetts.

Donald Rasmussen is Director, Philadelphia Teacher Center, School District of Philadelphia.

Lore Rasmussen is Director, Learning Centers Project, Philadelphia.

Colin Richards is Lecturer, Worcester College of Education and editor of *Education 3–13*.

Vincent Rogers is Professor of Education and Director of the Center for Open Education, University of Connecticut.

J. Salt is Dean of the Social Department, Polytechnic College, Sheffield.

Allen A. Schmeider is team leader for Teacher Centers, Office of Career Education, United States Office of Education.

James A. Sensenbaugh is State Superintendent of Schools, Maryland State Department of Education.

Barry Turner is a freelance writer and television broadcaster, specializing in education.

Willem van der Eyken is Senior Research Fellow of the Further Education Group at Brunel University.

Jack Walton is Co-director, Exeter University Institute of Education Resources Center.

Edward Yeomans is Director of the Greater Boston Teacher Center, and Associate Director of Academic Services, National Association of Independent Schools.

Chapter I

Introduction: A Manifesto for Change

Vincent Rogers

Surely there is no need for me to attempt to define or describe in these pages the phenomenon we have come to call "open education." Descriptive literature on the subject is vast and ever-growing. While we have not yet arrived at the precision some would like in our attempts to define openness, most of us (and particularly, I would think, the readers of this book) would accept Lillian Weber's summary statement that open education

> refers to the setting, the arrangements, the teacher-child and child-child relationships that maintain, restimulate, if necessary, and extend what is considered to be the most intense form of learning, the already existing child's way of learning through play and through the experiences he seeks out for himself.[1]

I should begin, then, with the assumption that we share a number of views about the nature of education and that we can therefore move on at once to the problem of the education of teachers.

John Coe, the perceptive, articulate head of primary education in the County of Oxfordshire in England, is fond of telling the story of Edith Moorhouse, one of the great early leaders of the movement towards informal education in that lovely county, sitting evenings at her home with a small group of primary headmistresses and teachers—knitting and talking about children. There were no elaborate lists of goals and objectives to be achieved, deadlines to be met, or tests to be given. Rather, there was good talk about children, how they learn and grow, and what this might mean to teachers.

Teacher education in Britain is obviously much, much more than Edith Moorhouse sitting, knitting, and talking with a group of teachers. The British have their teacher training colleges and their university departments of education, complete with required courses and electives, papers and examinations, "passes" and "failures."

Nevertheless, it is of the greatest importance that we recognize the qualities of informality, equality and mutual respect, intimacy, warmth, and responsiveness that were present in Edith's Oxfordshire cottage during these meetings. They do, in my judgment, symbolize some major differences between the directions teacher education has taken in England and in the United States.

Clearly, we see the origins of the "teacher's center" in these meetings. Similar events were occurring in Leicestershire, in the West Riding of Yorkshire, and elsewhere in Britain, despite the existence of "conventional" modes of teacher education. Why this happened (and is happening) in Britain on a reasonably large scale while this movement remains in its infancy in the United States can be explained only be examining a number of other differences between Britain and the United States in the way the educational enterprise is conducted.

For example, the British "Schools Council for Curriculum and Examinations," now generally referred to as "The Schools Council," was organized in 1964—about the same time that various American curriculum reform projects were being funded by the federal government in what we refer to as the "curriculum revolution" of the 1960's. Nowhere can the differences between British and American approaches to curricular and methodological change be contrasted more sharply. The Schools Council began with the basic assumption that each school should and would take full responsibility for the development of its own curriculum and pedagogy—based essentially on the needs of the children in a given local community. The Council would give every possible assistance in the task, but change begins in the local school. The contrast with American approaches during the same period needs no elaboration here—the story is all too familiar to most of us.

If curricular and methodological change are largely a local responsibility in Britain, so also are they almost exclusively the province of the professional educational community. The general public, the universities, and the educational publishing industry all played a relatively minor role in the evolution of British primary education as we know it today. This is not to say that parents, publishers, and university scholars had no influence on the shape of primary education in Britain. Rather, their influence was (and is) minimal by American standards, and it is still safe to say that local professionals—for better or worse—bear the burden of developing and improving primary education.

Curricular and methodological change came (and continue to come) in Britain on a local level—fostered and inspired by professionals. We must also keep very clearly in mind that when we say "professionals" we include in the most significant possible way the classroom teacher. The materials developed in the most famous of the Schools Council projects, the Nuffield Maths and

Science programs, are cases in point. (It should be pointed out at once that teachers, as members of development teams, played a major role in the development of these programs.) These materials are designed to stimulate teachers—to help them to grow and to become more flexible, spontaneous, and responsible for making day-to-day curricular and methodological decisions. The British have faith in the classroom teacher as the ultimate change agent; she is the *sine qua non* of meaningful, lasting change. This, too, contrasts sharply with generally accepted strategies for change in American schools.

Hand-in-hand with the development of a truly professional role for classroom teachers is the evolution of a similar role for the British "head teacher," or principal. Clearly, a good deal of the autonomy and flexibility of many classroom teachers stems from parallel freedoms and responsibilities for heads. As many Americans know, there are in England few citywide or countywide curricular or methodological decisions made that bind all of a district's primary schools to a given procedure or set of materials. The head is expected to take the lead in these areas of his school—and most of the heads who have provided the magnificent leadership we have seen so often in Britain's finest informal primary schools have utilized their own freedom to bolster the role of the teacher as a responsible, flexible, decision-making professional.

Perhaps a more subtle, yet no less significant, difference between the educational traditions in Britain and America involves what the British would call the "pastoral function." To quote Tim McMullen:

> Parents may cavil at masters' interference and excess of authority; masters may object to being involved in burdensome trivia about clothes and manners and hair and behavior on buses . . . whatever the objections, whatever the shortcomings, the fact remains that the intention of English schooling is more whole, complete, and inclusive than that of any other country.[2]

This concern quite possibly accounts for the willingness of many British primary school teachers to willingly take a broad view of education, valuing the total growth of the child and placing much emphasis on the role of art, music, dance, poetry, and drama—as well as on the "Three R's." Similarly, this may explain the British preference for small schools where teachers may get to know children (and each other) well, where there is much human response to children's problems and needs and where the possibility for assessing and aiding the total growth of the child exists more fully than it does in what the British sometimes call "the American factory schools."

In any case, the establishment view of education in Britain is child-centered and open. The Plowden Report gives a semiofficial blessing to the sorts of changes that have been growing gradually in British schools for thirty years. An open teacher may be encountering difficulty with a conservative head— but her battle is somewhat less lonely than it would be in most American schools because it is widely acknowledged that primary schools in Britain should be more child-centered, more informal. Clearly, this gives a kind of support and direction to primary teachers in Britain that is sadly lacking in our own schools.

These attitudes towards children, learning, curriculum, the role of the teacher, and the role of the head all contributed towards—indeed almost dictated—the development of alternate modes of teacher education in those areas where child-centered, informal education was valued in the schools. One result was the development of the teacher center in Britain as a viable, powerful, and effective force in the professional and personal lives of British teachers.

During the time that these attitudes towards children, learning, and teachers developed and took hold in Britain, a considerably different view dominated (and probably still dominates) American education. It would be difficult to be inclusive here but let me suggest the following as American attitudes, beliefs, and practices that appear to contrast sharply with British views and procedures:

(1) Despite talk of local initiatives and decentralization, we tend to make educational decisions on a systemwide (indeed, sometimes on a statewide) basis. We appear convinced that change can take place on a massive scale, and we still talk of "changing the schools" in Washington, D. C., Chicago, or New York. The federal government has never grasped the idea that monolithic approaches to any educational problem are seldom appropriate for all the children in a given community, and the principle of localism is simply not widely supported in the United States.

(2) American teachers and administrators are far more vulnerable to outside, nonprofessional pressures than are their British counterparts. The pressures may come from political groups, churches, or other special interests—as well as from the massive American education industry of textbook publishers and manufacturers of educational materials and equipment.

(3) We hold greatly differing views of the role of teacher and principal in our society. Teachers are not encouraged to act in truly professional ways, as decision-makers and agents for curricular change and adaptation on a local level. Therefore, many American teachers seem to lack the confidence, the

positive self-image, of their British counterparts. They are often told they are not very good—not very able—and many come to believe it.

Our principals do not generally have the power to behave autonomously in their schools as do British heads. Neither do they tend to see themselves as educational leaders; rather, they most often function as school managers, leaving truly professional decisions to those higher up in the administrative hierarchy.

(4) America's schools and colleges of education are dominated by essentially behavioristically oriented educational psychologists who tend to hold a rather narrow view of the learning process. American students at both the graduate and undergraduate levels are unlikely to study (unless they do so on their own) the views of Carl Rogers, Abraham Maslow, Erik Erikson, and others. Clearly, the general acceptance of such approaches as performance contracting, programmed learning, and behavior modification in our schools is evidence of the powerful influence of the behaviorists.

(5) Over the years we have built a vast educational bureaucracy in our schools. We have curriculum directors and coordinators, specialists of all kinds, assistant superintendents, and vice-principals, and so on. Clearly, some of these positions are staffed by very able people. Nevertheless, the overall effect has been the crippling of truly local initiative, the development of a subject-centered, atomized approach to education, and the creation of a largely authoritarian approach to the running of schools in most communities.

(6) Finally, teacher education in this country seems to reflect many of the problems outlined above. Surely it is authoritarian in nature, bureaucratic, rather narrow in its educational view, and unresponsive to the wishes of many of its constituents. There is a great deal of "change" taking place in teacher education today in the United States, but most of that change is based on quite conventional views of the purpose of schools and schooling and how children learn. Change is a good thing, then, if it does not challenge the dominant view of education. If it does, it is unlikely that the maverick program or project will be supported by those in decision-making positions.

One might examine, as an illustration, the widely heralded (federally and establishment supported) competency-based approaches to teacher education in the United States. At Weber College in Ogden, Utah, undergraduates are expected not only to acquire credits, but also to demonstrate competence in their chosen field (an objective that few would challenge). While students at Weber do, of course, have experience in schools with real children and teachers, and while they do occasionally work in groups and presumably engage in dia-

logue with their teachers and fellow students, much of the emphasis in the
Weber program is on the students' work with Weber Individualized Learning
Kits (WILKITs). Each WILKIT includes the following:

Title	—which identifies the topic
Introduction	—which provides the setting for the topic
Content	—which identifies the problems or considerations to be dealt with
Preassessment	—which assists the student to know his already attained level of performance
Behavioral Objectives	—which identify the behavior sought and at what level of proficiency
Learning Experiences	—which are suggested or required for meeting the behavioral objectives
Self-Evaluation	—which helps the student assess his progress
Proficiency Assessment	—which is used to determine if the behavioral objectives have been met[3]

The following are sample behavioral objectives extracted from viewing
WILKIT:

1. Demonstrate your comprehension of structural analysis skills by
scoring eighty or more points on the Structural Analysis Test.
(W-31 Structural Analysis Skills)

2. Display comprehension of the four functions which aid us in the
classification and understanding of the factors which account for
motivation, as measured by a teacher-designed examination with a
proficiency level of 80 percent. (W-13 Motivation and Learning)

3. Analyze the relationship to retention of recall, recognition, relearn-
ing, interference, nature of the stimulus, and intent to remember,
as measured by a teacher-made test with 80 percent proficiency.
(W-8 Transfer of Learning)

4. Respond to the group interaction of a classroom meeting in which
you will assume the leader role, as measured by a 75 percent agreement with the faculty advisor on a teacher-designed Summary of
Group Interaction. (W-21 Classroom Group Meetings)[4]

The total program for prospective elementary school teachers is as follows:

<u>Quarter Hours</u>

Education 195, [a "preprofessional" requirement]
    Introductory Field Experience 1
    WILKIT: Orientation (W-3)

Education 300, Fundamental Skills for Teachers 3
    WILKIT: Self-Concept (W-12)

Education 324, Basic Skills for Elementary Teachers 4
    WILKIT:

    W-57 Tutoring Techniques
    W-26 Reading Study Techniques
    W-35 Handwriting
    W-70 Media Equipment Operation
    W-14 School Health
    W-5   Growth and Development (may be waived upon
          successful completion of Family Life 150)

Education 325, Elementary School Curriculum I 6
    WILKIT:

    W-27 Reading Readiness
    W-28 Nature and Instructional mplications of
          Reading
    W-29 Reading Comprehension
    W-30 Basal Approach to Teaching Reading
    W-31 Phonic Analysis Skills
    W-32 Structural Analysis Skills
    W-33 Dictionary Skills
    W-36 Spelling
    W-38 Oral and Written Communication

Education 326, Elementary School Curriculum II 6
    WILKIT:

    W-6   Elementary School Mathematics I
    W-9   Elementary School Mathematics II
    W-42 Inquiry in Elementary Science
    W-43 Organizing and Planning for Teaching Elementary
          Science
    W-50 Social Studies in the Elementary Schools
    W-54 Elementary Social Studies Instruction
    W-40 Music for Children

Education 360, Instructional Skills for Elementary
                Teachers 4
    WILKIT:

    W-7   Principles of Reinforcement
    W-20 Instructional Resources: Evaluation and Use of
          Instructional Media

Given the framework, the educational view of those working in teacher education at Weber, the program is consistent and logical. It also suggests ways in which other colleges of education that share these views may make their own programs more precise and more individualized (in terms of pace or rate of learning) and perhaps more thorough.

We might contrast this approach, however, with excerpts from a description of a workshop for 60 teachers conducted by Sybil Marshall in Philadelphia, in the summer of 1971 (see Harkins, Chapter IV):

Geoff, working in the gym, sometimes with and sometimes without music, began our first sessions on movement. He began with a ball for everyone to bounce and then asked us to move around the room as we bounced it. Then to share a ball with someone else and then to move without the ball. The ease with which workshoppers began to move was a happy contrast to the conspicuous inhibitions of a few summers ago. Perhaps it is that many of these people had already had some experience with movement. Perhaps it is that our society has, in the space of a few years, come to value movement more and inhibitions less. Certainly part of what was working was that Geoff was very good at what he was doing and his calm sureness had a relaxing effect.

Ewart, who, among other things, is a professional illustrator, welcomed a group into the art room and invited them to do a representation of something from the riddles. Tools and materials were available in profusion: tempera, pastels, tiles, linoleum, fabric, twine, yarn, glass, plaster, paper of all sorts, styrofoam, wire, wood, cellophane, brushes, cutters, needles, cloth, screens—the ultimate remove from "a bit of rag on a stick." The contrast is interesting. The bit-of-rag approach had put the emphasis on the media by limiting the options and thereby enabled everyone to have an experience with one particular technique. Sybil's and Ewart's approach had made no mention of media, technique or materials although all had been made available in profuse variety. The emphasis had been on the message and the assumption had been that the message was sufficiently motivating to permit or force the workshoppers to assert themselves in spite of the techniques. Evidently, the inspiration had been sufficient: the work flowed quickly. By the end of the first day everyone had produced something. The diversity was impressive.[6]

Clearly, our first illustration (Weber) deals with an entire program, while our second illustration describes an isolated, month-long summer workshop. Nevertheless, contrasts in both purposes and procedures are striking.

The conclusion I have come to upon examining both conventional and innovative (in the Weber College sense) approaches to teacher education that dominate in the United States is that, for many of us, they are sadly lacking. We need, I think, teacher education programs at all levels that:

(1) Allow for the total personal development of the individual as a human being and as a professional. There is more to becoming a good teacher than the accumulation of a set of skills. Teachers need to express—to feel, to write, to dance, to move, to create—in nonthreatening, unpressured situations. Teachers need to rid themselves of the idea that "I cannot do, therefore I teach," because good teaching is doing in a hundred different ways. This clearly is tied up with the almost desperate need for teachers to develop self-trust, self-respect, and confidence in themselves as teachers and as people.

(2) Allow ample time for teachers to experience—not merely "learn about." In Art Combs' words:

This calls for the development of a *personal* philosophy rather than learning about philosophy, which is a very different thing. If it were true that knowledge and philosophy made you a good teacher, then professors of philosophy would be our very best teachers—and everybody knows that is not true. So we have to concentrate on helping students *develop* a philosophy instead of learning about philosophy.[7]

It follows then, that teachers need to feel comfortable with materials, to explore new environments, to develop talents and interests, to examine and reexamine purposes, to stimulate and be stimulated by others, to have the opportunity for study and sustained involvement, and to be constantly "in process," questioning and being involved inwardly and outwardly in dialogue.

This, it seems to me, is a manifesto for change—a demand for another way to help teachers grow—a rationale for the development of teachers centers in the United States. Such centers will and should take many forms as they evolve in the United States, but evolve they must, for there is little sustenance for many of our most thoughtful teachers in traditional forms of pre- and in-service education. The chapters that follow should do much to stimulate thought among Americans about the form and direction such centers might take in America.

Notes

1. Lillian Weber, *The English Infant School and Informal Education* (Englewood Cliffs, N. J.: Prentice-Hall, 1971), p. 11.

2. Unpublished report for the British Schools Council, June 1967.

3. Caseel Burke, *The Individualized, Competency-Based System of Teacher Education at Weber State College* (Washington, D. C.: American Association of Colleges for Teacher Education, 1972), pp. 11-12.

4. *Ibid.,* pp. 25, 26.

5. *Ibid.,* pp. 21-24.

6. John Harkins, *Bridge Building* (Philadelphia, Pa.: Friends Committee on Education, 1515 Cherry Street, Philadelphia, Pa. 19102, 1972). Not paginated.

7. *On Interpreting and Meeting Standards for Teacher Education* (Washington, D.C.: American Association of Colleges for Teacher Education, 1971), p. 3.

Chapter II

Supporting the Learning Teacher: An Overview of Teacher Centers in the United States and England

Marilyn Hapgood

It is commonly observed that teachers need ongoing support in the classroom. How to provide this support has been a thorny problem. In the United States the system of supervisors as support for teachers has failed, largely because the supervisor has been seen as judge, manager, and public relations expert rather than as supportive agent—"About the last thing the school supervisor has time for is teacher-training," Albert Shanker has remarked.[1] A supervisory support system can, however, be successful. The "advisory" as it has developed in England is a supervisory group in a local education authority or district; advisers have been effective because they are highly successful classroom teachers, chosen as teachers to work with teachers, and because they see their roles as helping ones, even, according to one adviser, as "pastoral."

A major move toward support in the American supervisory style would appear to be outside the realm of possible human and institutional change, although Lillian Weber in her Workshop Center for Open Education at City College in New York is working in this direction with a small staff, as are the Follow Through advisers at Education Development Center, Newton, Massachusetts, and others.

Currently being adopted on a much wider scale as a support system for American teachers are some Americanized versions of the British teacher center. In England a teacher center is a kind of local club where teachers receive support from each other and approval and funds from the local educational authority for requests for outside supporting persons. Theoretically, from a heightened sense of professionalism born of thinking out their problems for themselves, teachers begin to take on the roles of researchers, collaborators in research, and clinical observers of children learning. Jean Piaget has said that until teachers assume these roles they will continue to do what they do out of habit instead of conviction about the learning process (see Chapter III). He has also said:

> The illusions that teachers have in front of classes of children are that they are making themselves understood and that they are understanding. These are two illusions that must be dissipated. If they are going to be at the level of psychological understanding which they need to be good teachers, they must not only read about research but practice it.[2]

Teachers are beginning to value a high degree of involvement of the child in the learning process. This involvement is equally essential in the teacher's learning process, and is at the heart of the teacher center movement.

Teacher centers are very recent phenomena worldwide. In Japan, for example, the first center began about 1960, a direct outgrowth of Japanese teachers' informal "study circles" which continue today. Teachers could study any subject from "insects to moral education" and could belong to more than one "circle."[3] Initially, the teacher centers were begun for massive retraining of science teachers; in the last few years the training programs have been extended to include training for teachers in the social sciences, mathematics, and languages. (In science Japanese 14-year-olds, not streamed for ability, recently scored highest worldwide in achievement surveys announced by the International Association for the Evaluation of Educational Achievement.)[4] Japanese centers are financed for the most part by the local prefectures, are staffed by professionals in their particular fields and by experienced classroom teachers. Teachers who receive training at the centers go back to their own schools to teach colleagues what they have learned.[5] Bentley Glass, on a tour of the Japanese centers, pointed out that they were inquiry centers rather than centers for memorization and indoctrination, and told the following story about himself:

> At Gifu we were privileged to see the famous cormorant fishing in the Niagara River by torch light. The regurgitation of the undigested fish caught by the birds supplied a vivid parallel to our usual methods of teaching and examination, an analogy which I was able to use in subsequent lectures with humorous and apparently telling effect.[6]

In Holland, besides the central state pedagogical institutes and newer regional institutes for in-service training, there are now local teacher advisory bureaus in many of Holland's cities, locally funded. In Russia, a network of Advanced Studies Centers has been set up for teacher renewal. Sharpes reports, "the experience of teachers sharing in dialogue on new trends, theories, curricular developments and research is apparently having a tremendous impact on Soviet educational practice."[7] Teachers in Russia are paid to attend a center every five years.

In England, over 600 teacher centers have sprung into being in the last eight years, but they have roots that stretch back several decades. Woolley Hall, one of the fine residential teacher centers in England, was a pioneer with others in the movement over 20 years ago (see Clegg. Chapter IV). The recent rapid development of teacher centers in England is the result of the Science and Mathematics Curriculum Development Projects funded by the Nuffield Foundation in the early 1960's. The Foundation believed that classroom teachers should be centrally involved in curriculum development and set up regional centers where teachers could meet. From these beginnings and the beginning in 1964 of the national Schools Council, mainly teacher composed, came the current emphasis on teacher centers. These were strongly encouraged by the Council in an early working paper in 1965.[8] Between the publication of that paper and the publication in 1970 of a report of three national conferences on teacher centers sponsored by the Council, over 308 centers began (see Chapter V).

The 1970 report states that no one actually knows what the needs are that have led to such a multiplication of centers. Almost all are funded by local educational authorities and are theoretically run by teachers for teachers. The visitor, however, finds it hard to pin down the actual government of any one center since practices vary widely. Most centers are open after school and in the evenings, but many are open during the day. All are meant to meet some social needs and offer relaxation, comfortable chairs, a tea and coffee bar (one I visited offered liquor on occasional evenings), new periodicals on education, and a browsing library of professional books. Displays of children's work are often hung in a center; just as often there are publishers' displays. Several workshop rooms may provide carpentry tools, potters' wheels and kilns, looms, audiovisual machines, duplicating equipment (one well-known teacher educator I talked with in England suggested that what teacher centers have to offer is "a chat-in and a hardware exhibit"). Most centers have one or more rooms for lectures and discussions. Few buildings used by centers have been built for that purpose, and most are housed in adapted buildings. Most centers have a part-time warden who coordinates the affairs of the center and many have a full-time staff. The governing committees of English teacher centers, made up mostly of teachers, also include representatives of the local authority. Working rules suggested by the Schools Council in 1967 (see Chapter V) recommended small steering committees with "as full a representation as possible of local teacher opinion" from a total teacher population "catchment area" of between 400 and 800. These rules have in general been followed and English centers, though varied, appear more alike than the much smaller number of American teacher centers.[9]

The history of the teacher center in America is short and characteristic of the innovative groups that have fostered it. One of the oldest, the Follow Through Center at the Education Development Center, at Newton, Massachusetts, has been funded by the U. S. Office of Education since 1967. It has been most influenced by a number of Leicestershire educational practices (many materials, invitations to creativity, openendedness), and many people from Leicestershire have been in its advisory. The needs and ideas of teachers are very important in all the teacher centers it sponsors, exemplified by its Advisory Center in Philadelphia. Its teacher centers try to take their character from the local community.

The free-school movement in America has its counterpart in the free teacher center movement, perhaps best exemplified in the Teachers' Active Learning Center in the San Francisco Bay Area. This center maintains independence from schools and universities although it welcomes liaison; it has its headquarters on the second floor of a building in a light industrial area of the city and works from teacher-identified needs. It was begun by three teachers in 1969 and is currently funded by the Rockefeller Foundation (see Chapter VII).

Another kind of teacher center, the Teacher Education Center, a consortium pioneered at the University of Maryland, began in a cluster of public schools that were used for training student teachers. It became evident that the teachers who were training students needed opportunities for growth themselves on an advanced level. "The education of a teacher can only be started in a four-year baccalaureate program," states the official report sponsored by the Maryland State Department of Education (see Chapter IX). With the partnership of the local school systems, the colleges and the University, and the State Department of Education, 12 pre- and in-service training centers were created in Maryland by 1970. These were directed by university faculty and school administrators.

Still another kind of center exists in the greater Boston area. The Greater Boston Teacher Center sponsors many workshops for teachers held in schools and resource centers throughout the area; it has a small office headquarters in Cambridge and works cooperatively with many teacher groups throughout the country. Edward Yeomans, its director, has coordinated the outstanding workshops for teachers of the National Association of Independent Schools during the last five years. The Greater Boston Teacher Center has had continuing foundation support for its work and is working toward a residential teacher center in the future (see chapter IV).

The U. S. Office of Education currently sponsors four teacher centers—in Rhode Island; Washington, D. C.; San Francisco-Berkeley-Oakland; and Dallas. The Office of Education plan for renewal centers in each state has met with Congressional snags and may not ever be funded (see Davies, Chapter X). A plan to work through the National Institute of Education calls for teacher centers "on the British model" that will use " 'education extension agents' to stimulate the use of new materials and techniques. All the centers will be in areas where there is a concentration of disadvantaged children and each community will be asked to make a local needs assessment" (see Marland, Chapter X). The Dallas center now operating appears to be modeled on the University of Maryland cluster plan for training both student teachers and experienced teachers; the other three centers do not train student teachers.[10]

Although virtually all teacher centers in England are funded by local educational authorities, few in the United States are. One exception is the Philadelphia Teacher Center, directed by Lore and Don Rasmussen. It grew from a small learning centers project for children that started in a few inner-city Philadelphia schools in 1963-64. As teachers began to want to shape their own classes into partial learning centers, the teacher center was created. The center, which has had foundation as well as local financial support, is almost totally teacher and community oriented and houses in the same building a preschool and infant center and a school for junior high mothers. Everyone is welcome at this center and Lore Rasmussen speaks of it as a "womb to tomb" operation (see Chapter VII).

The literature on teacher centers is not voluminous. There are very few research studies to date on any center or any group of centers.[11] The literature is descriptive, argumentative, and most of it frankly states that teacher centers as an educational phenomenon are too new and too varied and changing even for full description. In this country, Schmeider and Yarger, on the basis of a recent study, suggest that many more teacher centers than generally recognized may already exist here.[12] Smith has studied state departments of education and reports that teacher centers are being studied at the state level in two-thirds of the states, have been legislated in four: Vermont, California, Florida, and Texas.[13]

The National Education Association is presently working cooperatively with nine pilot sites nationally to encourage "teacher centered development programs" in those areas, as well as across the country. Such programs, they insist, might be totally individualized, tailored to the needs of a single teacher.[14] The association believes that the "local" should "program and budget a portion of its fiscal and human resources to projects on instructional improvement."[15] The NEA has also advised that "teacher involvement in professional development programs will not take place unless this cause is championed and actively pursued by the teachers' professional associations."[16]

Stephen K. Bailey, of the American Council on Education, is a recognized authority in this country. He directed a conference on teacher centers sponsored by the Syracuse University Research Corporation in April 1972; his article in *Phi Delta Kappan* (see Chapter III) was widely read and quoted. Bailey has appeared before a Congressional committee to discuss teacher centers. He believes the British center to be the most important model and sees teacher centers as "cheerful, non-threatening clubs which could form the essential but presently missing link between innovative ideas and pupil performance in the classroom."

Since the British model most fully embodies the concept of teachers helping to guide their own growth, and since most writers about teacher centers at least pay lip service to this idea, we might see teacher centers as encouraging and supporting teacher self-education and autonomy and contrast them with teacher-training centers where programs for teachers are set up without consulting them. A true teacher center then should fulfill Audrey Griggs' definition: "to make the teachers feel professionaly strong enough to look at their own positions, discuss with colleagues, parents and pupils the direction in which they should go, work out together what is needed to make this possible and feel free and able to act on it" (see Griggs, Chapter VI).

An examination of the literature that treats the concept of the teacher center discloses some commonly debated problems. In fact, in typically English fashion a very civilized but heated exchange of views rages in that country about whether or not centers need to exist—while the centers flourish! Few of the leaders in teacher education I talked with in England could see great gains from the centers. One serious problem in both England and the United States concerns the apathetic teacher who is no more involved in self-directed learning in teacher centers than he or she is involved in any other educational innovation. Sybil Marshall expressed the general view of English teacher educators most concisely: "The teacher centers have made things better for the better teachers. It takes a long steady pressure to make teachers change—the teacher centers only just break the surface." The recently published James Report, *Teacher Education and Training,* recommends providing substitutes for all teachers for a term each seven years for the purpose of voluntary in-service training. Some currently existing teacher centers as well as colleges of education would be converted into "professional centers" for this purpose. The national government would share the expense of renewal training with the local educational authorities (see Chapter IX). In this country, Stephen Bailey has suggested that the Unity, Maine, school district program, now in its third year, could be widely emulated. Adopted as an economic measure, the plan calls for a four-day work week for children in schools, the fifth day given up to compulsory teacher training in a local teacher center. Teachers are given many choices and opportunities for initiative. Studies in Maine showed that children did not lose on standardized tests with their shorter work week.[17]

In England, heavy participation in in-service training during out of school hours is thought by some to be a demanding burden on teachers' time and energy. However, teachers flock voluntarily to centers there, and many think that voluntary in-service training has advantages over contractual in-service work. Amity Buxton, discussing her own San Francisco teacher center, expresses this point of view: "Here teachers act; they do not just receive. At the heart of the process is the teacher who identifies his own needs. It is he who is responsible for his own learning and action necessary to change . . . because attendance is not mandatory, resistance—a primary obstacle to learning—is removed. Freed from resistance, a teacher is open to interact with the learning environment and structured activities. He can focus on learning, on content, and on self-generated change in his own classroom" (see Chapter VII). But apathetic teachers seldom appear at this kind of teacher center. And many teachers who would otherwise appear at centers voluntarily are exhausted at the end of a day in the classroom. Some in England warn against "stereotyped" patterns of release which the James Report and its sequel, the White Paper, *Education: A Framework for Expansion*, might encourage. They urge instead more varied opportunities for "entitlement" a few weeks a year rather than one term every seven years. Both released time for a reason which is meaningful to a teacher and voluntary time for in-service work that is stimulating appear to be desirable.

A second problem concerns the advantages and disadvantages of large teacher centers designed to reach teachers from a number of schools, both primary and secondary, in a given area. In England it is reported that secondary teachers are more likely to use a teacher center, if they do so at all, in the convenience of their own school (see Schools Council, 1970, Chapter V). Many primary advisers and head teachers I talked with in England also believe that the proper place for in-service training is within a school; they view the Schools Council as concerned mainly with its own projects through promotion of the teacher centers, and they see these projects as remote from their own immediate problems (see Richards, Chapter VI). Others, in both England and America, state a strong case for nonparochialism in teacher education. Allan Schmeider, of the U. S. Office of Education, says, ". . . attempts to improve American education must place a high priority on overcoming the isolation and loneliness of teaching. It is probable that every classroom teacher does something better than every other classroom teacher; yet we are unable to take advantage of these successes because teachers simply do not have many opportunities to share ideas, problems, and solutions with one another. It is possible, therefore, that the greatest advances in education in the present decade could be gained through the finding of more effective means of linking the creativity, strength, and excitement of every classroom to every other classroom" (see Schmeider, Chapter X). Many in England see in the very heterogeneity of a center that draws people from a range of schools the advantage of understanding one's own problems better when looked at from another point of view; they strongly counsel secondary teachers to mix with primary teachers in the centers (see Schools Council, 1970, Chapter V; Hubbard and Salt, Chapter VIII). However some detractors rightly observe that some large centers have more facilities than are needed or used and that they attempt to "lay on" courses to justify their existence. One answer is the sensible policy of a large authority in southern England (which currently funds nine local teacher centers in various stages of development): "start things off usually in temporary accommodation and if the need is seen to be there, then step in and provide more permanent premises and staff" (see Griggs, Chapter VI).

A third major problem concerns the way advisory and college staffs can work with the teacher centers. In England, except for those teacher centers that have old traditions—like Woolley Hall, where advisers set up and direct courses teachers have requested (see Clegg, Chapter IV)—the advisories appear to have an ambiguous relationship with the autonomous teacher centers (see Griggs, Chapter VI; Owen, Chapter VI). At the conferences in England in 1970 on teacher centers there was considerable division of opinion on this matter; one strong group of people believed the initiative in teacher centers should rest in the hands of teachers; another equally strong point of view was that the centers required the "support of a programme of activities, making full use of the stimulus of national projects and of proven courses of training. . . advisory and college staff was an integral and indispensable part of the centre" (see Schools Council, 1970, Chapter V). A former Schools Council joint secretary, J.G. Owen, says, "too much autonomy for teachers led to a wallowing about. Teachers in England and Wales were, after all, neither accustomed nor trained to manage their own re-education" (see Chapter VI). This problem is critical. Reconciling these opposing views could be the task of the professional, autonomous teacher center with strong regional and national links to the in-service training institutions that virtually everyone speaking for teacher centers espouses. England has almost an embarrassment of riches in a long tradition of in-service courses through local authorities, Institutes of Education, Colleges of Education, the Schools Council, and more. The James Report asks for more cooperation among these agencies (see Chapter IX). Such rich opportunities for in-service training do not yet exist in the United States, and establishing any liaison between a school system and a higher education training system is difficult. Human relations in general have been cited in the Maryland Study of 1970 as the major problem in effecting linkages (see Chapter IX). Boucher, in reporting for a British publication on a center in Maryland, said, "Some teachers do not wish to be involved, some head teachers see a threat to their control over what is going on in their schools and do not readily accept the presence of the coordinator who has a responsibility, emphasized by the dual nature of his appointment, to persons 'outside' the school" (see Chapter IX).

In England, also, relationships between Colleges of Education and the teacher centers have been difficult ones. Traditionally, the Colleges of Education have expected the teachers to come to them; they have not gone to the teachers. There is increasing concern for better liaison between the colleges and the centers: "One is delighted to read . . . that fourteen Teachers' Centres and curriculum development committees have extended links with their neighbouring Colleges . . . the fact that this is *news* can disturb as well as please us. I for one would have liked to assume that they would have linked up with Colleges from the start. I know, too, that at meetings of College lecturers there have been expressions of regret, and indeed, resentment, that they have not been invited to join the teachers in the Centres and that, although individual lecturers have been involved, there has been no planned attempt to involve the Colleges as a whole" (see Evans and France, et al., Chapter IX). The problem, in the United States as well as in England, becomes less convoluted if colleges are seen in part as supportive agents for teachers in the field, as Lovegrove describes them:

> a college is also a local institution, often with close administrative links with the local authority, bringing to an area a sizable body of well qualified and experienced teachers and, in addition, buildings and resources that ought to play an important part in the professional life of the local teaching community.[18]

The teacher centers in England have also been somewhat exclusive in their communities. Most have invited neither parents nor students; perhaps it is not surprising that college faculties have not felt welcome. On this side of the Atlantic, some centers have welcomed parents, children, and, in fact, all comers (see Rasmussens, Chapter VII; Edelfelt, Chapter III). Teacher centers as community educational centers are a serious possibility in this country, are being more than occasionally mentioned in England (see Hubbard and Salt, Chapter VIII).

A move off-campus for American college and university education faculties to the schools or to teacher centers or to community involvement represents a shift that might not be welcomed by faculties. On campus, however, it is increasingly difficult for university staff to teach in one way while advocating that their students teach in another. Massive reform is being demanded in both education and teacher education. It would be "indefensible to call for change in schools if there isn't substantial change in the institutions that educate teachers" (see Edelfelt, Chapter III). The partnership between theory and practice that both Piaget and the Plowden Report advocate may be tantalizingly within sight (see Chapter III).

> If the stimulus is provided by industry, local education authority organizers, university lecturers, researchers, and H.M.I.'s, the initiative and responsibility for development must lie mainly with primary school teachers themselves. They must form working groups which exist not primarily to listen to lectures but for the discussion of experience and ideas and for practical work. The centres for teachers which are being established in some areas will fail in their object if they encourage either a passive attendance or attendance with the object of learning how to teach a programme. They must have as their main objective the encouragement of initiative and of imaginative and constructive thinking.[19]

What is the work of the teacher center? In England, it is felt to be curriculum development, and by some writers to be local curriculum development (see Working Paper No. 10, Chapter V; Ellison, Chapter VI). In the United States, the work of teacher centers is seen to be staff development (see Schmeider, Chapter X; Marland, Chapter X; Buxton, Chapter-VII). At least one writer questions that there is a difference between the two (see Griggs, Chapter VI). There has been gradual realization that a teacher's education is just beginning when she receives a diploma and that the nature of children, research in learning theory, and the widespread curriculum reforms of the 1960's demand pedagogical change based on wider and deeper understanding of all these by teachers. "It is clear from studies such as that by Goodlad and associates that curriculum and teaching as it exists in the total concept of school must be considered together"[20] (see Edelfelt, Chapter III). Piaget sees teachers thinking for themselves as the key to the problem (see Chapter III).

Teacher centers have responded to these needs. The Rasmussens' center in Philadelphia, for example, has been described as a "treasure house of new methods and materials that enable [teachers] to convert 'pencil and paper' style classrooms, which haven't changed significantly in a hundred years, into richly equipped learning laboratories where each individual child becomes an active explorer, with the teacher as his guide."[21] Imagine the teacher as an active explorer and you have the kind of teacher education teacher centers have become known for (see Harkins, Chapter IV). For purposes of both curriculum and staff development the teacher must understand learning by experiencing it herself. Teacher centers can provide the experiences.

Finally, what contributions can teachers make to educational theory and practice through teacher centers? These contributions involve partnerships in educational research with institutions (see Piaget, Chapter III), research in local studies that teachers can contribute to children's learning, and the resource banks of teachers' work that can be made available to others (see Hubbard and Salt, Chapter VIII; Mitson, Chapter VIII). The Leicestershire Educational Authority has pioneered in schools' work in resources for learning and has funded an Area Resource Center in a teachers' center.[22] The University of Exeter Institute of Education has a thriving Regional Resources Center for teachers, now in its fourth year (see Walton, Chapter VIII). Newham, a leading teacher center in London, has begun building up resources for and with its teachers (see Arnold, Chapter VI). The Nuffield Foundation has also funded a major project in resources for learning, cosponsored by the Schools Council. Their aim is to encourage "an agency to support teachers with a regular and reliable supply of appropriate materials."[23] In this country some teacher centers like the Workshop Center for Open Education in New York City, and the

Philadelphia Teachers' Center are beginning to publish work done by teachers which would be useful to others, and organizations like Zephyros in San Francisco periodically issue rich collections of resources for teacher members.[24]

The strong new theme of local environmental studies, learning from the resources of a community in the arts as well as in the sciences, is beginning automatically to integrate the curriculum in many English primary schools. For instance, Shropshire has taken groups of teachers out into the local envrionment for in-service training from the ground up (see Ellison, Chapter VI). London's History and Social Sciences Teachers' Centre offers courses like the use of archives in the classroom, industrial archeology, model making for history, and experiences like meetings with representatives from film production companies to "tell the producers what kind of film material they want for the classroom." At this center less experienced teachers are given opportunities to visit archives, museums, and schools then discuss their visits with experienced teachers. "The warden tries to keep teachers informed of new developments and thinking concerning history and the social sciences, while *Clio*, the Centre's newsletter, provides a further useful channel for doing so."[25]

Using community resources for teaching and learning has led to one suggestion of calling teacher centers "teaching resource centers." Cautionary advise comes from the Schools Council that too much emphasis on resources in centers will lead to overwhelming cataloguing problems as the centers are "swept off course by the needs of technology" (see Schools Council, 1970, Chapter V). Nevertheless, bending technology to human needs is felt by some to be highly worthwhile, and the Curriculum Laboratory of the University of London's Goldsmith's College has led the way through the maze.[26]

"Growing to greatness as a teacher is a long, and probably never-ending process (see Edelfelt, Chapter III). Can this process be promoted with efficient business and behavioral management methods? Or should the process be more concerned with enriching the lives of teachers and children for personal growth? Dewey believed that personal growth led to social growth for children and teachers:

> Speaking again from the most general philosophical standpoint, this authoritarian principle in education and the consequences that flow from it in the conduct of the school will never be effectively eradicated as long as the traditional notion prevails that the qualities of ideas are inherent essences. For it follows from this notion or doctrine that the education of teachers consists in transmitting to them certain collections of fixed, immutable subject matter which they

in turn are to transmit to the students under them. The educational regimen thus consists of authorities at the upper end handing down to the receivers at the lower end what they must accept. This is not education but indoctrination, propaganda. It is a type of "education" fit for the foundations of a totalitarian society and, for the same reason, fit to subvert, pervert and destroy the foundations of a democratic society.

For the creation of a democratic society we need an educational system where the process of moral-intellectual development is in practice as well as in theory a cooperative transaction of inquiry engaged in by free, independent human beings who treat ideas and the heritage of the past as means and methods for the further enrichment of life, quantitatively and qualitatively, who use the good attained for the discovery and establishment of something better.[27]

We need to keep in mind, as Morgan reminds us, that one of the most outstanding accomplishments in education in recent years developed primarily from the good practices of teachers: the British infants' school derived from "innovation and leadership by inspired teachers, not university research by large curriculum projects or intervention by education authorities or central government."[28]

Teacher centers can and almost certainly will be used both managerially and humanistically. There are indications that the Office of Education wants teachers to be in on the design of programs, and a national cross-section of classroom teachers has been meeting with Office of Education officials since early spring, 1972 (see Schmeider; Crosby, Chapter X). However, the direction of the grants from the Office of Education for planning and implementing teacher centers appears to be toward university staffs, curriculum developers, and consultants. "One looks at the list of participants in a government-sponsored teacher center conference and there is an overwhelming preponderance of university and 'curriculum expert' personnel. The few representatives of school districts turn out to be primarily curriculum supervisors, resource people, etc. One searches in vain for a few genuine classroom teachers" (see Pilcher, Chapter X).

While American centers continue in limbo, the English centers are busy examining the support and linkages teachers want and what others have decided they need (see Owen, Chapter VI). How far the Office of Education, or NIE, or states or districts, will follow the British model into autonomy for teacher centers is open to question; what is clear is that grass-roots teacher centers are not compelled to wait for government. Teacher centers are not the only way to support teachers in the schools, but they are one opportunity for teachers to provide support themselves.

Notes

1. Albert Shanker, "The 'Teacher Center': A Major Educational Advance," *The New York Times*, December 26, 1971, p. 17.

2. Richard E. Ripple and Verne N. Rockcastle (eds.), *Piaget Rediscovered: A Report of the Conference on Cognitive Studies and Curriculum* (Ithaca, N.Y.: School of Education, Cornell University, March 1964), p. 40.

3. M. Vere De Vault, "Teacher Centers: An International Concept," *Journal of Teacher Education*, Spring 1974, p. 38.

4. Joseph Featherstone, "Measuring What Schools Achieve: Learning and Testing," *The New Republic,* December 15, 1973, pp. 19−21.

5. Stephen K. Bailey, "Models from Abroad," a paper presented at the Teacher Center Conference, Syracuse, New York, April 13−14, 1972.

6. Bentley Glass, "The Japanese Science Education Centers,"*Science*, October 1966, p. 226.

7. Donald K. Sharpes, "Eye-witness Report: Soviet Teacher Education," *Journal of Teacher Education,* Summer 1973, pp. 116−117.

8. Schools Council, "Raising the School Leaving Age" (London: Her Majesty's Stationery Office, 1965).

9. The exact number of teacher centers in this country is not known. In late 1972 *Scholastic Teacher* compiled a guide to fifty teacher centers in the United States; a 1974 study at Syracuse University suggests there may be many hundreds today. (Sam J. Yarger and Albert J. Leonard, *A Descriptive Study of the Teacher Center Movement in American Education*, U.S. Office of Education, June 1974).

10. Mary K. Murphy, "Dallas: Renewal's in the Wind, *Scholastic Teacher*, September 1972, p. 11.

11. Note the excellent bibliographies in R.E. Thornbury (ed.), *Teachers' Centres* (London: Darton, Longman & Todd, 1973; New York: Agathon Press, 1974).

12. Allen A. Schmeider and Sam J. Yarger, "Teacher/Teacher Centering in America," *Journal of Teacher Education*, Spring 1974, p. 9.

13. Emmitt D. Smith, "The State of the States in Teacher Centering," *Journal of Teacher Education*, Spring 1974, p. 22, 24.

14. William J. O'Keefe, "Some Teacher-Centered In-Service Programs," *Today's Education*, March-April 1974, pp. 39−43.

15. National Education Association, "In-Service Education and Teacher Centers, Briefing Memo No. 3," Fall 1973, 4 pp.

16. National Education Association, "Teacher Centered Professional Development," 1973, 4 pp.

17. Murphy, *op. cit.*, p. 14.

18. W.R. Lovegrove, "Links Between a College of Education and the Local Teaching Community," *Education for Teaching,* Autumn 1968, p. 75.

19. Central Advisory Council for Education (England), *Children and Their Primary Schools*, (London: Her Majesty's Stationery Office, 1967) p. 239.

20. John Goodlad and others, *Behind the Classroom Door* (Worthington, Ohio: C.A. Jones, 1970).

21. Arlene Silberman, "Santa's Workshop for Teachers," *American Education*, December 1971, p. 4.

22. See Emmeline Garnett, *Area Resource Centre, An Experiment* (London: Edward Arnold, 1972).

23. Proposal from the Nuffield Foundation Resources for Learning Project, "A Co-operative Agency to Support Independent Learning," n.d., mimeograph. See also, L.C. Taylor, *Resources for Learning* (Harmondsworth, Middlesex, England: Penguin Education, 1971).

24. Bruce Raskin, "Teacher Information Exchanges," *Learning,* April 1974, pp. 66–69.

25. "Learning about People," *Times Education Supplement*, Feb. 15, 1974, p. 66.

26. See many issues of *Ideas* published by the Curriculum Laboratory, particularly October 1971.

27. John Dewey, "Introduction," in Elsie Clapp, *The Use of Resources in Education* (New York: Harper, 1952) p. xi.

28. G.A.V. Morgan, "Teachers' Centers," *The Urban Review*, July 1974, pp. 187–96.

Chapter III

Change Through Teacher Experience and Judgment

Introduction

The major purpose of this book is to awaken teachers to the fact that their initiative is vital to the total education process—that what they do or do not do is critically important to administrators, parents, curriculum reformers, university teachers of education, and especially to children. As self-evident as this might seem, most teachers do not genuinely believe it. Piaget has said:

> ... the schoolteacher is not thought of, either by others or, what is worse, by himself, as a specialist from the double point of view of techniques and scientific creativeness, but rather as the mere transmitter of a kind of knowledge that is within everyone's grasp. In other words, it is considered that a good teacher is providing what is expected of him when he is in possession of a general elementary education and has learned a few appropriate formulas that enable him to inculcate similar education in the minds of his pupils.

In Stephen Bailey's words:

> The underlying rationale for teachers' centers may be stated succinctly in terms of three interlocking prepositions: (1) Fundamental educational reform will come only through those charged with the basic educational responsibility: to wit, the teachers; (2) teachers are unlikely to change their ways of doing things just because imperious, theoretical reformers—whether successions of Rickovers or Illiches or high-powered R & D missionaries from central educational systems tell them to shape up; (3) teachers will take reform seriously only when they are responsible for defining their own educational problems, delineating their own needs, and receiving help on their own terms and turf.

Bailey, Edelfelt and Piaget in this chapter stress that the thinking of the teacher is indispensable to the success of any reform effort in education; that, indeed, no effort can succeed without teachers' wholehearted support and understanding. Roy Edelfelt believes the school should be an ongoing "laboratory of learning" for all who work there. This laboratory should include all the students, the parents, the teachers, the administrators, the teacher center staffs, and the nearby college of education faculties.

The vitality of education depends on teachers continually testing educational thinking, their own and others, and on trying out "ideas locally generated, as well as improving on, sharpening, and making locally relevant any innovation, from whatever source, which commends itself to the teachers in the area."[1]

As Albert Shanker has said, "In teaching as in other professions, the mutual stimulation of colleagues may succeed where outside criticism, supervision and prodding have failed."[2]

Notes

1. Schools Council, "Curriculum Development: Teachers' Groups and Centres" (London: Her Majesty's Stationery Office, 1967), p. 15.

2. Albert Shanker, "The 'Teacher Center': A Major Educational Advance," *New York Times*, December 26, 1971.

TEACHERS' CENTERS: A BRITISH FIRST

Stephen K. Bailey

Ever since DeWitt Clinton called America's attention a century and a half ago to the British infant schools as worthy of emulation, this country has derived policy nourishment from educational experimentation in the United Kingdom. In the 1960's the British open school received particular attention, serving as a basis for many of the reforms featured in the writings of distinguished American educators—including especially Charles Silberman's *Crisis in the Classroom.*

Perhaps the most significant potential British contribution to American education, however, is only now being identified and discussed: the development of teacher centers. British experience with these centers, at least in their present form, is a matter of three or four years only. But the idea is so simple, so obvious, so psychologically sound, as to make one wonder why teacher centers have not dotted the educational landscape for decades.

Teacher centers are just what the term implies: local physical facilities and self-improvement programs organized and run by the teachers themselves for purposes of upgrading educational performance. Their primary function is to make possible a review of existing curricula and other educational practices by groups of teachers and to encourage teacher attempts to bring about changes.

Stimulated by a working paper on school-leaving age prepared by Britain's Schools Council* in 1965, and by a variety of *ad-hoc* study groups and curriculum-development committees in the mid-1960's, teacher centers have mushroomed in the past half decade. Today there are approximately 500 centers located throughout England and Wales, over half with full-time leaders. The centers vary greatly in size, governance, scope of work, and the quality of tea and biscuits, but most of them are engaged in exciting and profoundly significant educational activities.

*The Schools Council is an independent body with a majority of teacher members. Its purpose is to undertake in England and Wales research and development work in curricula, teaching methods, and examination in schools, and in other ways to help teachers decide what to teach and how. The council is financed by equal contributions from the local educational authorities on the one hand and the Department of Education and Science of the national government on the other.

The underlying rationale for teacher centers may be stated succinctly in terms of three interlocking propositions: (1) Fundamental educational reform will come only through those charged with the basic educational responsibility: to wit, the teachers; (2) teachers are unlikely to change their ways of doing things just because imperious, theoretical reformers—whether successions of Rickovers or Illiches or high-powered R & D missionaries from central educational systems—tell them to shape up; (3) teachers will take reform seriously only when they are responsible for defining their own educational problems, delineating their own needs, and receiving help on their own terms and turf.

The more these intertwining propositions buzz around the brain, the more apparent their validity becomes. In the United States, for example, we have developed in the past several years a slew of educational R & D centers, Title III supplementary centers, and educational laboratories, each in its own way designed to discover and disseminate new educational truths. Most of these centers and laboratories have done important work. But the impact of this work upon continuing teacher performance (and pupil performance) in the classroom has been miniscule. And well before federal largess was directed toward inducing educational reform through a trickle-down theory, many state and local education departments and teachers colleges had developed curriculum-improvement supervisors charged with being "change agents" through workshops and in-service training. But the initiative was almost always from the bureaucrat or the educrat, rather than from the teachers themselves.

Few professionals have suffered more painfully or seriously from "being done good to at" than teachers. In spite of the fact that they are the ones who work day in and day out on the firing line, the definition of their problems, of their roles, of their goals, always seems to be someone else's responsibility: supervisors, parents, college professors, textbook publishers, self-styled reformers, boards of education, state and national education officials.

What the teacher center idea does is to put the monkey of educational reform on the teachers' own backs.

And they love it!

When teachers find out that they have their own facility where they can exchange ideas, learn from each other, receive help as they see fit, munch bread and jam and drink tea without the interruption of a bell or buzzer, they come alive. New ideas come from old heads, and the new tends to be sounder because the heads are experienced.

How does a teacher center work?

Let us look at an example.

One British teacher center in a county borough of roughly 60,000 population emerged from a "new math" project sponsored in 1966 by the Nuffield Foundation. The deputy headmaster, a mathematician, provided "crash courses" for teachers from both primary and secondary schools. From a very successful crash course experience, participating teachers urged continuation and extension of the general activity. The deputy headmaster agreed to serve as secretary of a committee of elected teachers and each school in the area was asked to nominate members. The cooperation of the chief education officer in the district was sought and he sent a representative from his staff.

The Schools Council report on this prototypic development (SC Pamphlet No. 1, 1969) says: "It was clear that the local teachers felt a need to come together to widen their experience and share ideas, not only in 'in-service' training, but in the wider area of curriculum reform. It was clear also that, such was the interest, they would be prepared to spend some of their own time on this."

Adequate physical facilities for the new teacher center were found in the form of an empty old primary school. The local education authority allocated 750 pounds for improvements. The facilities finally included a curriculum workshop for mathematics and science, a lounge, a small library, and the beginnings of a film collection. A part-time assistant acts as keeper of the schedule and as building superintendent. The program itself, however, is entirely teacher-initiated and controlled.

The Schools Council report on this particular center is studded with illuminating phrases:

"The center's first task will always be to stimulate and draw together local initiative."

"[Policy remains] . . . firmly in the hands of the teacher committee."

"The whole concept of a teacher's job is getting more complex . . . and the more complex it gets, the more necessary it will be to mobilize the expertise of the teachers."

"The teachers are asked to suggest the program of activities ['The committee is anxious to know the type of course you desire. Suggestions should be forwarded to the secretary. . . .']."

"Any group of teachers may use the building in and out of school time, for projects and meetings. All you have to do is book ahead."

". . . making locally relevant any innovation, from whatever source, which commends itself to teachers in the area."

"It is important that the center reflect local teacher opinion about the curriculum and test ideas locally generated. . . ."

These give the spirit and flavor of the entire teacher center movement. But the fact that initiative is local and is from the teachers themselves does not preclude valuable relationships with local educational authorities, with representatives of the national Schools Council, with nearby teachers colleges and universities. The centers' committees facilitate such relationships, but on a basis far healthier than has often obtained in the past. Gone are the traditional deferential attitudes and the superciliousness that have so frequently marked "workshops-organized-for-teachers" by educational reformers in official or academic-status positions.

What are the activities? In the teacher center noted above, programs have included, during school time: Nuffield Junior Maths (six meetings), junior science (six meetings), decimalization and the school (one day), infant environment (six lectures), maladjusted children (four lectures), and athletic coaching for schools (three days).

Typical after-school programs were: lecture-demonstration on understanding numbers, nine weekly meetings and discussions on how children learn, three lectures and workshops on visual aids, gymnastics and dance display, and devising a humanities course for leavers (those not planning further academic work beyond school-leaving age).

The teacher center also promotes and provides exhibits of new textbooks, programmed instruction, audiovisual aids, homecrafts and handicrafts, and student art. Promotional and informational activities (bulletins, newsletters, posters, etc.) are disseminated to keep all teachers and other interested people in the area informed about programs and exhibits. After-school experimental classes on family life, adolescent identity crises, and community problems are undertaken with selected students.

But reports on the activities of a single center should not suggest a rigid format for all such centers. The key to the success and the enthusiasm associated with the teacher center notion is control by *local* teachers. In consequence, center facilities and programs vary widely, depending upon the definition of need constructed by the local teacher-controlled center committees working intimately with local center leaders or "wardens." Some centers limit their curriculum investigations to a particular field like math or science; others attempt a wholesale review of the adequacy of an entire curriculum by grade or age; others have a strong social emphasis; still others feature outside lecturers and exhibits of new materials. Many centers feature formal in-service training courses; others stress informal workshops; still others provide facilities for self-study. Some centers are primary-school oriented; others draw heavily from secondary schools. Some attempt to draw in students, parents, supervisors, professors of education, and others directly related to the educational process; others keep such types at arm's length and relish the sense of teacher autonomy and the sense of dignity that come from self-directed accomplishments.

Tactfully, in the background, are the supporting services of the Schools Council: studies, reports, curriculum R & D, conferences, etc. The council leaders, including their distinguished staff of field officers, are exquisitely sensitive to the importance of teacher centers being locally operated and defined. The field officers of the Schools Council are themselves teachers loaned for short periods of time only to the itinerant functions of the Schools Council.

For the first time, local teachers are not low on the totem pole. They are prime movers in reforming an inevitably sluggish system. The reforms are not imposed by the arrogance of ministries, authorities, supervisors, or academicians. The reforms emerge from the teachers' own experiences and creative impulses. Through the field officers of the Schools Council and through the outreach of the local leadership of the teacher centers, important educational innovations from whatever sources can be scrutinized and tested; but, once again, this is done on the teachers' own terms and turf.

Who pays? Local education authorities and, through contributions of time and materials, the teachers themselves. Capital improvements, major equipment and facilities, and basic operating costs come from the education committees of local authorities. But without significant inputs of time and talent (as well as marginal voluntary donations to help defray the costs of social food and beverages), teacher centers could not exist—at least not in their present form.

Depending on the size of the center, annual budgets may run from a few to thousands of pounds. In some cases, where teacher centers agree to serve as area distribution headquarters for educational audiovisual materials, their local-authority budget may be sweetened substantially.

Experience with the center idea is still meager. But their stunning proliferation is testament to their meeting a felt need among teachers and among those who understand the futility of attempts to reform British education without the teachers' being directly and importantly involved.

In 1970, the Schools Council sponsored three national conferences on teacher centers in the United Kingdom. A total of 300 people attended. The liveliness of discussions and debates was indicative of the variety of opinions, experiences, and goals that inform the teacher center idea. The conference spectrum ranged from the total enthusiast to the cynic.

Among the most insistent questions raised at the conferences were the following:

How many of the center activities should be on an "in-school" as against an "after-school" basis?

Should the "wardens," or "leaders," of the centers be part-time or full-time? And how should they be selected and trained? Is a new kind of profession emerging (i.e., teacher center wardens)?

Should teacher centers encourage membership from those who are non-teachers?

Should teacher centers concentrate special attention upon the evaluation of, and experimentation with, new educational technology?

How can more teachers be induced to use the centers—especially the apathetic who need the centers the most?

What are the best methods for spreading the word of experts or even of "Charlies Jones's" good ideas?

The greatest problem seen by all members was the demand of development work on the time and energy of teachers. Although some of the work is presently done during school hours, much of it takes place after 4 p.m. The financial and logistical problems associated with this central issue are at the heart of the possibilities for the long-range success and survival of teacher centers in Britain.

Even at their best and most creative, teacher centers are still tentative. New regional linkages and national information networks will surely be needed to supplement local insights and resources. At the moment, there is an inadequate flow of information about what is going on in other centers and areas; and extant knowledge and research directly related to locally defined problems is inadequately collected and disseminated. The Schools Council is sponsoring a series of regional conferences this coming year in order to address many of these issues.

But the basic concept remains structurally and psychologically sound, and our British cousins have good reason for being enthusiastic.

Fortunately, the idea is beginning to catch on in the United States. Don Davies, acting deputy commissioner for development in the U. S. Office of Education, is actively promoting the notion of a major network of local teacher centers. Leaders in both the National Education Association and the American Federation of Teachers have shown considerable interest in the teacher centers concept.

Would it not be wonderful if, after years of telling teachers what to do and where to go, American educational savants and officials suddenly discovered that the only real and lasting reforms in education in fact come about when teachers themselves are given facilities and released time "to do their own thing"? Perhaps in the not too distant future, following the pioneering experiment voted by the Unity, Maine, School District for the fall of 1971, a four-day week for teachers in the classroom will be standard. On the fifth day, the teachers will be in their teacher centers, rapping about their common problems, studying new ways to teach and to understand students, imbibing a Coke or Pepsi, talking shop over billiards, and cheerfully allowing management to check off dues, parts of which will be assigned to defray the operating costs of the federally or state-funded teacher center facilities. Linked through regional associations, informed by the R & D activities of a National Institute of Education, teacher centers could form the essential but presently missing link between innovative ideas and pupil performance in the classroom.

THE REFORM OF EDUCATION AND TEACHER EDUCATION: A COMPLEX TASK

Roy A. Edelfelt

At the U. S. Office of Education, educational renewal centers are the new panacea being proposed these days for in-service teacher education. But if much is to be accomplished, it is imperative that pervasive reforms in both education and teacher education should accompany the establishment of such centers. This article spells out some crucial problems of pervasive reform and makes suggestions for essential strategy and process that should be employed if educational renewal centers are to be more than just another passing fad. The persuasion for reform is based on the following assumptions:

(1) Schools and teaching need radical reform.

(2) All segments of the teaching profession (especially teachers) must be involved in planning, carrying out, and evaluating reform in education and teacher education.

(3) Instruction and teacher education must be closely related.

(4) Teacher education should be a career-long enterprise.

(5) Teaching must have a career pattern.

(6) Parents and students must be involved in the reform of education.

Pervasive reform of education and teacher education in terms of these assumptions provides a challenge unparalleled in the history of education. Not only does such reform require an examination of the purpose and content of education, it also requires reviewing what teaching is and how one learns to teach. Not only does it involve a basic reassessment of how teachers are now prepared, it also prompts thinking about changing the whole character of the profession. Not only does it require specifying clear and valid goals for education and teacher education, it also calls for laying out process and strategy for achieving reform.

The idea of reform in education and teacher education is ripe. Laymen and students are demanding it. The human-services professions have become particularly attractive to the idealistic youth of this era. The current teacher supply-and-demand situation permits more rigorous selection of applicants and candidates in both training and employment. And both the public and the teaching profession are talking about accountability in education.

The problems central to reform of education interrelate elementary and secondary education with teacher education so inextricably that it is absolutely essential to deal with both at once. Education cannot be reformed if the personnel who serve it are not prepared to operate schools differently. The problems to be attacked cluster as follows:

(1) Most undergraduate and graduate professional study in education is in the context of the self-contained classroom, and largely oriented to standard academic subjects. It assumes a school that convenes five days a week for five to six hours on a 9:00-3:00 schedule for nine months of the year. The program, which takes place almost entirely in a school building directed by teachers and administrators, is based on textbooks and a few other materials. In both schools and colleges, the main mode of instruction is the lecture, which creates an overdependence on the value of dispensing knowledge.

(2) Students preparing to teach and teachers in schools represent middle America. They seldom include dissenters or protesters. They tend to be conformist and are forced into being conservative, middle-class models for the young to emulate. The experience of teacher education and of being a teacher imposes conformity, which generally means staying clear of controversial subjects (such as sex, drugs, non-Americanisms, and the morality of war), supporting the status quo, illustrating conventional behavior, avoiding expressions of feeling, playing it safe—not taking any risks. Although things are changing, there is still the pressure to be beardless, eschew miniskirts, wear coats and neckties, embrace suburbia, frown on four-letter words.

(3) Helping neophytes to learn to teach is undertaken largely through telling and showing how it should be done. A chance to try teaching under supervision is limited entirely to preservice teacher education (except for a few intern programs). Learning to teach is always inadequately supervised and seldom related to theories of teaching. Teacher education rarely includes a rigorous analysis of teaching.

Ironically, sharpening performance in teaching under supervision ends with preservice teacher education. Graduate study and in-service education are hardly ever designed to improve teaching performance (defined as the behavior of the teacher in carrying out his professional duties). Graduate courses, almost always devised by college professors, are a good example of something that someone else does *to* teachers. Too often, they are shoddily put together, vapid, dreary efforts. The very fact that they are separate, distinct pieces detracts from wholistic goals and achievement in developing better teachers.

Worst of all, there is no continuum of preservice and in-service teacher education and no incentive for doing otherwise. Preservice training terminates abruptly just as practice and in-service training begin. There is no gradual transition and no clear suggestion that growing to greatness as a teacher is a long, and probably never ending, process.

(4) The elementary and secondary schools, in which portions of teacher education take place, are not sufficiently experimental in innovative curriculum or new training and staffing patterns. For example, as far as staffing patterns are concerned, there are very few operational models of team teaching or differentiated staffing that are comprehensive in all the dimensions of those concepts. Few schools in the nation have programs of individualized staff development.

(5) There is little understanding of the philosophical and pedagogical changes intended in new curriculum developments. Curriculum projects in science, math, social science, English, languages, and other fields, which were conceived to engage the student in discovery, inquiry, concept development, synthesis, and application of knowledge, often turn out in practice to be merely changes in subject content. The same old methods prevail.

(6) Little has been done about defining and demonstrating new teaching roles. The literature presents some models, most of which emphasize levels of a teaching hierarchy. Almost nothing exists on different orders of teaching— that is, roles that differ without necessarily being more or less difficult, responsible, or prestigious.

If pre- and in-service teacher education are to prepare teachers for new developments in curriculum content, new concepts of school (e.g., nongraded school, open school), and new staffing patterns, these six problems present some hellishly difficult roadblocks. A teacher education program could work into all of these problems gradually, and that is how it may happen. However, it may be too late for gradualism, if educators are to exert initiative and leadership. If there is much delay, someone else will be calling the tune.

Part of the creed in education circles is that change is a slow process. But with the survival of the American public school at stake, there is no time to move slowly. We need to learn how to accelerate improvement. If we don't, other agencies and organizations will take over, and the survival of public schools may be in real jeopardy.

What To Do

Reform must begin in several places. But it is particularly appropriate to move at the college and university level because that is where the responsibility for and control of teacher education now rest. It would be difficult—and indefensible—to call for change in schools if there isn't substantial change in the institutions that educate teachers.

Such change calls, first, for altering what teacher educators can most easily control—professional education. Let us suppose this begins with organizing professors and students (undergraduate and graduate) into working teams: teams that study and work at changing curriculum and instruction; teams small enough to be manageable and to deal with individual growth (faculty and students); teams that work in public schools as well as colleges; teams that use experience as the laboratory for the study of psychology, sociology, anthropology, and education; teams that analyze and evaluate how each individual learns and teaches. Almost the total life of the becoming or developing teacher could be considered as the curriculum. The growth and development of the total personality could be the standard against which achievement is evaluated. Behavioral objectives would need to be established of course, and within the context of broad goals each team would need to develop its own. The very identification of such goals—and the testing of their adequacy—could be part of the learning experience.

The college program should, however, be closely related to and highly dependent on what is done to solve other problems. This would necessarily mean a better blend of liberal and professional education. Professors will need to work at developing *people* who will be teachers rather than the patchwork approach of attaching addenda to students as they pass through courses. It also requires input from the community and the school. It would mean testing what is learned against the reality of live situations and it would involve students and teachers alike in the political process of governing themselves and promoting change. Most important, it should include the student of teaching, whether he be prospective teacher or practicing professional, in determining what he studies, how he learns, and what he becomes.

The selection of people to man education should be accomplished in very different ways. In every team there should be a balance of different ethnic and social-class groups. There should also be students and teachers with a range of talents who represent different types, from conformist to nonconformist, liberal to conservative. Selectors should seek out people with some qualities such as creativity, insightfulness, sensitivity, curiosity, tenacity, and so on, already developed, but they should also try to identify those with potential. A good deal of screening will happen through thoughtful, deliberate self-selection.

The program should include the kind of evaluation and self-evaluation that seeks to test aptitude, potential, adaptiveness, and all the other qualities the team establishes as behavioral goals—all of these in terms of performance criteria. It should be designed to stretch and broaden students of teaching socially and culturally. It should be more than reading about subcultures, ghettoes, deviates, the handicapped. Teachers should work with many types of people in a variety of settings. Experience again becomes a selector. The basic and controversial problems of man should be confronted in depth and directly. Students of teaching should be participants in a variety of dynamic living situations. Decision-making and scholarship should become more than an academic matter. Teachers who are students of teaching would focus on learning and analyzing what they do and what they can do. They should be encouraged to test, analyze, and develop their own teaching style.

Much of what such study will involve hinges on developing a total concept of education, getting at what elementary and secondary schools are all about; analyzing the way schools reflect, serve, lead, and respond to their communities; ascertaining the teachers needed in such schools; planning how such teachers can be developed; and developing the specifications for staffing patterns.

We need, then, to establish teacher education schools (the current terms, "teacher centers" or "renewal centers," might be synonymous with teacher education schools)—that is, elementary and secondary schools or settings adjacent to schools where the education of teachers takes place concurrently with the education of children, schools in which the community, the school, and the college have reached some mutual agreements (contracts) about common and individual purposes. The specifications for such an operation include the following:

(1) The school district, the local teachers association, and the college would specify their purposes and mutual commitment.

(2) The school would be a laboratory for learning by all who work there. The teacher education dimension would be as important to the learning of regular faculty as to prospective teachers and college personnel.

(3) The curriculum and modes of instruction would be worked out and tested against the broad goals established by parents and the public. Educators would attempt to involve parents as much as possible in all dimensions of the school program. Wherever possible, professional decisions would be explained and discussed with parents, who would be helped to recognize the complicated and individual nature of learning, the uniqueness of their own and other children, and the meaning and value of their school's measures in

relation to the normative measures typically used to assess individual achievement.

(4) Many prospective and junior teachers (all salaried) would be included on school faculty teams to make possible a much more individualized program of learning for youngsters.

This concept of school (for youngsters) would develop curriculum and organization that would get away from group, lockstep learning. (This does not mean eliminating sequence in learning, nor does it mean destroying curriculum organization.) A program would be designed for each student; time, materials, and approaches to learning would be arranged, used, and evaluated to fit the learner's purpose and needs—but not in isolation. It would not be an approach that caters only to selfish needs or that pampers the student. It would be a live, realistic nurturing of individual growth and development in the context of the society in which the student lives. It would be based on the assumption that much is not known about what a student needs to learn, and certainly all students need not learn the same things. The focus would be on learning how to learn; on developing productive, positive attitudes about learning; on intriguing the student with the intellectual process; on the application of thinking processes in solving human problems; on developing skills and knowledge that have purpose and that cultivate human satisfaction; on human-relations skills; and on fostering self-understanding and personal adequacy. Education would include much more than traditional in-school learning. All students would take part in planned work-study programs. Many outside people, agencies, and institutions would be used as learning resources and experiences. School, no longer considered just a place for education, would extend far beyond the physical plant. It would then become an idea, not a place. It would be conceived of as a context in which people (students and faculty) live, work, and learn. In one sense, it would be an experience for its own sake—social, psychological, intellectual, physical, and esthetic. Planning for all this requires some rearranging and some reeducation—for students, teachers, and parents.

Unless some effective evaluation devices to verify learning in terms of these goals are built and used, a lot of people, including teachers, are going to be very critical, and rightly so. Whatever program goals are devised, teachers, students and parents must be involved, and there must be ways to assess the degree to which goals are achieved. Descriptive data will also be needed, particularly to report and assess process. If process and human encounter with ideas and people are major school goals, evidence will have to be presented that such a curriculum has learning outcomes of value.

Obviously present school staffing, existing approaches to teaching and curriculum, and attention given to teacher education in schools do not fit the kind of school described above. Some sample schools needs to be developed, capable of demonstrating various concepts of what a school might look like. Taba,[1] Joyce,[2] McKenna,[3] Mallery,[4] Silberman,[5] Weber,[6] and Bussis and Chittenden[7] provide illustrations of how teachers in such schools might function. Peter Dow[8] develops a fascinating approach to curriculum and teaching.

It is clear from studies such as that by Goodlad and associates[9] that curriculum and teaching as it exists in the total concept of school must be considered together; and further, that the elements of curriculum and teaching must deal with program organization, decision-making, curriculum organization, teacher roles, and other considerations related to time, space, climate, and resources as they exist in schools. Chart I, *Illustrations of Possible Models of Schools,* gives more details on what must be included in the total concept of school. And the possible models include alternatives other than the one advocated in previous pages as a desirable model.

It is not important that teachers or laymen accept a single concept of school. There should undoubtedly be alternatives. What is important is that teachers, students, and parents who are most directly concerned with a school have a part in shaping what it becomes and that teacher training in service, in addition to contributing to general enlightenment, is directly related to developing skills for specific undertakings.

Getting to work on school purposes requires getting organized for the task. This is both an organizational problem and a teacher education task. There needs to be precise thought about various teaching and supportive roles and how people (teachers and others) learn to create such roles. Having described roles in terms of program and purpose, some testing needs to be done to discover levels of complexity. For example, some are direct-encounter roles, such as lecturers, discussion leaders, demonstrators, seminar leaders, coaches, tutors, or performers. Some roles require more training than others. Some roles are more difficult than others. Some should be rewarded more than others. Can we dissect and analyze the elements of these roles? Can such roles be taught? They must be, if teacher education is to make any sense.

There are, of course, other orders of roles—such as diagnostician, strategist, evaluator, consultant, guide, or programmer—and the same questions can be asked about these. To what extent are the direct-encounter roles separable from this second set? How can they be put into combination? Does any combination of roles logically fit together? Is there some reasonable vertical hierarchy in terms of difficulty, artistry, or prestige?

Roles such as manager of the learning environment, planner of curriculum or student experience, or learning guide add still other dimensions. The organizational hierarchy of team leader, assistant teacher, intern, teacher aide, and so on, suggests still other role dimensions. How is an organizational hierarchy role related to teaching roles? Can prestige levels be assigned to organizational, confrontation, and managerial roles? How should salary be assigned to these various roles?

Colleges preparing teachers cannot deal with role differences in isolation from schools. Value differences and difficulty differences need to be tested in performance situations. Testing the difficulty of various roles will require considerable research. Most important, though, is that in-service education cannot proceed very far unless there is more focus on the roles various teachers take and how they can be prepared for them.

So the teacher education school is essential. There have been ideas like this before—and too often they have remained on the drawing board or in the literature. The new USOE interest in teacher renewal centers provides a chance to get action. How can this be approached?

Strategy and Process

Government agencies, national and state, are already working out agreements (contracts, planning grants) with higher education and local school districts to get educational renewal centers under way. Ironically, even with all the evidence from teacher institute programs, curriculum development projects, Triple T, and others, there is almost no involvement of teachers in the planning of teacher renewal centers. Teacher organizations at the national level, AFT and NEA, were contacted almost after the fact to provide input in planning renewal centers. State and local teacher organizations remain ignorant at this time as to what the whole idea is about.

The issue is more than involvement for political purposes, to get input and concurrence so that teacher organizations support rather than resist establishing renewal centers. The issue is also that renewal centers for teachers cannot succeed if they are not by the teacher, of the teacher, and with the teacher. Teachers are tired of being done to, of having innovation imposed, of being led or pushed into in-service training. They are suspicious and resentful from too many experiences with education personnel who don't teach but who devise schemes and content with little teacher input that teachers are expected to embrace and apply. The university master's degree program is the best illustration of the type of study that is usually piecemeal, haphazard, and imposed. Encouragement of intrinsic motivation for professional development

CHART I

ILLUSTRATIONS OF POSSIBLE MODELS OF SCHOOL

	Model A	Model B	Model C
Primary emphasis	Subject matter and skill development primary; academic subjects have priority	Intellectual, emotional, social, physical, esthetic development	A productive life experience for students during years spent in school
Learning decided by	Learning developed sequentially by experts and professionals	Learning developed along individual and personal lines depending on the student's ability and interest	Learning determined by students, with consultation of teachers, parents, and community contact people
Content determined by	Curriculum content dispensed by teachers and texts and workbooks	Content drawn from all sources of knowledge, depending on problems a student or students are attacking	Content incidental to learning, emphasis on learning how to learn, to inquire, on making decisions or drawing conclusions, encounter with experience as it comes up their major determinant
Curriculum organization	Curriculum organized around subjects, courses, or disciplines	Curriculum organized around the individual development of each student	Curriculum organized around the experience students have, the problems they face
Teacher's main function	Teaching involves directing student learning along prescribed lines	Teaching includes any form of interaction with students which is designed to assist learning	Teacher mainly a sounding board, a constructive critic, a resource person

	Model A	Model B	Model C
Criteria for learning	Evaluation of learning largely by paper-and-pencil, teacher-made, or standardized tests	Evaluation of learning employs multiple devices for assessment, with emphasis on behavioral change and self-appraisal	Evaluation of learning based primarily on student-developed goals—assessed by students as well as faculty and community-involved people
Schedule for school learning	School day 5-5½ hours, five days a week, 175-190 days a year	"School" extended to any hours devoted to learning—in or out of school under the auspices of school	School serves as the base from which work-study program extends—essentially calendar is developed for the individual and includes the entire year
Organization of students	Students organized into classes, taught in classes, and grouped by age and academic ability within age	Students organized in groups or individually, in terms of purposes—determined by students, teachers, and parents	Students organized sociometrically, this balanced with teacher having some options to organize for new exposures
Organization of teachers	Teachers organized in faculties by grade level in elementary and subject at high school level	Teachers organized into teams, including a variety of types or personnel, professional, paraprofessional, and ancillary people	Teachers organized and reorganized periodically—for students' benefit and to ensure their own vitality and challenge. Central guideline is bringing together a vital, productive, stimulating team

has too seldom been fostered for American teachers. The time is right to emphasize intrinsic motivation, and this must begin with teachers working on their own problems, indicating their own needs.

Therefore, planning for renewal centers, or teacher education schools, must involve more teachers and include teacher organizations. More important, the plans or guidelines developed for teacher renewal centers must provide for teachers a central role in the governance of such centers. Guidelines for teacher education schools (as described in this paper, one type of renewal center) should include provisions such as:

(1) The staff should include everyone from teacher aide to senior professor, and governance of the center should be the right and responsibility of those who use it.

(2) Teachers should work individually, but also in groups, to study and solve problems.

(3) Study and research should be an integral part of the usual school operation.

(4) The community (parents and laymen) should be deeply involved.

(5) Many community agencies and institutions should work with the school.

(6) Adequate money and the readiness to gamble with new and different ideas should be evident.

Author's Epilogue

Having said all this, I must come back to remind myself that whatever is done with teachers and students, whatever new roles are developed, our primary goal is to free and nurture the individual in his growth, our top priority is to foster self-fulfillment, our major dream is to help every man gain an awareness of himself. Teachers, though grounded in fact and based in science, must still lean hardest on that element of being we call artistry. That is the pivotal function in teaching, and I submit that any plan for teaching or learning which does not value artistry above mechanism and system will become humdrum and banal.

Notes

1. Hilda Taba, *Teaching Strategies and Cognitive Functioning in Elementary School Children.* U. S. Office of Education Cooperative Research Project No. 2404 (San Francisco, Calif.: San Francisco State College, 1966).

2. Bruce R. Joyce, *The Teacher and His Staff: Man, Media, and Machines* (Washington, D. C.: National Commission on Teacher Education and Professional Standards, National Education Association, 1967).

3. Bernard H. McKenna, *School Staffing Patterns and Pupil Interpersonal Behavior: Implications for Teacher Education* (Burlingame: California Teachers Association, 1967).

4. David Mallery, *New Approaches to Education: A Study of Experimental Programs in Independent Schools* (Boston, Mass.: National Council of Independent Schools, 1961).

5. Charles E. Silberman, *Crisis in the Classroom: The Remaking of American Education* (New York: Random House, 1970).

6. Lillian Weber, *The English Infant School and Informal Education* (Englewood Cliffs, N. J.: Prentice-Hall, 1971).

7. Anne M. Bussis and Edward A. Chittenden, *Analysis of an Approach to Open Education* (Princeton, N. J.: Educational Testing Service, 1970).

8. Peter Dow, *Man, A Course of Study* (Washington, D. C.: Curriculum Development Associates, 1971).

9. John Goodlad and others, *Behind the Classroom Door* (Worthington, Ohio: C. A. Jones, 1970).

RESEARCH AND THE TEACHING BODY

Jean Piaget

In the period between 1935 and 1965, in almost all the branches of what we term the natural, social, or human sciences, one could quote the names of great writers, men of international reputation, who have revolutionized, more or less profoundly, the branches of learning to which they have devoted their labors. Yet, during that same period, no great pedagogue has appeared whom we can add to the list of eminent men whose names provide our milestones in the history of education. And this raises still another problem.

It is a problem, however, whose terms are not limited to the period in question. If we glance through the tables of contents in the various histories of education, the first observation inevitably thrust upon us is the very large proportion of innovators in the field of pedagogy who were not professional educators. Comenius created and ran schools, but he was by training a theologian and a philosopher. Rousseau never held classes, and though he may have had children we know that he did not occupy himself with them to any extent. Froebel, the creator of kindergartens and the champion of a sensory education (however inadequate it may have been), was a chemist and a philosopher. Herbart was a psychologist and a philosopher. Among our contemporaries, Dewey was a philosopher, Mme. Montessori, Decroly, and Claparède were all doctors of medicine, and the latter two were psychologists as well. Pestalozzi, however, perhaps the most illustrious of the pedagogues who were purely and simply educators (though he was a very modern one), invented nothing in the way of new methods or approaches, unless we allow him the use of slates, and even that was simply for reasons of economy. . . .

One of the important events in pedagogy between 1935 and 1965 was the French project of reforms that gave rise to the "observation and guidance phases," which sprang directly from the work of a commission guided and inspired by a physicist and a psychologist-doctor (Langevin and Wallon).

There have doubtless been examples in other disciplines, too, of fundamental inspirations being contributed by men who were not "of the profession": everyone knows how much medicine, for example, is indebted to Pasteur, who was not a doctor. But medicine in its broad outline is nevertheless the work of doctors, the engineering sciences have been constructed by engineers, and so forth. So why is pedagogy so little the work of pedagogues? This is a serious and ever-present problem. The absence or scarcity of research on the results of scholastic instruction that we were emphasizing a moment ago is only one particular case. The general problem is to understand why the vast army of educators now laboring throughout the entire world with such devotion and, in general, with such competence, does not engender an elite of researchers capable of making pedagogy into a discipline, at once scientific and alive, that could take its rightful place among all those other applied disciplines that draw upon both art and science.

Is the reason inherent in the nature of pedagogy itself, in the sense that its lacunae are a direct effect of the impossibility of achieving a stable equilibrium between its scientific data and its social applications? This is something we shall go into later, in the light of the fresh problems that have arisen between 1935 and 1965. We shall answer in the negative, but before examining the theoretical questions it is indispensable to begin by giving due importance to the sociological factors, since it is as true in this case as in every other that a science cannot develop other than as a function of the needs and stimuli of a social environment. And the fact is that in this particular case those stimuli are to some extent lacking and the environment not always favorable.

We shall, of course, return to each of these problems—the position of which has been perceptibly modified since 1935—but the question for the moment is that of the situation of the teaching body with regard to research, and of the social obstacles that prevent teachers from engaging in such research into fundamental educational problems.

The first of these obstacles is that the public (which includes certain educational authorities and an appreciable number of the teachers themselves), being unaware of the complexity of these problems, does not know that pedagogy is a science comparable with other sciences, and even a very difficult one, given the complexity of the factors involved. When medicine applies biology and general physiology to the problems of curing diseases it need not hesitate about the aims to be attained, and it employs the already advanced sciences while itself collaborating in the development of the intermediary disciplines (human physiology, pathology, pharmacodynamics, etc.). In contrast, when pedagogy seeks to apply the data of psychology and sociology, it finds itself confronted with a tangle of questions concerning not only ends but also means, and it receives no more than modest aid from its mother sciences, since those disciplines have themselves still not made sufficient progress, and it has still to constitute its body of specific kinds of knowledge (an educational psychology that is more than a merely deductively applied child psychology, an experimental didactics, etc.).

In the second place, the schoolteacher is constrained to conform to a set program and apply the methods dictated to him by the state (except in certain countries such as, in principle, Great Britain), whereas the doctor, for example, is answerable more to his faculty and to his professional council than to a ministry of health or hygiene. It is doubtless true that ministries of education are mainly staffed by educators, but they are educators filling administrative posts and therefore have no time to devote to research. And it is also doubtless true that such ministries often take the precaution of founding and consulting research institutes (such as the pedagogical academies in Eastern countries together with the many laboratories attached to them), but this still does not alter the fact that the specific intellectual autonomy of the teaching body itself still remains extremely restricted, throughout the world, in comparison with that enjoyed by the other liberal professions.

In the third place, if we compare the societies formed by educators to those formed by the medical or legal professions, to societies of engineers or architects, and so on, in other words to all those professional associations within which the representatives of the same discipline—even though they are "applied" disciplines as opposed to the so-called pure sciences—engage in shared study projects or exchange discoveries, one cannot but be struck by the prevailing lack of scientific dynamism in these bodies of frequently specialized educators when discussing exclusively intra-union problems.

In the fourth place, and this is doubtless the essential consideration, there are still many countries in which the training of teachers has no connection at all with university faculties: secondary school teachers alone are trained at the university, and even then almost exclusively from the point of view of the subject they are going to teach, their pedagogic training properly speaking being either nonexistent or reduced to an absolute minimum, while primary school teachers are trained separately in teacher training colleges that lack entirely any direct link with university research. We shall return later to the changes in ideas and institutions in this respect during the past 30 years, but it is important to note at this point what a deadly effect the traditional system has had upon educational research: first of all, it has left future secondary teachers in ignorance of the possibilities of such research (when it could produce such very fruitful results in secondary education in the fields, among others, of mathematics, physics, and linguistics); and second, it has helped to make the teaching body of the primary schools into a sort of introverted intellectual class apart, deprived of its rightful social recognition, a situation made worse by the fact that primary teachers are thereby cut off from the scientific trends and the atmosphere of research and experiment that could have injected new life into them had they been brought into contact with university teaching.

One phenomenon, the seriousness of which cannot escape notice and which has been becoming more and more clearly apparent during recent years, is the difficulty of recruiting primary and secondary schoolteachers. The XXVIth International Conference of Public Education placed on its agenda in 1963 the problem of "the struggle against the scarcity of primary teachers," and it became quite clear on that occasion how general the problem is. This, of course, is above all an economic question, and if we were able to grant teachers salaries equivalent to those earned by representatives of the other liberal professions, we should thereby increase the rate of recruitment. But the problem is much wider and in fact concerns the educator's position in social life as a whole: that is why it is so closely linked to our central question of pedagogical research.

The truth is that the profession of educator has not yet attained, in our societies, the normal status to which it has the right in the scale of intellectual values. A lawyer, even one of no exceptional talent, owes the consideration in which he is held to a respected and respectable discipline—that is, the law, whose prestige corresponds to clearly defined ranks among university teachers. A doctor, even one who does not always cure his patients, represents a hallowed science, the acquisition of which is a lengthy and arduous process. An engineer, like the doctor, represents a science and a technique. A university teacher represents the science he teaches and to whose progress he devotes his efforts. What the schoolteacher lacks, in contrast to all these, is a comparable intellectual prestige. And the reason for this lack is an extraordinary and rather disturbing combination of circumstances.

The general reason is, for the most part, that the schoolteacher is not thought of, either by others or, what is worse, by himself, as a specialist from the double point of view of techniques and scientific creativeness, but rather as the mere transmitter of a kind of knowledge that is within everyone's grasp. In other words, it is considered that a good teacher is providing what is expected of him when he is in possession of a general elementary education and has learned a few appropriate formulas that enable him to inculcate a similar education in the minds of his pupils.

Thinking in this way, it is very easy to forget that teaching in all its forms raises three central problems whose solutions are still far from being found, and of which we are still even bound to ask ourselves if they ever will be solved except with the collaboration of our teachers or of at least a section of them:

1. What is the aim of this teaching? To accumulate useful knowledge (but useful in what sense?)? To teach students to learn? To teach students to innovate, to produce something new in whatever field is concerned, as well as to know? To teach how to check, to verify, or simply to repeat? And so forth.

2. Once these aims have been selected (and by whom, or with whose consent?), it then remains to determine which branches (or sub-branches) are necessary, irrelevant, or contraindicated for the attainment of them: branches of education, branches of reasoning, and above all (something that still remains absent in a great many programs), branches of experimentation that will help to form a spirit of discovery and active verification.

3. The appropriate branches selected, it remains lastly to acquire sufficient knowledge of the laws of mental development to be able to find the methods most suited to the type of educational formation desired.

Chapter IV

Teacher-Initiated Learning: A New Kind of Teacher Education

Introduction

The new teacher education is based on modern learning theory, mainly Piaget's. It follows the premise that nothing is learned that is not learned actively—"transformed by the actions of the learner." Groups of teachers can thus learn very little about teaching children by sitting passively in a lecture hall or seminar room. The teacher must learn how to teach children by observing and studying them and by confidently going ahead, actually proceeding with an experimental plan, as Piaget would have it, either of her own or in collaboration with theorists. Hence there is the fusion of theory and practice that is essential if education is to "take its rightful place among all those other applied disciplines that draw upon both art and science." As Piaget has written:

> . . . The same reasons that have rendered our school system inadequate have also led to the inadequacy of the social and (as an indirect consequence) of the economic position of the teacher.
>
> These reasons may be summed up by saying that our school system, as much under left-wing as under right-wing regimes, has been constructed by conservatives (from the pedagogic point of view) who were thinking much more in terms of fitting our rising generations into the molds of traditional learning than in terms of training inventive and critical minds. From the point of view of society's present needs, it is apparent that those old molds are cracking in order to make way for broader, more flexible systems and more active methods. But from the point of view of the teachers and their social situation, those old educational conceptions, having made the teachers into mere transmitters of elementary or only slightly more than elementary general knowledge, without allowing them any opportunity for initiative and even less for research and discovery, have thereby imprisoned them in their present lowly status. And now, at the moment when we are witnessing an educational revolution of great historical importance, since it is centered on the child and the adolescent, and on precisely those qualities they possess that will be most useful to tomorrow's society, the teachers in our various schools can command neither a science of education sufficiently advanced to permit personal efforts on their part that would contribute to the further progress of that discipline, nor the solid consideration that would be attached to such a scientific, practical, and socially essential form of activity . . .

> From every point of view then, the problem of teacher training constitutes the key problem upon whose solution those of all the other questions examined until now depend.[1]

As can be easily imagined, this view of teacher training will not meet with universal enthusiasm in this country. The teacher is simply not thought of as one who can learn to proceed scientifically as well as practically and intuitively to educate children. In fact, there are those in teacher education who do not believe that teachers can exercise wise autonomous judgment. For an example, ask any small group of school administrators if they believe teachers should be allowed to run their own teacher centers. As Edward Chittenden states:

> ... [to support teachers] try very truly to respect the teacher for where she may be at that point in her own teaching and to really mean this. . . . The approach in so far as possible is to treat the teacher in the way one would like the teacher to treat the child, and that is with respect and with interest in the original contributions of the teacher.
>
> Toward the end after our visits we drew the general conclusion that there should be two kinds of questions that one asks when visiting a school. One is, to what extent are the children moving into a kind of a central decision-making role? The other question, not independent of the first, is to what extent is there movement of the adult from a role of a curriculum follower to a thinking, mature behaving, resourceful adult? The approach of the advisor-consultant should be to identify a starting point with the teacher and to work with that and not come in inadvertently or consciously proclaiming a whole set of generalizations (Piagetian or otherwise) which a teacher "should" use.[2]

Although there are healthy variations, the new teacher education is based on discovery and decision-making on the part of the learner-teacher who will be learning all her life. It assumes that the teacher will want to provide a milieu for children of discovery and decision-making, as well as to encourage children in the self-confident behavior that makes thinking for oneself possible. The Leicestershire approaches to teacher education, and in this country the outstanding National Association of Independent Schools workshops described by Edward Yeomans in this chapter, begin with active workshops equipped for many ideas in the curriculum areas: science, math, art, reading, and so forth, then try to integrate ideas that may originate in one area into the others. Another active approach, perhaps more naturally integrated, is Sybil Marshall's thematic one described by John Harkins in this chapter, which begins with one idea then attempts to extend it into every area of the curriculum.

Both approaches are mirrored in the extraordinary work of English primary teachers in classrooms: Sir Alec Clegg here describes teacher education in the West Riding that has led to remarkable expressive work by children in writing and art, exemplifying perfectly, in the words of the Plowden committee, that "slow building up of teachers, best done on small courses, ... perhaps the most difficult and the most rewarding aspect of in-service training. We have seen its results in some of the most distinguished primary school work in the country."[3]

In Oxfordshire, and elsewhere, Robin Tanner, Her Majesty's Inspector and one of the great teacher educators of England, used similar methods in working with teachers with a further emphasis on life lived fully and richly by adults. Van der Eyken and Turner have described his work illuminatingly, and the work of primary children in Oxfordshire is a constant testament to it.

Notes

1. Jean Piaget, *Science of Education and the Psychology of the Child* (New York: Orion Press, 1970), p. 124.

2. Edward Chittenden, "Symposium: Problems, Issues, Questions, and Application of Piaget's Theory." Conference, Application of Piagetian Theory to Education: An Inquiry Beyond the Theory. (New Brunswick, N.J.: Rutgers University, Graduate School of Education, 1970). Quoted in Milton Schwebel and Jane Raph, *Piaget in the Classroom* (New York: Basic Books, 1973), p. 279.

3. Central Advisory Council for Education (England), *Children and Their Primary Schools* (London: Her Majesty's Stationery Office, 1967), vol. I, p. 359.

AN INSPIRED ADVISER, ROBIN TANNER

Willem van der Eyken and Barry Turner

In Oxfordshire, Robin Tanner spent the first few years establishing himself among the schools in the country, visiting them regularly and getting to know their teachers. One young headmaster, David Evans, whose school Robin Tanner helped to transform ("It looks like a public lavatory, doesn't it?" he had said when he first saw it) described the effect of his personality: "Robin Tanner had talked to me about William Morris, who had lived nearby at Kelmscott. I knew hardly anything about this. "Aren't you lucky," he said. "You can take your boys and girls to Kelmscott Manor and enjoy for yourselves Morris's block-printed hangings, the great Kelmscott Chaucer, and get the atmosphere of that strangely evocative house."

"But I put off going there; and then, one day, I did take the children. I shall never forget it. We set to work at once, learning about what Morris stood for, cutting and printing blocks, making books, drawing native plants like the snakeshead fritillary, and assembling a display of craftsmanship, lent by Robin Tanner and his colleagues about the work of William Morris. We just never looked back after that. We were away.

"Slowly we changed the entire appearance of our three classrooms. More than that, we changed our conception of educating children. There was not a single child who could not win some mastery over one craft or another. It was as though something of that sense of standard and of quality at the heart of Morris's way of life had communicated itself to those children. Even the infants created patterns on cloth by the age-old process of tie-dyeing, starch-resist, and discharge. The younger juniors gathered wool from fences and hedges, which they carded and spun—making their own spindles and also using an old spinning wheel. They dyed their yarns with native dye-plants which they collected, and they started to weave on looms they made themselves. The older juniors not only printed wallpapers and textiles with their own blocks, but engraved patterns on boxwood, using the tools of the adult engraver, and with these they printed cover papers for the books they made.

"What I find surprising is that each succeeding generation of children builds on and adds to this tradition that started in the late Fifties. We even have an indigo vat at school now!"

It was with young teachers like David Evans, George Baines at Brize Norton and now at Eynsham, Tom John at Tower Hill, and some young women teachers that, from 1956 to 1964, Robin Tanner worked and shared his message. The message was simply that education should be designed around the child, for him, according to his nature and his needs. "It can't be an easy path, you know," he used to tell them. And he meant it, for what he wanted from them was a sharper awareness of the world around them, of their attitudes to young children, and of their own sensibilities. Apart from encouraging ruthless honesty ("If you're really honest, you're unassailable," he would tell his teachers), Robin Tanner achieved a great deal by bringing groups of them together, socially and unofficially. There were dinners and long talks at the Lamb Inn at Burford, where he always stayed. Or a meeting at David Evans' home at Sherborne in the Windrush valley, or a day with his family at his own home at Kington Langley, where the talk might range from ways of propagating plants, or how to make a syllabub, to a current volume of poetry, choosing a carpet, the political situation, or planning a French holiday. By breaking down the insularity common to many village schools (and not only village schools!) he was, consciously or not, creating an elite among the teaching profession. For the first time, for most of these teachers, they felt part of a special vocation. "He gave me a new dignity," said Tom John, "and that meant that I, in turn, gave a new dignity to the children I taught. We felt terribly important people. After all, here was one of H.M. Inspectors taking us out for poetry readings and dinners, and driving us into the country to see old churches and carvings, and sharing his own collections of art treasures with us. I wasn't being taught, exactly; I was being educated."

A great deal of this work was done in Robin Tanner's private time, in the evenings or the weekends. For him, there was no division of time, no "work periods" and "rest." He often quoted Lawrence Binyon's line "Nothing is enough" to prod and cajole further efforts from his team. He himself spent endless hours on his correspondence, on discovering new works of art and craft for the many displays and exhibitions that he organized in schools and colleges, and in the preparation of the many courses that he gave for educationists both in the county and at national level. In 1960, for example, he ran meetings on handwriting at Watlington, Leafield, Chadlington, Kingham, Ascot-under-Wychwood, Witney, Charlbury, and Long Hanborough and ran a course on the study of nature at Cowley Manor in Gloucestershire. The following year there was another conference on school gardens and one on the exploration of the natural environment at Charney Manor in Berkshire. In

1962 there was one of his famous Dartington courses on "Movement with Art and Poetry," an Oxfordshire discussion on "Living in a New School," more poetry readings, and a special celebration of William Morris.

At these conferences, the highlights were the exhibitions created, sometimes by Robin Tanner himself and at other times with Christine Smale, one of his close colleagues. During his holidays on the Continent he and his wife, Heather, created their private collections of baskets—their garage, where they hang from the rafters, looks like some displaced African marketplace—of woven and printed materials, of pots of all kinds, a vast collection of calligraphy, of books and prints, of jelly moulds, straw hats, and even of corn dollies, made by countrymen from straw at harvest festivals. Christine Smale was also an avid art collector, particularly of costumes and nineteenth-century domestic craftsmanship. Together, they would start preparations for one of their exhibitions a day or so before any major course began, completely transforming the building in which it took place.

From the voluminous boot of her car, Christine Smale would produce bonnets and crinolines, early dresses of frail sprigged muslin, Victorian knickknacks, old photographs and letters, lace, velvet, feathers, and brooches. From Robin Tanner's big station wagon he would haul antique and modern chairs, pictures, printed textiles, living and dried plants, baskets, wine jars, brass rubbings, eighteenth- and nineteenth-century waistcoats, prints, and carvings, together with vast rolls of white corrugated card for mounting the displays. For many hours before any conference, they would be busy, with pins and rampions, placing these objects in arrangements designed to stress certain aspects of colour, design, or texture.

Every member on the course would have received, some weeks before it began, a programme of suggested undertakings from which they had to choose one to pursue at the conference. A typical case was a conference held at Dartington Hall early in 1964, "Art and Craft—Their Place in Secondary Education." These were a few of the themes put before the teachers:

> Even in the depth of winter the gardens at Dartington never look forlorn, dull, unclothed. Explore some of the many reasons for this, making numerous drawings to demonstrate your points. . . .

> In the Great Hall and also in the medieval Solar a number of old, rare, costly and beautiful things are placed. There are banners, tapestries, carvings, furniture. Make a book or folio of descriptive drawings of those you like most. . . .

> Study the many stone steps and stairs about the Hall and Gardens,

and also the cobble and flagstone paths, particularly those in the court-yard. The stone work of the garden walls and buildings is worth noting, too. . . .

Lichens and mosses flourish in the moist, warm South Devon climate. Stone, slate, bark, wood are all friendly hosts for different kinds. Get inside this miniature world. . . .

In the architecture of Dartington, surface texture plays a significant part. Make rubbings and annotated drawings of both old and new in-stances—not forgetting the church tower. . . .

From the exhibition in the Great Hall make a history of English waistcoats. . . .

Such a daunting programme—there were about 30 items to choose from—was intended to occupy only three days of a ten-day course, but if a teacher, bewildered and not a little put off by the enormity of the tasks provided, failed to produce a reasonable piece of work, Robin Tanner was never disap-pointed. "It really doesn't matter," he would say. George Baines, on his first conference at Woolley Hall in Yorkshire, began making some faltering draw-ings and then threw the result into the wastepaper basket in disgust. Robin Tanner pulled the crumpled paper out again, sat down with him and began to move a pencil over the work. "I think we can probably do something here," he said, lifting the drawing to a new and acceptable plane. George tried again, and found, as he himself later explained, that he could draw.

"You are all artists," is how Robin Tanner would begin one of his talks to a group of teachers. He was challenged about this once from the audience. "Really, not an artist?" he asked. "Does someone else buy your clothes?" No, said the teacher, he bought his own. "Well, only an artist could have bought that suit!"

During such conferences, the teachers became aware that art and craft were not merely satisfying occupations or pursuits; that behind the obvious there lay an intricate and deep philosophy which would be pursued through readings of prose and poetry, and by endless discussions on the need for and the mean-ing and rightness of art. ("Why do we all respond to that perfect proportion we call the Golden Mean? Why do we prefer a portrait lighted from the left? How did the inevitable shape of a spoon evolve? And why can't we tamper with it?") Robin Tanner would quote Jacquetta Hawkes, where she asked:

Where did [the makers of these flints] discover this rightness of form, a rightness we still recognize a quarter of a million years later? Did it perhaps, and does it still, spring from memories, deep in the un-conscious, of natural forms observed and participated in during the vast stretches of our pre-human evolution? Is it these memories, these inherited prejudices, that make us say: this is right—the relation between this tapering point and this curving butt are so perfectly satisfying as to possess a kind of life of their own? It may be we are moved by such an inheritance, or it may be that as creatures of this world we are swayed by the laws of its construction and existence. I do not know how we come to possess them, but I am sure these aesthetic convictions of ours, these ideas of formal rightness, are bonds between the human mind and the universe in which it is lodged. They are also bonds between ourselves and our remote forebears, having passed from brain to brain, from their time until our own, in an unbroken mental process spanning all human history.[1]

Robin Tanner himself, stressing always the importance of quality in everything that was done for and with children, saw this strand of human consciousness as lying closest to the surface in childhood. For this reason he complained, loudly and at length, about the spuriousness and artificiality of much that was brought into primary schools. He spat out the word "plastics" with particular venom, and once argued that the only object that had remained true to its origins in many schools was the wastepaper basket, a simple willow construction. "But now some schools are even embroidering raffia daisies around their basket!" he exclaimed, throwing his hands in the air at the travesty. On another occasion, he threatened to write an exposé of the "Gift Shoppes of England," for which he had a particular horror. "The trouble is that if it were ever printed I should be prosecuted for obscene libel."

Quality was all important, he felt, because young children had eyes and feelings to understand and almost identify themselves with the true nature of things, and so to abuse their direct gaze was to commit a crime. That was why, he argued, a school should be a "good place," a "wholesome, shipshape place of truth and beauty," and every teacher, in whose trust lay the development of childhood, should be dedicated to the fight for this ideal.

It was this concern with the true, the real, the genuine that caused Robin Tanner to seek the assistance of practising artists in his contacts with teachers. Many were his personal friends, and they came willingly to help: the potters Bernard Leach, Lucie Rie and Hans Coper, the block printers Phyllis Barron and Susan Bosence, the architects Mary and David Medd, the craftsman-teacher Ewart Uncles, the historian Grant Uden, and the educational pioneers Dorothy and Leonard Elmhirst. All of them came to join forces, uniquely, with fellow inspectors like Christine Smale and Geoffrey Elsmore.

[1] *Man on Earth* (The Cresset Press, 1954), p. 9.

At the end of these gatherings, "I felt about three feet up in the air," one teacher remarked years afterwards. "I was literally a changed man. It was impossible not to be. I sat down and wrote letter after letter to Robin. What about this? What about that? Should I try such and such? Why didn't we do this or that? and every time, by return of post, in the italic handwriting which he tried to instil in all of us, back would come the replies. Probably every person on the course was writing to him, too, but he always found time to write back, to keep us going. And then, perhaps four or six months afterwards, we would have a reunion. Nothing to do with the Ministry, or with his official work, but just a private social affair, where we would talk and meet him and he would keep up with events and find out how we were doing. It was a lonely business sometimes, you see. On the course, there were perhaps thirty of you all with a common purpose, but when you left with your vision, you might be the only one in your county with any idea of what you were talking about."

As his retirement approached, Robin Tanner more than ever looked ahead to what had still to be done. "Education has a very long tail," he explained. "A very long tail!" The Department of Education gave him a touching farewell, but his real sendoff took place in the hall of Tower Hill School, Witney. Educationists from all over the county came to the event, and the large school hall could hardly cope with the crush.

After the tributes, he rose himself. It was an occasion when any man might have been tempted to look back. But he refused. His subject was: "Where do we go from here?" and he drove his colleages on with a long list of all the work that waited to be done.

"Will it ever end?" he asked them. "No, there is no end. And that's the joy of it."

WOOLLEY HALL AND IN-SERVICE TRAINING IN THE WEST RIDING

Sir Alec Clegg

There are some educational tasks which can be discharged quite admirably by in-service training in sessional courses—short or long. For the transmission of information or the consideration of techniques they are effective and convenient. Often they bring together whole staffs of infant, junior, middle, and/or secondary schools and provide an opportunity for each to learn of the others' aims and methods. Frequently, however, sessional courses attract disparate gatherings of teachers at varying stages of experience and understanding and thus invite precisely the same educational limitations as class teaching or the public lecture. For this reason, the Chief Education Officer began to turn his thoughts towards the development of residential courses in which it might be possible to exploit the advantages of continuous association and thus give greater attention to the "why" rather than the "how" of teaching problems. Only in premises suitable in design and furnished appropriately to the purpose did it seem likely that one could detach teachers from their day-to-day responsibilities and provide an atmosphere conducive to relaxed and informal discussion.

The old hall at Woolley, near Wakefield, was adapted to be opened in March 1952 as a college in which in-service training could be provided for all connected with the County Education Service. Since that time it has been progressively improved and extended by a series of minor building and maintenance works. At present it offers comfortable boarding accommodation for more than 50 teachers and the necessary tutorial, administrative, and domestic staff. In addition, there are a handsome library, music and conference rooms, a purpose-built hall for movement and drama, and a series of studios for art and craft. An environmental and rural studies centre has been established in the grounds with a classroom/laboratory, livestock and horticultural areas, greenhouses, and an extensive demonstration apiary. More recent extensions have been provided in addition to a specially equipped centre for the training of school caretakers as well as display areas, general purpose rooms, a well equipped workshop, and additional bedroom accommodation. The college has a bar and social area which also serves as a canteen for some day courses. Not least appreciated by teachers are the extensive grounds and gardens with facilities for tennis.

The importance of the residential nature of our courses cannot be under-estimated. It allows the concentration of discussion and sharing of ideas to develop well after the programmed sessions and without the distraction of travel, home, and family responsibilities. The social as well as professional re-lationships which are formed can last long after the course has dispersed. This is a vital ingredient to help bring about a change of attitude and understand-ing to work with children.

The existence of excellent physical provision is of vital importance to the value of the work of Woolley Hall, but this does not in itself create an effective programme of in-service. A major factor is the availability as tutors of a strong team of advisers who are in daily contact with teachers and who are capable of answering their needs. The team is large and contains within it people with a wide variety of concerns and expertise. It is impossible to overestimate the contribution made by this powerful team to all the aspects of in-service train-ing at Woolley Hall.

The influence of the Warden of such a residential establishment used for this purpose is of the utmost significance. To contribute to the development of an enlightened code of practice, the Warden must be directly involved with every stage of the courses as they are planned and conducted at the college and must subject all that is done to sensitive and critical scrutiny. In recent years the changes of thought and attitude which teachers have brought to courses at Woolley Hall have moved away from methods of instruction to the way children learn. There are increasingly more "non-subject" courses than there used to be. The courses that ten or fifteen years ago would have been devoted to particular aspects of the primary school curriculum are now in-creasingly being replaced by courses which involve a combination of activities which concern children's experience and learning. More courses are examin-ing the relationships between areas of study which traditionally were separate, such as art and science and mathematics. More courses involve practical and first-hand study. Whilst the majority of the residential courses are Friday to Sunday and Tuesday to Thursday, there is an increasing need to extend some of the courses by one or two days to enable the work to go to greater depth as well as to allow more time for the teachers to know each other well enough for frank and more extended discussion. The midweek residential courses are particularly valuable for visiting schools and observing children as an integral part of the course. Teachers themselves are increasingly taking an active and responsible part as tutors and lecturers on the courses. For a teacher to have to speak to his peers about what he does or to lead a group of colleagues is a daunting but exhilarating ordeal; but if he comes through it, his own standards (which are high, otherwise he would not have been invited to act) are likely to rise.

The demand for courses at Woolley Hall is such that its use is committed for at least a year ahead. In the educational year 1971-72, more than 5,000 teachers have applied for courses, two thirds of them for residential courses and the remainder for day courses in the college. Nearly 150 teachers have met regularly during the year for Saturday or evening sessional courses in the specialist teaching areas within the college and grounds. Many of the increasing number of sessional courses held throughout the county are closely related to what is done at Woolley, serving either as preliminaries to or enlargements of the more concentrated residential courses. More than 350 caretakers have been trained on three residential or eighteen nonresidential courses, using the college and the specially equipped caretakers centre in the stable block. Over the years these courses for caretakers have had far-reaching effects on the quality of this aspect of the school service.

There have been, in recent years, a number of courses held jointly with teachers from other counties, including Hertfordshire, Oxfordshire, and Wales, and other countries, including Germany, Norway, and the United States.

We have been fortunate in having a committee prepared to assist financially in mounting a not inexpensive addition to the service, as well as governors and managers who are well disposed towards releasing teachers as may be necessary for training. Of all the ventures on which the committee has embarked none has proved more effective or brought greater benefits to the service than the work of Woolley Hall. About the value of continued support there can be little doubt. It is surely significant that in certain areas of the West Riding where 20 years ago there was thought to exist a special need for the training of teachers there is now to be found educational work of a quality and distinction rarely to be found even in the most favoured areas of the country.

In writing to the Education Officer, H.M. Inspector said:

> The indirect benefit West Riding children derive from the in-service training provided for their teachers at Woolley Hall is not so easily assessed but it is far reaching. Woolley is undoubtedly contributing very significantly to the quality of work in your schools and there is ample evidence that its influence is spreading, and rapidly spreading, throughout the West Riding. Not only are you concerned with the periodic

refreshment of teachers and the fostering of educational experiment, Woolley Hall is increasingly a place where all concerned with education in the West Riding, the two wardens, teachers, your C.C.I.'s, your officers and my colleagues, meet frequently to discuss freely and cooperatively educational problems and their solution. If the facilities provided by Woolley Hall did not exist, educational progress in the West Riding would be much slower, and many of your enterprises might not even have started. It is the double interplay between Woolley and the schools, and between the schools and Woolley which I find so impressive in the in-service training, not only of teachers but of all who take part at Woolley Hall.

The Education Officer along with all of his colleagues who have had any part in the development of in-service work in this college, believe that Woolley Hall is the most effective means the Authority has of developing its educational force.

How Does the News of Change Spread?

So-called change can be brought about by imposing it on schools, just as so-called education has in the past been brought about by imposing it on children. In either case, the effect in many instances is a lack of conviction, a lack of sincerity, and inert and sterile results.

At worst, a group of pundits remote from the classroom think great thoughts as to how improvements shall be brought about, and these are then accepted by the school authority and "required" by them from the schools. Even if this does not occur quite so blatantly, there are always promotion-seeking teachers who are prepared to mount the current bandwagon and do what the pundits or the paying authority say should be done. Where the punditry is less blatant, groups of teachers are brought together in authoritative conclave,and they decide what shall be done by their fellows. Again, the doing of it becomes an official requirement.

Both of these procedures court ultimate failure. Either of them, however, and particularly the second, may achieve a measure of success. But real progress in education is best brought about when it is drawn convincingly and sincerely from good practicing teachers. One of the great joys of administering education in an area the size of the West Riding of Yorkshire, with its 12,000 teachers, is that any day its senior officers can see teaching genius at work. Indeed it is one of the major aspects of their job to see that good ideas spread. How is this best done?

Initially, "punditry," as I have called it, was well to the fore in the minds of those who prepared the weekend and midweek courses Woolley Hall was providing. Experts told the teachers what to do.

Soon, however, those who ran the courses realized that what they were doing with the teachers was the opposite of what they were recommending the teachers do with their pupils. Very rapidly the ways of handling the courses changed. Formal lectures were reduced; discussion groups and seminars were increased. As often as possible, teachers were put in learning situations where they were conscious of an inadequacy similar to what their pupils so often felt. They painted and modeled and explored the environment at their own level of competence, and in this way their sensitivity to children's needs and their knowledge of their own capacity were both greatly enhanced.

The demand for the use of Woolley Hall by advisory staff wishing to raise standards and spread good practice was very heavy. More and more, however, they came to realize that the best way to raise standards and spread good practice was to get good, practicing teachers to say what they did with children and what happened to the children with whom they did it.

I remember once listening to a slow-speaking, not very articulate, not very spectacular headmaster who spoke quietly and with the utmost sincerity of the work he was doing in his school. He showed some children's work and talked with conviction of the children who had produced it. It was very moving, and as we went out of the room after the talk, I heard one rather brash and inadequate teacher say to another, "Well, what's good enough for Old Hanson is good enough for me." I felt we had made one small step forward.

It is important that such a center, which can be—and in the case of Woolley Hall was and is—the powerhouse of the area, should receive the direct concern and attention of the head of the service. Believing this as I do, I am always present when the program of courses for the year is compiled. In the early years, I was present when the warden and the director of the course discussed what they were going to do. Some of the questions I invariably asked were: What does the course aim at achieving? How do you propose to achieve it? What staff do you propose to employ? What talks will they undertake?

I learned early on that it is fatal, for example, to place before a group of indifferent teachers an exponent of outstanding brilliance. Some will hate him, many reject him, and about all will disbelieve him. These are the only reactions available to them if they are to retain their self-respect in the presence of this luminary. The right practice is to place before any group someone who is just far enough ahead of them that they have every hope of catching up with him.

It is of paramount importance, of course, that the teachers themselves should have a major say in many of the courses. In the case of Woolley Hall, every year we have called in a number of teachers associations and put at their disposal not only Woolley Hall itself but any of the advisory staff of the Authority whose help they want.

A course, however, is not enough. It has to be followed up. A teacher who has paid for his weekend at Woolley and learned much from it may be hesitant about taking the first step in his own school. He needs encouragement, and this comes best from visiting advisers who know about the course and the kind of inspiration, understanding, and advice that it proclaimed.

What should be the approach of such an adviser? The most gifted exponent that I know of the art of drawing the best out of the schools that he visited was an adviser who, when he entered a school, however poor in quality it might be, would look around until he could find something he could commend and that might, if developed, prove productive. He would praise the teacher for it, invite the head to see it, and leave the school with the idea that the school would be a better place if there was more of it. At his next visit, there *would* be more of it, and the teacher who had produced it would have begun to think why it was good, and his insight and understanding would deepen.

As the teacher developed, he might be invited to address a group at a teacher center. The result would be apprehension, support, and encouragement, much thought, and a growing confidence which would eventually affect the whole school. It is in this way that schools wax and flourish and give birth to new and effective ways. It is a slow process; but it is sure, sincere, and founded with a firmness that seldom results from an attempt to improve from above by new blanket techniques.

There is a world of difference between new ways born of conviction and new ways introduced by those who mistake the shadow for the substance and who, having jumped upon the bandwagon, find that they cannot play the instruments.

The Rights and Wrongs of Change

I would like now to state what I believe to be the right conditions for successful change and then to list the signs of a poor school in which change is needed—or in which it has been attempted but has not been understood.

The first requirement for change is that one or two people must work as "encouragers" and advisers. They should be people who have proved to themselves, by their own work in the schools, the benefits of change. They must be sensitive, patient, undoctrinaire, and unauthoritarian people who will avoid all temptation to impose rapid change on schools; rather, they will look for growing points in each school and move on from there.

These people must accept the fact that to enlighten and develop the dull mind is the real test of a teacher, and that the purpose of education is to get the best out of all children and not merely to provide a rich diet for the gifted few.

They must be persons whom teachers will enjoy having in their schools. The advisers themselves must have sufficient humility to recognize that many of the teachers with whom they work will be far more gifted as teachers than they have been.

They must be able to recognize high standards of achievement and to discern what has inspired them. They must understand the subtleties of obtaining such standards by awakening in children a desire to produce their best and to take a justifiable pride in it, rather than by imposing arbitrary standards on children.

They must have a center in which to do in-service training, a center to which teachers will enjoy coming and where they are made welcome. Such a center should serve as an education powerhouse throughout the area in which it is situated. It should be a place that is well equipped with teaching resources that are available for inspection by teachers who attend the courses. But those who direct the center must be fully aware that right personal relationships and right attitudes will do more for education than all the gadgets, kits, tests, workbooks, imposed discipline, and rules in the world.

The program of such a center will consist of a certain amount of "chalk and talk" by acknowledged experts whose main function is to stimulate discussion. More time, however, will be devoted to interchanges among teachers; the center will be a place where teachers explain to each other what they do, describe how the work they display was produced, and tell what happened to the children as a result of producing it. In the center, there will be an ever-changing display of children's work.

The center will be the base for learning that will affect teaching. Here, teachers will paint and model and write and make music and explore the environment at their own level. In doing so, they will grow in their understanding of children's problems.

In the preceding paragraphs I have identified some of the conditions for successful change. Let us now consider the signs in a school that betray *the need for change.* There are many such signs, of course; here are some of them:

- the acceptance of low standards
- work poorly displayed and labeled
- only the best work displayed
- litter, untidiness, noise
- torn and tattered books
- too much reliance on competition
- children of varying abilities, backgrounds, and maturity all being taught the same thing at the same time
- fear of bare walls
- walls covered with tawdry commercial illustrations
- walls covered with a display of children's work which has not been changed for months
- shabby display tables
- jam jars for flowers
- sentimentality
- meaningless projects
- jargon without thought
- workbooks that demand little of the teacher and are mere filling of blanks or underlining by the child
- following the fashion
- indiscriminate use of handwork and gadgetry
- failure to build on the strengths of the staff
- attempts to measure aspects of learning not susceptible to measurement
- change for the sake of change
- failure to recognize that change must come gradually
- change that lacks both understanding and conviction.

The preceding list suggests some of the signs in a school that indicate the need for change; there are other evidences of failure that are far more difficult to eradicate or to avoid. One of these is the influence of social pressures. At any time and in almost any country, schools are subjected to sometimes fierce social pressures. In England, the 11 plus examination afflicted the primary schools and inhibited development. It is no coincidence that development has taken place as the 11 plus pressures have been removed. At the secondary stage, however, the public external examinations at 16 and 18 plus still dominate what is taught to the quick learner and corrupt what is taught to the slow.

In the United States, I had the feeling that pressures from the universities, social pressures exerted by parents and alumni, pressures exerted by the graded system itself, and pressures of competition all tended to make teachers teach relentlessly as they themselves had been taught. Moreover, it seemed that the administration often dared do no other than support these pressures, all of which stem from a status-controlled structure of society as hierarchical in its way as anything we find in England.

Such pressures are fierce. Interestingly enough, their impact varies from one segment of society to another. In England at the present time, we have the seemingly odd situation that change in the schools is most likely to succeed in areas where parents are really intelligent and knowledgeable about education and seek change when it is necessary, and in areas where parents don't know enough or care enough to ask questions about change. It is in the middle areas of suburban social aspiration that change is resisted and that schools are pressured to groom and train traditionally for the great rat race of life.

Let me conclude this section with the response a teacher made to a question that I raised. The teacher was working in an informal school, and my question was: "How do you maintain standards when so much of the decision making is left to the children who work nowadays so much more on their own and at their own pace?"

He replied thus: "It seems to us that high standards of academic achievement were obtained of old for just the same reason they are obtained today— somebody was determined on getting them. Yesterday, it was a matter of command; today, it is much more a matter of influence. But there would not be high quality results in either situation unless objectives had been clearly defined."

We must be careful, I think, in our efforts to assess the achievements of today and those of yesterday. Sometimes I wonder if we may not be comparing today's worst with yesterday's best. If, however, the level of achievement drops because of the new ways of learning, I must suggest that, for one thing, the teachers have lowered their expectations. They have failed to convince the children of the necessity for choosing that which is right and pursuing it with discipline. Here, of course, the teacher's example gives us the important clue. To my mind, education is something to do with learning *together,* and if the adult leader does not lead, or opts out of giving guidance, or leaves the children to initiate, choose, and decide without his constructive influence, then morale will decline and there will be an awful lot of underachievement. The teacher's job, among other things, is to inspire. He can only do that if he is there in the thick of it—and enjoying it; there can be no virtue without enthusiasm.

We must not forget the headmaster's influence either. His job is to inspire the staff with what is possible, and he must help make sure that goals are very clear.

A lot of woolly thinking and jargon have been associated with modern methods of education and have done damage. One of the culprits, I believe, has been the notion that you must "let the child follow his own interest." This worthy and excellent idea often ends with a full stop, and the whole point is then lost. The injunction should continue ". . . and work together with the teacher toward a clearly understood objective."

About two years ago, I had the beneficial experience of looking into some half a dozen or so "progressive" schools in the south of England. In the interests of freedom, the children were often to be seen going about quite happily, and there was certainly a friendliness and easy social grace between staff and children. But nowhere did I see much evidence of disciplined planning toward worthwhile objectives, and that, in my thinking, is essential if learning and growth are to take place.

What Have We Gained from the Revolution in the Primary Schools?

When we seek to answer this question, we must keep clearly in mind just what we want. If what we want is the learning of the basic skills and the ability to acquire information from books, we have gained something—but not all that much. If we broaden our goals, however, to include freedom to learn by exploring, choosing, and making judgments; an eager interest in nature and in human society; the ability to express personal ideas and feelings fluently, forcefully, and, as occasion demands, imaginatively; the development of self-respect and of compassionate regard for others; and the capacity to enjoy those great aspects of civilization designed to be enjoyed—such as music, art, and literature—then there is no doubt at all that the newer ways are vastly superior to those that preceded them.

Perhaps the first and most important gain derives from the fact that because the child learns from his own explorations, he's *eager* in his learning. Artificial goals, such as the competitive lists, merit marks, and examination results, then tend to be redundant. Once this situation comes about, the well-endowed child is no longer exalted beyond his desserts; the endeavors of the least able are more easily cherished; the self-aggrandizement of the quick in the presence of the slow and the envy of the slow for the quick are both reduced. Each child makes his mark and receives "that recognition which our natures crave and acknowledge with renewed endeavor." This is a quotation from a statement made a hundred years ago by a school inspector who knew then what we must continue to keep in mind: We all crave recognition; it is the spur to nearly all our endeavors.

In the "new" schools, the individual can't be lost in the mass. The talking and listening that go on in the early years are part of the love that is the start of life for all pupils. Painting, drawing, acting, modeling, singing, and dancing offer to our children the beginnings of an enjoyment of beauty that later enriches adult life. The opportunity pupils have to learn from natural phenomena gives them their first acquaintance with scientific truth. Thus it is that love and beauty and truth are changing our schools, and we are moving away from the obedience that is so important in the Old Testament law to the truths of the New Testament which affirm "that knowledge puffeth up, that charity edifyeth, and that love is the fulfilling of the law."

One of the interesting aspects of the changes that are taking place in my own county, the West Riding, is that they are completely spontaneous, as far as I can determine. I know the schools in which the changes began and I know something about how the ideas spread—and what has happened had nothing at all to do with "educational philosophy." I don't believe that the people who started the changes had ever heard of Caldwell Cook or Dewey. They owed nothing to the progressive school movement of the 1920's and 1930's. What is most interesting, however, is that the good educational theorists and philosophers of the past would have given full support to the people who are making today's changes.

Support would have come also from many other people, because the newer ways lean heavily toward the esthetic and moral convictions of many thoughtful and sensitive and compassionate persons. The new ways, for example, agree with Plutarch that the soul is not a vase to be filled but rather a hearth that is to be made to glow. They agree with Erasmus and his love of the liberal arts; with Rabelais in taking Gargantua through the meadows and over grassy places to observe all that grows; with Montaigne in urging that the child observe the curious in his surroundings; with Locke in his opinion that learning must be had but as subservient only to the greater qualities, with Rousseau in his avoidance of verbal lessons; with Goethe who said that to digest knowledge, one must have swallowed with a good appetite; with Ruskin who held that the spirit needs several sorts of food, of which knowledge is only one; with Whitehead in his condemnation of inert ideas and his conviction that every child should experience the joy of discovery; with John Dewey in much that he said in *Experience and Education*; and certainly with a great deal that is set out in

The Humanities in the Schools, a little book published in the United States in 1968.

To be a bit more specific about our gains, I would say that children certainly express themselves in painting and writing and dramatic movement as they never did in the days of formal instruction. In mathematics, they may not manage the grotesque calculations of our grandfathers, but their understanding of the whys and wherefores of mathematics is far greater than it used to be. In one of the schools that I know best, the quality of teaching is completely upsetting the national norms. The really significant gain, however, is the dramatic change in children's behavior, and how this has come about is something that I cannot readily explain.

One thing I know is that the changes in our primary schools are affecting the human spirit just as much as they are affecting the human mind, despite the endless succession of pressures that conspire to focus our attention on what can be measured to the neglect of what cannot. Perhaps I had better explain what I mean by "spirit," an archaic word that has dropped out of fashion in this age of measurement. My spirit deals with my loves and my hates and my hopes and my fears and my ambitions and my enthusiasms and my enjoyment of what is beautiful. My mind tells me that 6 times 7 is 42; my spirit responds to the kindness of my friends. As I see it, when the human spirit is wrong, it makes for evil and cruelty and strife and warfare. When it is right, it makes for generosity and compassion and nobility.

The education of the mind is relatively easy. We bring it about by the processes of mathematics and science, by manipulating the facts of history and geography, and by all our school programs where measurement is so important. We bring in effective gadgetry to make these programs more efficient, we build splendid buildings, and we write textbooks. Education officers and superintendents of schools evolve new systems of organization. And 90 percent of all this business is aimed at the mind. We overvalue the mind and extol its products—from the two times table to the technicalities of the space program. We let these things take on more importance than the actual growth and development of the child himself.

And since the things of the spirit are impalpable and cannot be measured, they are difficult to deal with and are conveniently put aside. As we all know, the result is that the growth of knowledge and mental acuity has far outstripped the growth of humanity and compassion and other manifestations of the qualities of the spirit.

The kind of teaching and learning that is developing in our best elementary schools does not exalt mind over spirit; it starts and ends with the individual. From the outset, the child is thrown on his own resources. Once this happens, initiative and sensitivity and determination and many other qualities emerge as by-products of the learning process. The child learns to recognize and value his power of expression, and this power of expression is central to the new forms of learning. Sensitivity to beauty in a variety of forms is deliberately cultivated. And more and more, the teacher comes to realize that what really matters is not the quality of the picture that the child has drawn or the excellence of the writing he has produced but what has happened to the child during the process.

THE TEACHERS' WORKSHOP IN THE UNITED STATES
A Sense of Direction in Teacher Education
Edward Yeomans

We in the United States are not by any means without a history of growth
and change in education. If we could peel away a few layers of prejudice
toward the progressive education movement, some of which are justified, we
would find a very strong, very indigenous strain of interest in the scientific
study of learning going on in the 1920's and 1930's. The pamphlets and books
that were written then have the same quality of quest and zest that one finds
in current works on open education. The teachers' workshops that were held
by the Thirty Schools as part of the Eight Year Study, were not unlike the
English workshops that I have described.

The results of the Eight Year Study would have given us a sense of direction in the 1940's. We have just begun to recapture it 30 years later. The Study
showed that students do better work when their interests are enlisted, when
they share in the enterprise, and when the content has meaning for them.*
Instead, we were diverted, first by World War II, then by our fear of technical
inferiority, then by the Cold War—and so an important demonstration was all
but forgotten.

Quite in character, the English held to the philosophy which we both
shared before the war and implemented it as rapidly as they could afterward.
Fortunately for us, we now can go to get help in sorting out our jaded theories
by visiting their classrooms and reading their documents. Fortunately, indeed,
for they have preserved for our view a philosophy that owes as much to John
Dewey as to Froebel and Montessori, which is to say, a philosophy essentially
pragmatic, democratic, American.

How has America responded to this view? By a sense of kinship, partly.
There is nothing alien to our culture in seeing children who are active in the
pursuit of learning—however rare this sight may be in our own schools. We
respond warmly to achievement, even when accomplished in the absence of
external rewards and punishments. Our Puritan ancestry still frowns upon

---

*It also showed that teachers, for their part, do a better job when they feel themselves
to be a part of an evolutionary process in which no one has all the answers.

75

much prominence of music, art, and drama in the curriculum, but we are beginning to give these subjects houseroom, if only in the servants' quarters. Furthermore, there are distinct overtones of the country schoolhouse in our view of the integrated day, and what could be more normal than that? The mixed ages, the older children helping younger ones, the do-it-yourself tradition of build your own fires and make do with whatever comes to hand—these are strong bonds indeed.

At a time when our schools are turning the young against intellectual and artistic interests, not only in the ghetto, but in the suburb as well, we see with some amazement a generation of English boys and girls from every walk of life moving into higher education with enviable preparation, as well as anticipation. Here is something to ponder, for when we discount in full the differences between the cultures, the things children learn before they come to school, the proportion of students who expect to go to college, there still remains that sense of kinship with the idea, as well as with the people involved in it. To the extent that this is true we are not so much "importing" or "transplanting" a philosophy that is alien to our soil as rediscovering patterns that are native to our climate when understood, appreciated, and cultivated with the care that the English have used.

The National Association of Independent Schools, having shared with other early visitors a period of fascination with English primary schools, became convinced that there was, within the concept of the integrated day, an important lesson for American education—a lesson to be examined no less in independent schools than in public schools, no less in urban schools than in suburban schools. How best to do it? A few teachers and school heads could arrange to be sent, or could go on their own resources to visit schools and see for themselves, and they did. Many were stimulated by the series of articles in the *New Republic* by Joseph Featherstone in 1967, by the Plowden Report in that same year, and by other books and pamphlets.

It was clear, however, that we needed the first-hand experience of teachers and heads of schools against which to judge our own, over a reasonably sustained period of time. The result was the NAIS Workshop on the Integrated Day, held in Cambridge for a period of four weeks in July 1968 and described in the booklet *The Wellsprings of Teaching* (NAIS, February 1969). Under the able direction of Roy Illsley, then Headmaster of Battling Brook County Primary School, Leicestershire, this workshop set a general pattern which has been followed successfully ever since. Among the components of this pattern are the following:

● participation encouraged from public and independent schools equally; in groups of two or more from a school

● a nonresidential session of four weeks during the summer

● enrollment limited to 60, with a staff of five or six

● a learning environment similar to that of the integrated day which encourages participants to learn from one another, as well as from the staff, the materials, and the books

● children not a central feature of the workshops, in the belief that teachers need time to be away from children and with other adults.

Workshops were held the following summer in New York, Philadelphia, and Washington, D. C., as well as in Cambridge. These followed the basic plan of the first one, with one exception: two British co-directors were in charge of each, one of whom brought particular experience with children of 5 through 7 years of age, the other with children of 8 through 11 or 12. Also, the local staffs became somewhat larger to include people having special skills, including music, dance, mathematics, science, language, social studies, woodwork, art, and dramatics.

These four workshops were studied by a team from the Harvard Graduate School of Education, who sent questionnaires to the participants and visited some of them in their classrooms. This study pointed to a number of strengths, as well as weaknesses, in our general plan, among them the following:

● of the one hundred respondents (52 per cent of the total who attended) almost two thirds rated the workshops as excellent

● 82 per cent reported that they had changed their teaching as a result of the workshop

● almost as many believed that the workshops should be "better organized" or "more directed" as felt that the open-ended nature of the workshop was valuable.

Recommendations of the team included greater attention to the special needs of minority groups in staffing future workshops and in planning the daily programs; care lest the premises and facilities of the host school appear too elaborate to people from less favored schools; that each center provide some form of follow-up, leading as directly as possible to an advisory service on some regular basis; and that an administrator be included in the group of teachers from a given school who attend a workshop.

The Philadelphia workshop was reported in print in a pamphlet entitled

Box-Breaking, by John Harkins, and on film: *Side Streets,* by Oliver Nuse. The pamphlet quotes a participant:

> In my eighteen years of teaching kindergarten, I must admit I have made some changes but I need a new viewpoint to carry me through the next eighteen years. Our children come to kindergarten so much more informed than ever before as a result of our nursery schools, Get Set programs, and television. Motivating five- and six-year-olds becomes a major task. Having heard so much about the success of the English Infant School, I am happy to have a chance to get first-hand knowledge about its operation.

And another:

> I sense my own work pattern—involvement, intense effort with some aspect of a problem, and a working it through (greatly helped if others are interested), and then collapsing for a time—I am played out. A pendulum swing. Gradually, I get moving forward again. Many children must work like that, too. Again, the importance of messing around becomes clear. I intend to watch for work patterns emerging in the children, individually, and try to learn to capitalize on them—or rather, I guess, to support them at the crucial places.

And finally:

> As far as I can recall, out of the many courses in teacher training institutions, this has been the only time where I have experienced a learning situation in adult terms and have been led to feel the real learning involved. The real impact for me was a very personal experience which could only have occurred in a free environment such as was provided. I learned very dramatically the joy and self-confidence that can come from a creative experience and I fully intend to help my next year's class to attain something of this feeling of accomplishment.

The film gives visual substance to many of the activities that are described in the pamphlet.

By chance a student, Joyce Olum, from Swarthmore, visited the Philadelphia workshop, became intrigued, and decided to carry out her own follow-up visits to teachers who had attended. Her purpose was to see in what ways and to what extent the teachers had changed their classrooms and their styles of teaching as a result of having attended the workshop. She also wanted to find out what obstacles teachers were running up against.

Not surprisingly, Miss Olum found a high correlation between successful change in the classroom of a participant and the support—or lack of it—given her by the administration, parents, and other teachers. She saw great diversity in the styles of the classrooms. She heard many explanations for the limits that had been put upon change by teachers who, had they felt free to do so, would have made more rapid changes. Among those most frequently mentioned were standardized tests. Many teachers, though convinced of the benefits to children of open education, could not bring themselves to ignore test scores as valid measures of their children's work, and hence of their own as teachers.

Miss Olum has some interesting things to say about the role of the specialist teacher in an open classroom. She saw clearly the dilemma arising from the need for special competence on the one hand and for an integrated schedule and program on the other. She also saw difficulties arising from the practice of "ability grouping," which is common in both public and independent elementary schools. She sums up as follows:

> But given that one thinks the Integrated Day is a good way of teaching, the question becomes: "Was the workshop an effective way of introducing the Integrated Day to teachers?" Judging from the effects I have seen on the teachers and schools I have visited, my answer is "yes." Of the twenty-eight classroom teachers whom I observed or to whom I spoke, eleven or twelve seemed to have been powerfully affected by the workshop and to have changed their whole way of teaching as a result of it. One or two additional teachers were making extensive use of the Integrated Day, but I gathered from them that they had already been using it before the workshop, so one cannot give the workshop all the credit for it. About five teachers were making some use of the ideas from the workshop and were using the Integrated Day approach some of the time, but had not gone all the way with it. And about ten teachers seemed to have remained relatively unchanged in their teaching methods and to be making little or no use of the Integrated Day.
>
> This means that of the twenty-eight teachers I observed, nearly half of them had been radically changed in their approach to teaching by the workshop. Considering what a big change that means, that's a pretty high proportion. And over two thirds of the twenty-eight had been at least somewhat affected.

The following summer there were nine workshops under NAIS auspices. While each one followed the familiar pattern, there were interesting variations along the way. For example, the Rochester (N. Y.) workshop invited a group of day-care children to come in three times to work with the materials. Some participants helped the children by choice, while others went on with their own work.

The Washington, D. C., workshop accepted twenty paraprofessionals preparing to be teachers' aides in the Morgan Community School.

There were workshops in Greenwich, Atlanta, Cleveland, Detroit, and Chicago, as well as in the same cities as before. Public schools played an important role in each one, from sharing the costs to providing participants and staff. Graduate credit was extended by the University of Massachusetts to any participant who wished to apply and pay for it—and 125 people did.

A VISITOR'S REFLECTIONS

But organisational and curricular changes are merely vehicles for a much more fundamental change. The really important thing is the professional growth of the teachers, and thus the establishment of a climate conducive to such growth. We can see curriculum reform on every hand. The game is not too difficult to play with expert players now prepared to participate. Yet the new curriculum materials often fail to touch the child in ways that really matter and do not seem to have affected teachers to any marked degree. Their self-image is much the same, and many accept new materials passively. There is little evidence that curriculum reform has led to the formation of a climate of professional growth in which teachers themselves innovate, make decisions about education, and have the ability and skill to turn ideas into practice. Professional growth involves freedom to integrate in new ways, freedom to make mistakes, and freedom to be one's self. It leads to variation, to an untidy pattern of development, rather than a neat array that can be easily assessed. In Leicestershire there are some signs that professional growth of this kind has occurred, although it is by no means complete and there is much that still needs to be done.[1]

THE QUESTIONS that recur to a visitor in Leicestershire are: (1) "What are the basic components of the Integrated Day?"; (2) "Are they transferable to children of different backgrounds and cultures?"; (3) "How much retraining of teachers would be necessary in order to transfer them?"

Students of the Eight Year Study of the 1930's[2] will recall a considerable similarity of framework between that experiment and the present plan in Leicestershire, the main difference being that our secondary school graduates were closely observed during their years in college while no such research scheme is presently in effect for graduates of the Leicestershire schools. The significant fact about the Eight Year Study, for our present purpose, is that 30 secondary schools were allowed to send their graduates to some 200 colleges without College Board exams or other entrance requirements in terms of content. In place of such requirements the colleges agreed to accept the Headmaster's or Principal's recommendation based upon the student's school record. This agreement was comparable, in effect, to the elimination of the Eleven-Plus Examination, for the 30 schools in the Eight Year Study were then free to teach as they believed that adolescents should be taught, without the pressure of external requirements, the competition, the rewards or punishments, and the other paraphernalia of a university-dominated preparatory school. The fact that the graduates of these 30 schools performed at superior levels in college in practically all respects when compared to the control group, who continued to prepare in the traditional manner, has been widely ignored in America, but not in England. The curricula that were chosen by various schools in the Eight Year Study made relatively little difference to the record of their graduates in college. What seemed to matter most was that the work was relevant to the students' lives, that choice could be exercised and interest exploited, and that studies could proceed in depth. Those schools among the 30 which offered the most encouragement to learning in these ways sent on to college students whose work was superior to that of the others from the experimental group of schools, as well as from the control group.

I kept being reminded of statements from the Eight Year Study about the nature of children, and the interaction between children and adults, and the significance of communication between teachers and administrators. I also recalled the ideals of our progressive schools: their faith in "problem-solving" and in "learning by doing," their belief in allowing each child to learn at his own rate and to his full capacity, their wish to balance academic work with creative and imaginative activity, their desire to make the school a microcosm of the community. As a headmaster, I had felt the pressures for academic achievement that impinge increasingly upon the elementary school from the secondary school, and upon the secondary school from the colleges, and upon all teachers from parents, and even from children, who had in mind certain definite attainments that presumably accompany entrance into certain definite institutions. I had seen the ways in which schools respond to these pressures by tightening up the schedule, increasing the expectations for work to be covered, raising the entrance requirements, reducing the free-choice activities, increasing the homework, tightening up the testing and grading systems. The net result has failed to produce in students a craving for learning or an undiminished curiosity, but has produced, rather, a growing alienation from school and college work, rebellion against authority, and for some, a search for relief in the contrived introspection of marijuana and LSD. We are entitled to ask whether, in the pursuit of academic excellence at the expense of other values, our schools are losing touch with the nonconformists, the individualists, the poets, and the dreamers among their students, and also whether we are feeding the conformists with such a surfeit of intellectual vitamins that they are losing respect for our pills and us alike.

The genius of Leicestershire, it seems to me, is that they have so far avoided formulas, systems, and conformity. They are not out to prove one theory called "learning by doing," or another called "the ungraded primary," or a third called "programmed instruction." Instead, they have studied all theories and have drawn upon those that seemed relevant to their situation, with classroom teachers being the judges of what is relevant. It is this key role of the teacher, aided by the Advisory Center, that is unique in Leicestershire. Our Progressives never achieved the integrated day in the elementary grades, partly because we did not have the many structural aids to learning that are available now and partly because we have been fascinated by methods of grouping children for optimum learning. Having the former and being less constrained by the latter, the people of Leicestershire have discovered that learning is enhanced when there is individual, rather than group, initiative and responsibility and that genuine choice of activity is accompanied by genuine involvement in activity.

This is not the doctrine of Froebel and Piaget only; it comes close, if I understand it, to the doctrine of Marshall McLuhan as well. There is little conflict for children in the Leicestershire schools between the media of communication inside of and outside of school. Both provide a full range of opportunities for absorption and inventiveness. There is room in both for emotional life, for fantasy, for speculation, and for art, as well as for intellectual discipline. There are few boundaries that separate one kind of experience from another, authority from observer, work from play, child from adult, or school from life.

Finally, what changes must take place within teachers to enable them to teach in the manner of the integrated day if they have been accustomed by training and habit to teach in the manner of the scheduled day? Clearly, this cannot be a superficial shedding of one technique and a putting-on of another. Nor is the presence of equipment in the classroom any guarantee that a teacher will trust herself, or the children, enough to use it properly. This is the weakness of all kits, systems, and devices for improving the curriculum: those who invented them have had all the fun of dreaming them up, testing them in classrooms, and perfecting them. Teachers, having no such creative investment in the device, may use it badly or not at all, depending upon the appeal of a competing gimmick.

The integrated day is an outward result of an inward feeling about children, adults, learning, growth, families, community, and life. It was shared by enough people at the outset to take root. It is now spreading to those areas which have made room for it by removing the contraints of systematized, competitive learning. It attracts and holds good teachers, for it offers growth to the teacher as well as to the child. It can flourish only where the conditions are right, and one of the conditions is that teachers be given the same initiative and responsibility that are desired for children.

No school that adheres rigidly to the graded sequence of an external authority, be it the state syllabus or the NAIS "definition of requirements," can say to its teachers: "Here is your equipment. Now let's convert to the integrated day." The ambivalence would be too great. The experiment would collapse.

Instead, it would be wiser to begin the process of change in the youngest classes of the elementary school by ungrading, by equipping a few rooms, and by removing most of the scheduled periods. As children became accustomed to the variety of choices and teachers had time to prepare for the widening span of achievement among individuals, the process could extend slowly to the middle grades with some likelihood of success.

Many of the people who are presently teaching in the junior schools of Leicestershire have come from formal, conservative schools. Several of them told me that it required a difficult adjustment on their part to accept the teaching philosophy of the integrated day. They had come to depend upon traditional routines and structure as a background for their daily function as teachers. However, they found it possible to develop different routines and structures within the new situation because they believed in it. They work harder than they did, but they enjoy it more, and they are sure that the children are learning more than they did under the older methods.

There have been some who could not, or did not wish to, change their methods. I saw some excellent teaching of the formal kind in some junior school classrooms. In one school, formal work in groups is done during the first part of the morning; individual activity occupies the rest of the day. In one school, the first two days of the week are planned on a relatively formal basis. Wednesdays and Thursdays are for individual work, and the week ends as it begins. Flexibility of this kind, and respect for individual differences, in teaching as well as in learning, are characteristic of the Leicestershire point of view.

Interest in the integrated day is beginning to spread to American elementary schools, and there are now several schools that are adapting it in various ways. Not only is it necessary for the teachers who are immediately concerned to understand and want this arrangement, but the parents and those teachers who will receive the children in a year or two must understand and want it too. There can be no "instant" integrated day. It must come, if it comes at all, as an evolutionary process in which much study and trial-and-error are involved, just as it came in Leicestershire.

Notes

1. L. G. W. Sealey, "Looking Back on Leicestershire," *ESI Quarterly Report,* Spring/Summer 1966.

2. See Edward Yeomans, "Adventure in American Education," *The Independent School Bulletin,* February 1967.

A TEACHER WORKSHOP IN PHILADELPHIA

John Harkins

Preface

In 1969 I attended a summer Workshop in Creative Education and wrote a report about it called *Box-Breaking*. The workshop held last July (1971) was similar in many ways. It, too, had leadership imported from England, funding from the same sources, and participation by many of the same schools. The participants in both workshops were interested in the pursuit of successful patterns of elementary education now variously called open classrooms, informal methods, or integrated day. They were and are the new progressives.

Since the workshops were so similar, it has been suggested that I call this report *Son of Box-Breaking*. But time changes the appearance of things, and growth changes the needs that we feel. The educational scene looks different in 1971. Breaking the boxes of a curriculum regimented into isolated parts was and still is important, but as schools have gained more experience with doing so, it has become increasingly apparent that the emphasis must be on what we build with the formless pieces. If a man has spent his life in a strait jacket, it is necessary to remove the jacket. But it is not sufficient.

The evils of contemporary American education have been amply cataloged and fully bemoaned. The time has come for building the bridges between the recognizable islands of excellence. Then, perhaps, we can explore the uncharted and turbulent waters.

For the 60 people from 19 public and independent schools who spent the month of July 1971 at Friends Select School participating in the Workshop in Creative Education, a kind of bridge was built, a bridge between our own experience and commitment to education and the wise leadership of Sybil Marshall, who guided us into what she had learned from her experience and commitment.

This article is a verbal blueprint of that bridge.

DRAMATIS PERSONAE

Sybil Marshall . . . . who was a director of the workshop, is known in America for two books, *Adventure in Creative Education* and *An Experiment in Education.* In England, she is also known as a BBC storyteller, a lecturer in Education at The University of Sussex and a director of workshops similar to that described in this report. She is, above all else, a teacher.

Ewart Oakeshott . . . . who was also a director of the workshop is known as the author and illustrator of many children's books dealing with historical customs or equipment, such as *The Knight and his Armour.* He is also an antiquarian, a museum lecturer, and a passing fair baritone.

Geoffrey Saddler . . . . head teacher of the Owston Skellow Middle school in Doncaster, England, came to the workshop to share with us his experiences as a teacher of movement and an all around schoolman.

LaRue Taliaferro . . . . (Tolly) the coordinator of the workshop, who did all the arranging and purchasing and scheduling and details that made it work so smoothly.

Mary Chapple . . . . of The Friends Committee on Education, who has been producing these workshops for three summers by raising the funds, and putting the basic staff together.

Terrence Farley . . . . principal of Frankford Friends School, who will be surprised to see his name in this list since he came as a participant. He assumed the responsibilities of a leader for the musical part of our final festivities.

Note:

John Harkins . . . . who wrote this report, has been very much a part of the program in 1969 and 1971 as official recorder and in 1970 as host when the second workshop was held at Germantown Friends School where he is head of the Lower School.

The Workshop

It is an old maxim in educational circles that some teachers have had ten years experience and other teachers have had one year of experience repeated ten times. Summer workshops are designed to help teachers avoid the latter category. They are designed with children in mind, the children who are going to be taught by the teachers who go to the workshop.

The need for workshops is clear if you consider the typical professional routine of elementary school teachers. After their college training and practice teaching, they are hired by a school and closeted with a succession of classes of children. They have no privacy and yet they are essentially alone in their work. Many teachers live out their lives with the only new professional inputs being a new batch of children each year and slight variations on the curriculum. There are antidotes to this poison. There are professional visitation days (one or two per year), a variety of team teaching arrangements, curriculum supervisors or activist administrators who sometimes get involved, faculty meetings, professional journals, in-service courses, and graduate study. For some teachers, these things suffice. For most, they do not. Some teachers cannot or do not make use of them. Some schools cannot or do not provide them. It's a sketchy and inadequate pattern.

The workshop held in July 1971 under the leadership of Sybil Marshall was, for a group of 60 teachers and administrators, a new and powerful antidote. For a month we had responsibilities to no students except ourselves. We had opportunity to immerse ourselves in a variety of materials and learning experiences without the pressure to apply them on Monday morning. We were adults, experts even, but we were allowed to approach new areas of learning as children do. That is not to say that we were treated like children but that, like children, we could enter areas new to us and experience the learning process as students rather than as teachers.

Experiencing the learning process was the core of the workshop. We learned a lot of history and painted a lot of pictures and made a lot of models and so forth. Their value is in the experience that produced them and what we learned from the experience. This was a workshop with a philosophy behind it and experience is at the heart of that philosophy. This was a coming together of 60 people who believe that Chinese proverb:

> *I hear and I forget.*
> *I see and I remember.*
> *I do and I understand.*

This was not the first such workshop. It was the third in Philadelphia. There have been over 20 in the country in the last four years all loosely affiliated through the National Association of Independent Schools. There have been countless predecessors in England. It is interesting that they are run so differently each time.

Considerable thought has been devoted to the best way to begin a workshop. The conclusions have been varied although most of the problems to be faced are the same. They are a four-week coming together of 50 or 60 people who have not previously worked together and in most cases do not even know each other. How should they spend the first day?

One workshop made up four different groups of randomly selected workshoppers and scheduled them into two sessions with each member of the staff: dance, art, math, and so on. The theory was that each workshopper would get to know a dozen other workshoppers quickly and would also be quickly and systematically exposed to the various members of the staff, their facilities, and their expertise.

Another workshop put all the participants in a few classrooms and told them to arrange, decorate, and designate them for their use during the summer. "Make it into a classroom, not for children, but for yourselves." That finished, they were sent out of the room to find and catalog resources in the community that could be of assistance to them. The members of the staff diligently avoided leadership roles in the ensuing arranging and searching.

One workshop loaded all the participants into a schoolbus, drove them to the other side of the city and dropped off groups of four in residential areas which they did not know. They were then instructed not to use any money unless they earned it that day and told to get themselves to a particular address in another city 15 miles away. Some gave blood to earn money; some cleaned a pizza oven; most hitchhiked. The experience was initially frightening to many of the workshoppers but enthusiastically endorsed by all once they had safely arrived. The objectives had been to let small groups of strangers get to know and rely on each other and to present everyone with a new and difficult task that they could approach and accomplish.

Another workshop started with the dual premise that everyone has the capacity for creative expression in a variety of media if only they have sufficient experience and skill to feel comfortable in those media and that if teachers are going to help children gain experience and confidence in a particular medium, they must have it themselves. The workshop staff decided to give that experience systematically to all the workshoppers by starting them off at the same point. They were given a piece of string and a bit of rag and told to go outside and find a small stick. With rag tied to stick, they were given black powder paint, a pile of old newspapers and some water and instructed to make some designs or paintings. The results were far more esthetic than any of the workshoppers anticipated and when cropped and mounted on black construction paper they were really quite satisfying.

For their next set of paintings, they were given a regular paintbrush. Then plain white paper was added. Then white powder paint. Then a choice of white or black paper. Then blue. Little by little elements of the painter's craft were added until, in the space of two weeks, the workshoppers had accumulated a systematic pattern of experience. The artwork on display by the third week of the workshop was very impressive in quantity, variety, and quality.

These four workshops were all successful. The various participants all felt that the first day had been a crucial part of the eventual success. "Call me Ishmael" isn't necessarily a better way to begin a story than "Once upon a time," but it certainly gets things off to a different start.

All of this by way of introduction to say that Sybil Marshall began our workshop in a most unusual way: with a lecture. It was the last thing any of the assembled workshoppers ("I hear and I forget") expected. Sybil talked for more than an hour about her concept of creative education as it had evolved in England. She called it variously informal education or progressive education and specifically avoided or rejected the phrase "integrated day." She immediately outflanked those American teachers who had noticed some silly things going on in the name of "open classrooms" by confessing that there had been some excesses in England and that it had been necessary in some cases "to put the brakes on ever so slightly." She urged us to learn from the British experience, mistakes included. But she balanced this with a stirring testimonial to the need for removing the regimenting formalities of some classrooms and the glorious freedom that had emerged from most of the classrooms where this had been done. Then, lest we misread her as a libertine, she stated her conviction that the teacher must assume the responsibility for inspiring and leading the children into interesting work, vigorously pursued and reaching high although individualized standards.

It was an exquisitely balanced statement: informed, eloquent, and precise. We all knew where Sybil was and therefore knew where we were too. We were at a workshop being run by a master teacher.

In the second half of her talk she explained her preference for working within and around a theme that could cut through the traditional subject disciplines. The theme could be almost anything although some themes proved more fruitful than others. But since it must be something, the teacher should choose it in advance so that materials and references can be gathered. Sybil had done this for us. Tolly had gathered the materials and references. We were to be introduced to our theme through seven pieces of paper which were then distributed. The first one looked like this:

> Forsaken by my father and mother
> lifeless yet not dead.   No form had I then
> but life was in me.   So a kinswoman
> took me and kept me   covered and warmed me
> cloaked me in comfort   gave me protection
> careful and loving   as to her own.
> Under her shelter   I forged my fashion
> foreigner fierce   and stranger unkind.
> My benefactress   housed me and fed me
> till in full strength   I fared far afield;
> and for her labour   lost all her loved ones,
> lost her own children   dear sons and daughters.

Sybil explained:

> We chose this topic so you could all begin at the same point. It's
> all in English so you can decode it. I'll give you no further help. Maybe
> you'll appoint a leader to report back to us all. Remember that you'll
> be in the position of so many seven-year-old children.

We were then assigned to one of six groups to approach the task of decoding. We worked at the seven sheets for a half hour. Some groups made considerable progress; some made none. All had their fancy caught.

When we reassembled as a total group, it turned out that our collective effort had solved six of the "coded messages." The first, printed above, was a cuckoo. The last and most difficult had to be given to us: a one-eyed man selling garlic.

> . . . It had only one eye   though it had two ears.
> Two feet it had, and   twelve hundred heads . . .

What we had been working on were Anglo-Saxon riddles, a popular art form in the seventh century. Our theme was to be the Anglo Saxons.

The choice had been neither arbitrary nor precipitous. Sybil had been planning to run a workshop in Philadelphia in the summer of 1969 and had to postpone it because of health. In March of that year, she had written to the organizers of that workshop:

Our theme, in which we are soaked at the moment, is best explained thus: if you and a team of American teachers were coming to give English primary teachers a month of something they only had at present vague ideas about, you would probably choose a topic in which Red Indians appeared. We are returning the compliment . . . our "savages" are the Anglo Saxons, who, since they were descendents of the barbarians that overran all Europe . . . are probably all (white) Americans' forebears as much as ours!

We trust you won't allow yourself to be put off by what looks like a dry, too-English topic as our theme. Please take our word for it that this practically unknown period of history is absolutely fascinating. We have been working on it for almost two years for a publisher who is going to put out our scheme for team teaching by thematic methods next year. I shall be able to bring a few bits and pieces of the test material with me, which will be a great help to getting things going with a swing in the short time at our disposal. I didn't really want to have to disclose our theme because I feared you might be disappointed: so I beg you to take notice of the Anglo-Saxon proverb "Never judge a day till the sun sets," and give us the benefit of any doubts you may feel. After all . . . my teachers at Doncaster didn't think they were going to get much out of "New Appleton House"!!! (*Adventure in Creative Education*). I shall probably be accused of working your teachers to death . . . I usually am!

The theme was a happy choice. It was rich in literature and history and led easily into related work in movement, art, and music. It was a subject in which Sybil and Ewart were experts and therefore in a position to be able guides. It was also a subject relatively new to most of the workshoppers. It had two drawbacks. First, from this side of the Atlantic, it did not seem very interesting, as Sybil had predicted. Therefore, for the 1971 workshop it was decided that the theme should not be announced in advance. Only Tolly was informed of the theme ahead of time so that she could gather appropriate resource materials. Sybil was able to announce to the group on the second week of the workshop:

You were given an experience of subject matter new to most of you. Now this was quite deliberate that we held up and didn't let on to you before the workshop started what you were going to study because if we had said that we were going to put on the workshop about Anglo-Saxon culture a great many of you wouldn't have been here. You would have said, 'Oh no, I wouldn't be interested in that,' and yet once you've been sort of pitched into the deep end of it you showed us by Friday how interested most of you have become. You've been caught in fact. Now do think about this with regard to your children. It's all very well to say you want to do what the children want to do and so you do, but do they always know what they want to do? Their amount of experience is after all limited and they won't be able to say whether they like it or not.

Very often, once you have started, the enthusiasm spreads and they get caught by it. It's worthwhile remembering that you can't always start from where the children are and what the children want or whether this is a fair or good way of starting. The fact does remain that there are a great many things that are completely outside their experience at the present to which you want to introduce them and you find a way of catching their enthusiasm.

The other possible difficulty with the theme was relevance. Here we were in a city that is highly sensitive to social issues, running a workshop for a variety of teachers, some white, some black, some teaching in ghettos. Anglo Saxons are not folk heroes in Philadelphia. There was some question about the wisdom of focusing for a month exclusively on Anglo Saxons. The stateside organizers of the workshop wondered whether the focus should not be counterbalanced by a pre-workshop series on African or Asian culture or in some way diluted. Sybil sent her veto across the Atlantic. She knew it was not necessary.

We had been "caught" before lunch on the first day. "Caught" in part by the riddles, but also charmed by Sybil herself, her scholarship, the good sense of her introductory remarks, and the pleasant charisma of her personality. She immediately proceeded to build on her good start. First was an assignment for each of us to compose a riddle about some common item in 20th-century life, to be ready two days hence. The assignment was undertaken the same day and by the following day the walls were beginning to disappear beneath the posted riddles of 60 workshoppers. They were collected and publblished. In a shrewd move guaranteed to have us study each other's work, Sybil offered a prize to the workshoppers who could guess the answers to the largest number of riddles. Here are two samples. ("All in English so you can decode it. I'll give you no further help.")

I keep that which none has seen, though glances flit my way uncountably.
Jeweled, fragile, plain, sturdy, I am fixed in motion.
Why do you beseech me for more of that which I had not, and never had?
Your eyes or fingers alone may tell my tale; but some, in disbelief, do crave my monotonous song whispered in an ear.

—Gloria Bush

No arms have I, but one long leg
Slender & smooth, ever toe-pointed.
My fairest feature—tresses well trimmed.
In seeming silver, the hairs are held,
Skillfully serried, cunningly kempt.
Water I love, and many strange potions
Drink I deeply, yielding them up
For beauty's boon or just for joy.
One doom I dread—the grip of glue.
It locks my locks, it dries, I die.

—Barbara Bell

After lunch on that first day, we were divided into three groups and "assigned" on a rotating schedule to spend an hour in three different rooms with the three staff members.

Sybil spent her hour working in a story telling and discussion session, starting out with the legend of Sigmund's sword in an adaptation written by herself. Her motive, as she commented later that day in a staff meeting was to "stuff them full of stories so they'll have lots to work on."

Geoff, working in the gym, sometimes with and sometimes without music, began our first sessions on movement. He began with a ball for everyone to bounce and then asked us to move around the room as we bounced it. Then to share a ball with someone else and then to move without the ball. The ease with which workshoppers began to move was a happy contrast to the conspicuous inhibitions of a few summers ago. Perhaps it is that many of these people had already had some experience with movement. Perhaps it is that our society has, in the space of a few years, come to value movement more and inhibitions less. Certainly, part of what was working was that Geoff was very good at what he was doing and his calm sureness had a relaxing effect.

Ewart, who among other things is a professional illustrator, welcomed a group into the art room and invited them to do a representation of something from the riddles. Tools and materials were available in profusion: tempera, pastels, tiles, linoleum, fabric, twine, yarn, glass, plaster, paper of all sorts, styrofoam, wire, wood, cellophane, brushes, cutters, needles, cloth, screens— the ultimate remove from "a bit of rag on a stick." The contrast is interesting. The bit-of-rag approach had put the emphasis on the media by limiting the options and thereby enabled everyone to have an experience with one particular technique. Sybil's and Ewart's approach had made no mention of media, technique, or materials although all had been made available in profuse variety. The emphasis had been on the message and the assumption had been that the message was sufficiently motivating to permit or force the workshoppers to assert themselves in spite of the techniques. Evidently, the inspiration had been sufficient: the work flowed quickly. By the end of the first day everyone had produced something. The diversity was impressive.

The staff did something important "after school" that day. After the workshoppers had gone home, they spent hours mounting and matting and hanging and arranging the products of the day's efforts. Their objective was to display one piece of work from each "student" and to display it to advantage. Plaster castings were propped against a piece of bright felt. Paintings were mounted on a complementary color of plain paper. Everything was arranged so that the cumulative effect was pleasing.

Some Americans were surprised by the emphasis that the British placed on the importance of proper display. Teachers trained in the states had usually been taught this lesson all too well but it was as a part of a larger lesson and the larger lesson has been, for the most part, rejected. The larger lesson included bulletin boards with titles such as "OUR BEST WORK" and a collection of the prize test papers, ugly and boring to anyone except the few prize pupils who got their glory from a 97 percent score on a long-division test. The lesson included the basic premise that if a work was worth hanging up, it was worth the respect of proper mounting and a pleasant overall display.

As one workshopper said:

> I was taught in normal school all that business about matting and I used to do it in the public schools but when I went to a private school, I saw they just had stuff stuck up any old way and when I got to the second private school it was just the same.

The emphatic message being sent from across the Atlantic was that the display areas were not for prize papers but for everyone's papers and that everyone's papers deserve the respect of proper and esthetic display. This is a kind of structure, a kind of insistence on quality and standards. Geoff Saddler likes to have at least one bit of artwork from each student displayed in the classrooms. Sir Alec Clegg, Chief Education Officer of the West Riding schools, speaks of display as one way of obtaining "that recognition which our nature craves and rewards with renewed endeavor."

One cannot help but think of some of the classrooms on the American scene. They have achieved a comfortable sense of informality; they have avoided the more overt forms of competition; they have given children free access to the materials; and with their emphasis on process instead of product, they have made children feel free to work creatively without the pressure to have it done by some appointed minute. Still, with all these virtues, one tends to find the room cluttered with half-finished work of low quality. Good motives get lost and good materials abused by quick and half-hearted efforts which somehow find their way to the floor. Such classrooms would benefit from the expectation of display. It's a case of the leadership coming from the teacher in the form of high expectations and thereby creating a tone for the whole classroom.

Gordon Hill commented, during the summer workshop of 1970, that it was time progressive educators stopped watching children putting two sticks together sideways and calling it an airplane. "It's depth, that's needed," he was always saying.

My own experience on that first afternoon of Sybil's workshop was representative not of the other workshoppers but of the two-stick-sideways child. The power of that lesson did not hit me that day as I worked, but in a cumulative fashion, every day thereafter. I must explain that I am one of those graphically damaged persons who goes through life announcing that I can't draw. I have confirmed my own diagnosis by systematically and deviously avoiding all opportunities lest I demonstrate my incompetence instead of merely confessing it, a strategy nicely explored by John Holt in *How Children Fail*. True to form, I hit upon a way to fulfill the "assignment" without drawing. I focused on the metrical form of the Anglo-Saxon riddles and rendered it in abstract form. I used torn construction paper to represent the two parts of each line. I used a curly bit of yarn to represent the alliteration contained in each part. And I used cellophane to represent the two beats that occur in each half of the line. You could see through the cellophane to the other parts. It was a coward's way out, retreating to poetic form, which I know something about, and running away from the challenge of picturing a cuckoo or a swan. Nevertheless, if I do say so myself, it was a kind of representation and, to me at least, it was interesting. While focusing on the abstracted intellectual part, I neglected the next level of challenge, which should have been to render my abstraction with pleasing or interesting graphics. I chose my colors carelessly. I pasted sloppily. I arranged the whole thing so that it was unbalanced and, to put it bluntly, ugly. I really wasn't thinking about the ugliness and probably hadn't noticed it, for I had been interested in the subject and had been pleased with the abstraction. I suspect that I was the first one done.

I took it to Sybil (child to teacher?) and asked her if she could solve my riddle. After a hint or two, she did. I was curious to know what she would do then. I was hoping she wouldn't make me focus on the design because I didn't want to fuss with that. I guess I expected her to want to talk about the metrical form of Anglo-Saxon poetry. I would have been comfortable talking about that. She did neither. She simply said, "Now you must find a way to display it properly." It caught me totally off guard. Here I had been playing my devious game so well, filling up the appointed time looking involved and getting my jollies out of what I was already familiar with and Sybil had, retroactively, changed what I had assumed were the rules of the game. My "thing" wasn't for looking at. No one could make sense of it without already knowing what it represented. Nor was it anything that I had expected to go on existing. What Sybil was saying, in effect, was that graphic things are to be looked at, that student work is not to be taken lightly—not even by the student—and that she was going to give it the respect of display whether I expected it or not. May I suggest, in retrospect, that such a message is a good one for teachers to send to children.

Sybil said it more explicitly in her talk on visitor's day:

> I see a great many schools in the course of my normal job and I must say that I get uncomfortable when I see a child bring a composition book to me on which page after page has got a little rather poorly executed picture at the top and then a story started, perhaps three lines. It breaks off in the middle of a sentence and the child has turned over and the same thing's happened on page after page. This would be explained by the teacher in charge of those classes that the child had found something else so interesting that he had to leave off and go and do it. I mean, I might find something very interesting to do at this moment instead of finishing this talk, but you wouldn't be very pleased. . . .
>
> This is one of the sort of moral things that children have to be taught. What is worth doing is worth doing well. What is worth starting is worth finishing.

It's a lesson I'm learning, although I hadn't learned it all that afternoon. I rigged up a sleazy way of hanging the thing and left the scene so I could take notes about other people's troubles and progress. When I later discovered that a Grand Display was being planned, I snuck back and destroyed it because I was ashamed of it. Still, the issues had registered with me and I kept thinking about them. Two weeks later, when someone else was confiding about her inhibitions in art, I confessed that I had destroyed my first day's effort and discovered that she had too. We wondered how many others had surreptitiously found the trash can down the hall just before the things were collected for the display. It couldn't have been many because the display that appeared the next day was massive. One might wonder who learned more from that display: the regulars whose work was given "that recognition which our nature craves" or those cowards, like myself, whose natures, at that moment, craved anonymity.

I had an extremely valuable experience on that first day in the art room, but there is no way anyone could have predicted it. My experience was, in fact, almost exactly the opposite from the experience that Sybil and Ewart had planned. On visitor's day, Sybil talked about the difficulties teachers have in setting up experiences for children:

> Now let's look at the function of the teacher. Every teacher here has a dual function; one is to be the organizer of situations in which children may gain new experience. The other is to TEACH with a capital T and large capital letters, the skills and techniques without which they cannot do anything with the experiences that they have gained. I had to be careful about saying "To organize those situations in which children may gain experience." I cannot say "to give children experience." You can't. You can only lead them to it and let them take from it what, at that moment they are ready to take. It may be a very valuable experience to them.

> You may organize an expensive trip in coaches to the nearest zoo or factory or, in our case, take a trip to London and pack in the Tower of London with all its history and the magnificent architecture of Westminster Abbey, show them where the Queen lives, the changing of the guards—and all these things. You bring them back to their rural country village and, in the old days, the next day they would have to write about it, And Charlie would have seized his pen and said "Yesterday we had a trip to London on a bus. I had three bottles of pop and four packages of potato chips. And I was sick down Mary's back on the way home!"

> One has to accept and admit one's limitations in giving children experience.

Many workshoppers were surprised that our second day should also begin with a lecture. Lectures are out of fashion, especially in a workshop directed by one of the pioneers of the discovery method, especially for a group of teachers who see the teacher-dominated classroom as one of the weaknesses of contemporary education, especially for a workshop in a continuum of workshops, most of which had shunned lectures. One British workshop director had written to the stateside organizers:

> So, in the beginning I propose no lectures. Let the teachers be thrown on their own resources as soon as possible. If the first day or two could be given over to "having fun" in the various rooms with no commitment at all, followed by an "educational visit," I think that this would prepare them for the theme—more of which later.

That had been in 1969. Now, in 1971 the needs seemed different. Sybil wrote to Tolly in May of 1971:

> I am sending you also herewith a plan of the kind of programme we propose. I have given this a great deal of thought and I think I shall have to explain it to you just a little, in educational terms. I am getting more and more concerned about what is happening to "informal methods" in schools in this country, particularly in the open-plan schools. "Freedom" has indeed turned into a "kind of anarchy" and the "integrated day" seems now to have led to a programme that is so completely unstructured that instead of encouraging alert and enquiring minds by allowing the children freedom to work at things they like, it is simply turning out youngsters with a magpie collection of odd facts. The basic skills and techniques of recording and symbolisation are being used so bittily that the children are lacking essential practice in them and—perhaps worst of all—the children are not required to see a job through and finish it properly before starting another. I find this fault with _____ school, good as it is. I certainly find it with _____ that we visited together and see that the tendency is growing worse with every month that passes. I have therefore reintroduced quite a lot of *structure* into my programme for the teachers in Philadelphia.

> I hope that this will in no way limit their freedom. What it means is that I am keeping control of what is pumped in in some sort of logical sequence, in order to give them plenty to work on for what they give out. I have therefore divided each day into three sessions: two in the morning, one long one in the afternoon. The first short session each morning will be a "class" session and take the form of some kind of talk on an educational principle that we are using. . . .

The contrast between those two suggestions is more than a difference between the two directors. The difference reflects what in America we would call an educational backlash. The word is too strong. Sybil had said in her opening remarks on the first day that we

> should profit from British mistakes. . . . Standards have been allowed to fall in some places and it's that shred of partial truth that gives the *Black Papers* their power.

The *Black Papers* she was referring to were a pair of vitriolic booklets edited by C. B. Cox and A. E. Dyson. They are a categorical rejection of most of the educational reforms in England in the past decade.

The attacks have not been unanswered. Sybil herself, in a part of one of the Answers (*Red Paper,* Islander Publications, 1970), also gives some indication of why our workshop should begin with academic substance:

As Tennyson remarked, a lie that is partly the truth is a harder matter to fight than an outright falsehood. Ten years ago, when the changes in primary education now lumped together under the umbrella title of "progressive methods" were in their early stages, I was writing an account of what I myself had discovered about them from practical experience: "If they (i.e., the formal teachers) stick their stalls long enough, however, they may find that their methods, like an old coat, will come back into fashion. If that is so, it will have been caused by a revolution against these greater enemies of real modern education, the people who embrace anarchy in the name of freedom, and who find it convenient to believe that no timetable and no record book mean, in effect, no work. Let no young teacher reading this get any false values from it. To control a class in freedom, to learn with each child instead of instructing a passive class . . . is the most exhausting way of all of doing a teacher's job."

There has been the same kind of reaction in America. While the 1970 workshop was going on, *Saturday Review* published an article praising the "open classroom." Its title, chosen by the editors, not by the authors, was *A Little Bit of Chaos.* That must have seemed like an encouraging word to the editors in 1970. During the summer of 1971, the same magazine published an article, *The Open Classroom: Save It from Its Friends,* containing a specific rejection of chaos. Brakes were being applied "ever so slightly" here in the States as well, not just to slow down the chaos but to temper the naive jargon that has come to be associated with the "open classroom."

Everyone involved with the movement toward a new progressive education in the States can think of a classroom, or in some cases a school, that has embraced "anarchy in the name of freedom." The professional, parental, and even political battles which ensue invariably focus on the words "structured" and "unstructured." In the opinion of this writer, at least, the words are inflammatory without being productive. Classrooms will have structure, not by administrative edict or popular demand, but by simple inevitability. Everything has structure, a jellyfish, a pontoon bridge or an afternoon in the sandbox. Schedule a few dozen people to spend their school year together in a classroom and some kind of structure will evolve even if it is not imposed. Take away the classroom, take away the student and teacher roles, take away the schedule, and still a structure will evolve. Take the most extreme of situations and call your institution a non-school and it will still grow some structures that the non-students will live with. Teachers that attempt to have no structure in their classrooms will find that they have structure aplenty—bad structure. The oft-debated question of whether to have structure is empty.

The real questions are: Who created the structure and why? How effectively does it meet the needs of those who live with it? Is it a limiting, inhibiting structure or an opening and generative structure? How rigid is it? Is it a bridge or a parking lot?

Sybil and Ewart and Geoff came to America to give us the benefit of some of their experience with building structures that were free without being anarchistic, that were inspiring without being regimenting.

Surprised or not, we began our second day with a lecture. Ewart who is, among other things, a museum tour leader and professional lecturer on archeology, told us about the extraordinary archeological dig known as Sutton Hoo. Sutton Hoo was a large burial mound located in East Suffolk and excavated in 1939. To the surprise of some and the delight of historians, the mound had been, for 13 centuries, the repository of Anglo-Saxon artifacts: a well-preserved helmet, a sword, some jewelry, and the imprints of the decayed remains of fabrics and a boat. Ewart came equipped with color slides of these and other related antiquities as well as his own considerable knowledge and fascination with the subject. By the end of an hour, his love for the subject had proven contagious and our involvement with the theme had broadened from literary to historical and artistic. In the process, we also caught some sense of the mystery and adventure related to the strange fact that although Sutton Hoo was a typical seventh-century burial mound, complete in most respects, there was no sign that anyone had ever been buried in it. Our artistic endeavors were given the added impetus of a rich and, for most of us, new set of patterns and stylistic variations, particularly the articulated interlacings so characteristic of the period.

As the Anglo-Saxon riddles had been followed by the invitation to imitate, now the slides were followed with the invitation for each of the rotating groups to do something in the art room that related to the morning's slides. The suggestion was that we should not attempt to produce anything final or definitive, but simply to experiment with one of the designs or patterns we had seen.

The resulting session in the art room was interesting. We assembled not knowing what we were going to do. Ewart spent approximately one minute making his suggestion, then wandered about the room for another minute or two and then managed to slip unnoticed out the door. Everyone knows how chatty art rooms are. When filled by teachers, they are usually a fair imitation of a cocktail party. But on this afternoon, no one talked. No one asked for special materials or advice about how to do this or that. Somehow, everyone got right to it. The impression was that each of us had in fact already zeroed in one one of the designs during the morning's lecture and had been waiting for the chance even though no mention of such a suggestion had been made earlier. Ewart wandered back in again after 20 minutes and evidently approved of the effect of his absence. He left again. After another 20 minutes he returned and found people ready to chat about their rough sketches, ready to speculate on materials or techniques. The whole session proved extremely generative. The designs worked out in that afternoon appeared and reappeared throughout the workshop. They were knitted, painted, woven, carved, welded, drawn, sewn, and even done in needlepoint. Workshoppers went back to the slides to confirm or revise their memories. They sought out books on the subject. They approached some of the designs with geometric precision, others with historical accuracy, and some with modernistic adaptations. The designs became one of the ongoing threads that ran through the whole workshop.

The first (four-day) week had been a *tour de force.* We had received a theoretical defense of the thematic approach on the first morning. By the end of the third day we had also had a demonstration. By the end of the week we were immersed.

One might question whether those three main lectures would be applicable to children. Sybil would be drawn into no such dogmatic disputes. She suits her approach to the needs and capacities of her "students" and since we were adults, we had no difficulty with a few lectures. The situation is very different from that of the teacher in September, who has ten-year-olds and a whole year to work. We had 19 days and it would have been foolish to ignore the abilities that we had as adults.

Neither the workshop nor this report should be construed as an argument for the renaissance of lecturing. The lectures were, after all, simply a starting point, an efficient way of infusing a vacuum with raw but interesting substance. The bridge that had to be built was founded on that substance, but constructed out of our experiences.

Those first three days had set the foundation for the whole month. There was the over-riding theme of the Anglo Saxons, introduced at first through the strong voices of scholarship but quickly augmented by readings, writings, sketches, models, and a variety of discovery activities. Throughout the month the theme was reinforced by more talks from Sybil or Ewart, talks now on more specialized areas of the theme and typically for smaller, self-selected groups. Those things that augmented the theme sometimes diverged from it temporarily to lead where they would, into weaving or silver-soldering or puppet-making. And these activities took on a life and meaning of their own. Workshoppers formed interest groups that met frequently to pursue one or more of these activities. Sybil soon gathered around her one group that could not have enough of her approach to literature and story-telling and another group that wanted instruction and practice in Chancery script. Geoff met daily with a group that was especially interested in movement and also another group, nicknamed "The Reluctant Painters," who had been somewhat inhibited by the massive display of talents coming from other workshoppers. Ewart formed a small group of individuals who wanted to know more about ships or weapons or architecture in the Anglo-Saxon period. Ewart is, among other things, an expert on the history of naval architecture and ancient weapons.

In addition to these groups, everyone had at least one private project going, most of them based on the design they had developed on the second day. In regular staff meetings and by dint of much planning at night, the staff managed to help the workshoppers keep all of these juggled projects in the air at once. It was, indeed, "the most exhausting way of all of doing a teacher's job." Lore Rasmussen commented later that the strongest single element was the example that Sybil had set for teachers by the diligence with which she planned and the freeness with which she gave of herself.

By the end of the first week, the workshop was running well. A conservative gambler would have taken the gains and quit, letting the workshop run out its time on what appeared to be a highly successful pattern. Sybil's experience in running workshops indicated otherwise. First of all, she predicted a general slump in intensity and morale unless things were changed. Secondly, she predicted that we would end with a whimper unless we made specific plans for a bang. At a staff meeting after the first week, she introduced an overall scheme for the rest of the workshop. Parts of that scheme were not made known to the workshoppers until two weeks later, but the pattern had been there from the start. The changes were not reversals, they were additions. Sybil still wanted groups, but not the original assigned ones. She wanted self-selected groups to be formed to work on a project connected with the theme. Beyond that, she wanted things and groups that had been imposed during the first week:

> Basically, I think we want to let up on some of the structure next week. You know we have structured it pretty solidly this week. I think now we want to begin to take off some of the controls.

As she explained in a staff meeting, she wanted the structure to begin to evolve from the workshoppers:

Well, by this time, you see, I would have thought that there will be other kinds of things starting up all the time. For instance, the moment we have a drama group starting up, they're going to want clothes. They're going to want props. They're going to be making their own props. The moment you get the puppets going, you've got the scenery to paint. And the people who are making ships or ship models are going to have to weave their own sails and possibly dye them. And so on, you know, there are going to be a lot of things thrown in the moment the groups start. Meanwhile, such things as Ewart's oil painting could be set up in a room and people who want to could go to him. And I'll have my Italic writing. But you know, I think we should be running our heads into a kind of unnecessary danger by taking too much notice at the moment that there are some people who haven't caught on because there are going to be so many more things tossed in.

Sybil collected the entire workshop together on Monday morning of the second week. She reviewed where we had been and some of the justifications for it. She gave us some more theory about the nature of thematic work, now that we had had a sample of it. And finally, she assigned each of us the job of forming or joining a group that would undertake a project within the framework of the Anglo-Saxon theme.

During a coffee break later that morning, the groups started to form. Some seemed to have snapped into existence. A few seemed more like the reluctant coming together of those who had not, for one reason or another, joined any of the other groups.

It becomes impossible, at this point, to follow the chronology of the workshop. That is a tribute to the independence of these self-selected groups. One group designed and executed an enormous mural depicting a scene from Beowulf, surrounded by a variety of Anglo-Saxon designs and artifacts. It was executed in every material available. ("There is no such thing as creative materials; there are only creative ways to use material. All materials are creative.") The mural used beer-can rings, government surplus shrapnel, paint, wool, and so on. The task took four people about ten days, working perhaps a third of each day until it was erected amidst general applause during the last week.

One group took an Anglo-Saxon myth and based a play on it. Another group sewed a tapestry of the traditional mead-hall scene. Another group rendered a similar scene three dimensionally, building the mead hall out of pillars and thatch. The most painstaking group set out to build a viking ship. Their standards were very high. After extensive research and endless geometric calculating, they began a true masterpiece worthy of proper display in a museum. Unfortunately time ran out before they could launch it. (The theory was that their water-soluble glue would be safe in the Schuykill River.) Even so, the half-built ship was a very satisfying accomplishment. The puppet group was probably the best-received project of the workshop. They wrote a script based on an Anglo-Saxon legend. They built exquisite puppets and performed superbly. Their crowning touch was a caricature of Sybil in the role of narrator.

The success of the group projects was spread unevenly. Perhaps the few difficulties are as instructive as the more common successes. One group had to abort their plans when several key members were called away temporarily by administrative duties related to their own schools, an appropriately characteristic event for school people. A few people felt obligated to complete their project for the sake of others in the group even though the original fire was burnt out. I suspect that a few people chose to avoid joining a group although I do not know their motives. I've wondered since whether their not joining a group proved as instructive for them as my not joining the Grand Display in the first week. ("One has to accept and admit one's limitations in giving . . . experience.")

After the formation of the groups, there were no major changes in the pattern of the workshop until seven days before the end. There were special events: a trip to a stained glass studio and factory, a visiting weaver, a visiting jeweler and silversmith, an interruption for the arrival of hundreds of visitors on visiting day, and a visit from one of the directors of the Springside workshop in Philadelphia, Janet Baines, who came to speak about the teaching of reading in the open classroom. These were one-day events. In most cases, they sparked some workshoppers into new areas of exploration. Still, the main threads of the workshop remained: regular groups that met for special interests (Italic writing, movement, oil painting, stories, etc.), the project groups that met to build their boat or write their scripts, and a diverse and prolific amount of individual work.

Everyone was happy with that arrangement. Everyone except Sybil and Ewart and Geoff. On the afternoon of July 22, with the group assembled at the conclusion of the Anglo-Saxon play, Sybil announced a new major thread and a new piece of work for all of us. We had been together for 13 days. There were six to go. People were busy, involved, even preoccupied with one undertaking or another. There was too much to do. For a few moments, it seemed as if we were going to have a revolt. The scene reminded me of a high-school class claiming they could not read *Silas Marner* this week because of a test in algebra tomorrow and a big history paper due on Monday and this was the weekend when they took the College Boards.

Sybil stood her ground. She was going to have no workshop end with a whimper. There was going to be A HAPPENING and everyone was going to be in it. The plan was risky but simple. Everyone was assigned at random to one of three groups: movement, music, or drama. Anyone who had extensive experience in one of the three areas was to be disqualified from that area. Collectively, we were going to put together an audience-participation performance of the story of the conversion of the Anglo Saxons to Christianity. The three groups were to work independently within the framework of a general plan and the whole effort was to be put together only once—at the performance.

Terrence Farley, who is the principal of a small school and also a music teacher, was drafted as the leader of the music group. Under his direction, the group wrote and rehearsed four songs. The first was a game couched in the myths of the old religion:

Great King Odin of Asgard
Yggdrasill so high
Reaching to the sky
The first one, the second one, the third follow me.

The next was a lullaby:

Dinogad's smock is pied, pied,
Made it out of marten hide
Whit, whit, whistle along
Eight slaves with you sing this song.

Next was a chant, rumored to have magical powers, based on the ability of nine herb sprouts that could cure nine poisons. Finally, there was a Christian chant, suitable for the first Christian procession in the Anglo-Saxon portion of England. Those in the music group had only a vague notion of how these songs would be interwoven with the efforts of the other two groups at the final Happening.

The movement group evolved a series of movements, some of them dances to be performed for the audience, some of them a kind of stylized mob action designed to bring the rest of the workshoppers into the show.

The drama group wrote and rehearsed the story of King Edwin and the conversion of Northumbria to Christianity, a story filled with adventure and intrigue of national significance but centered on a few people. (The story is from Bede, translated and amplified and soon to be published by Sybil

Marshall.) Only Sybil, Ewart, Geoff, Tolly, and Terrence Farley knew how these disparate groups were going to pool their efforts for the final Happening. Until that time, it became a daily assignment for each Happening group to meet and work on their part.

A curious but perhaps enlightening thing happened in the last few days of the workshop. People started going back to things they had dropped earlier, or, in some cases had noticed but never taken up. One of the puppeteers, for instance, had been immersed in the preparations for the puppet show. When that job was over and there were just a few days left to the workshop, she got back into papier-mache. Evidently the spirit of "the show must go on" had pushed her into the puppet show, right past a project that caught her private fancy. Now, with the show finished, she could get back to the more private urging. Another workshopper who had been busy with four oil paintings finally seized the opportunity to do a plaster casting in sand. This kind of work had been done the first day by some others, but she didn't have a chance to try it until the pressure of groups and the first fires of oil painting had cooled. The cast of the Anglo-Saxon play each immersed themselves in individual efforts: batik, a loom, a mask, and some writing. Double moral for teachers: save time for self-initiative, and don't despair if the bait is not taken on the first cast.

The last week of the workshop was filled with culminations. How did we ever build so much in a period so short? Plays and puppet shows were put on; murals were erected and models displayed. On Wednesday of the last week we had an Anglo-Saxon feast: beefy barley soup, biscuits, handchurned butter, cheeses, and a flat yeasty mead.

On Thursday we had the Happening. Sixty people spread themselves throughout the cavernous undecorated gymnasium. Sybil offered a few introductory comments, saying she didn't know if it was all going to work or not, when she knew perfectly well that it was going to work exactly as she had planned it. It was a strange mixture of feelings at work on everyone. We were all audience; we were all participants. We all did those things we had rehearsed and were all drawn into other things that we had not rehearsed. In style and pace, it was casual, even playful, as we delighted in our own impromptu piecing together of previously unmatched parts. But we were moved by the sight and involvement of our newly acquired skills applied to a story that we had made our own. The Happening really served as a kind of commencement, a culmination and celebration of ourselves and what we had learned in the workshop.

When it was over, we were slow to leave. First, we all sat around and sang songs, some from the Happening as a cast party might review their triumph, and then old favorites with new verses made up on the spot to pay the tributes that we all wanted to pay.

On our last day, we met once again with Sybil in the auditorium. There were tributes and thanks and last-minute announcements before Sybil gave her final words. Part of them contained a new definition of our workshop:

> Anything new that you learn that you take back to your classroom is only approximately half of any in-service training. The other half is made up of two things. One, that you get to know your colleagues, colleagues that, in the rather lonely task of teaching, you very rarely have an opportunity to know. And you're thrown together for a length of time long enough really to get to know your colleagues as people, as teachers with other ideas. You learn from each other. You rub off some of your spiky corners gathered during a hard year. You feel yourself again a member of a group all with the same problem. And this I know is very valuable.

> The other part of it is that if you do things that you enjoy and you enjoy doing them as I know you have done, you go back refreshed. It is to Geoff that I owe this because during the time that he and I were together, with Geoff as the student and I as the leader, in Doncaster six or seven years ago—at one point in the term Geoff was struggling to do something. I don't know what it was now, but he was enjoying it tremendously and he looked up at me and he said, "This isn't recreation. This is re-creation." . . .

> Now I don't know how much you've learned that you're going to take back to your classroom, but I could feel the other two things in my bones.

We then had the final announcements on the riddle contest. Each riddle was read and answered and correlated with previously submitted guesses. Carol Farley won the prize (two of Sybil's books) with 30 right answers. Coke Hewitt and Mary Davis were runners up.

Our last luncheon was a cooperative affair with covered dishes that added up to a modern feast. It was less educational than the Anglo-Saxon one, but tastier. Afterwards, there were gifts and thanks and goodbyes and, once more, a great reluctance to leave.

People clustered around to talk, to plan, to consider running another workshop next year. Could we have it in England? Could we charter a plane? Could Sybil and Ewart and Geoff come back to Philadelphia? Then there was more singing and finally "Auld Lang Syne." The nostalgia was thick.

And that was the end of the workshop. Those were the events that happened. About 60 people together for 19 days. What does it all mean? What can it accomplish? How can anyone evaluate it? There is no plan for a controlled or scientific evaluation of the workshop or its effect on teachers although subjective reactions abound:

... The second day of the workshop I tried to make a sandcastle and messed it up (after working a long time on it) because I didn't know how to use the materials. I *vowed* never to let that happen to a kid in my class ...

... Indeed, I felt that, at ong last I was emerging from the cocoon that had encased me ever since my art teachers of my childhood and youth had impressed on me what a dud I was. Of course, the implications of this in my own dealings with children were clearer than ever ...

... The insights gained by being forced into the position of a learner in totally new areas of attack completely exposed in a group can't help being carried over sympathetically into the classroom ...

... The major accomplishment of the workshop for me was to give me the time, supervision, and support to do things I've never done—things I "knew" I was no good at. Especially *movement* I started very self-consciously. But some confidence came—and movement became my favorite daily activity. But more than feeling good, I saw why movement is so important—action, expression, rhythm, creativity. Jumbled together: enjoyable. Geoff was superb—you could always sense his enthusiasm for our efforts. I did movement several times with a group of five neighborhood kids and I look forward to bringing it to my class this year ...

... Of the many things that I gained from the workshop, perhaps the most immediately important is a plan of approach toward my classes. I teach Language Arts to four groups of students who are on a 45-minute schedule. One of my constant worries has been how to approach this subject and all it involves without feeling fragmented. During the first week of the workshop I suddenly had a sense of how Sybil was dealing with us and a plan came to me of how I might develop my own themes within my own classes ...

... We all benefited from hearing Sybil and Geoff speak of the need for limits. I know we at our school have experimented with all kinds of limits. But to have our ideas about a kind of clearly defined approach to the "open classroom" articulated and underscored is very helpful and should send us into a classroom with a stronger sense of how to apply our own approach. ...

... I enjoyed very much meeting people from other schools and knowing something about the public school system from the teachers I met.

At the same time I got to know one of my own colleagues much better and I think this new relationship will be stimulating during the school year as we exchange ideas about how we are applying our new experiences. . . .

. . . The theme surprised me but showed that how you go about learning is much more important than what specifically is being learned . . .

. . . I have been motivated to work more closely with the children—to try to divest myself of some of the stupid administrative chores which have nothing at all to do with education.

. . . One of the most rewarding moments to my mind was Terry Farley's face during the singing of his hymn, when he realized that he had the whole gym full of folk completely in his hand. His whole experience of the workshop, maybe, led up to that ten minutes; and he'll be a bigger man and a better teacher ever after because of the confidence in himself he found. Is not that the answer to all the questions? Confidence?

. . . The remaining need is to continue all this—informal follow-ups in schools, group meetings, a newsletter. Follow-up is essential to consolidate our gains. I've cried with joy at this experience. I don't want it to stop at that.

. . . I have nothing to say but the highest praise for all concerned. The scholarship, humor, interest and organization displayed was fantastic and so inspiring and renewing. The projects were incidental to the friendships and self-renewal. Many thanks. Thanks. Thanks. Thanks.

Somehow, neither these reactions from the workshoppers nor my chronicle of the events can capture what the workshop really was. My chronicle is simply a record of the pivotal public events. Their reactions are only partial revelations of private response to those events. The real test of a workshop is not whether people say thanks, which they all did, nor whether the happening was a happy success, which it was, but whether the teachers go back to their schools as better teachers. Right now, there are over a thousand students who are giving the workshop its real evaluation.

There is another way of looking at the workshop, less thorough, but perhaps closer to the heart of the matter. The Anglo Saxons are obviously not essential to what happened. One could imagine and plan a workshop that had all the same essential ingredients on a variety of subjects: fish, kites, Kansas, or costume balls. What had really happened in the month of July is that a group of teachers had become a group of students. Each of them had become his own case study in how students learn; each of them had been immersed in a style of education; each of them had been tempted into new areas and new ways to learn.

Sort out the particulars of Sutton Hoo and oil painting, and the more general aspects of that way to learn still remain. There must be an initial structure of some sort: a challenge, a temptation, an inspiration, a starting point. There must be a variety of ways of following that initial impetus (movement, music, writing, arts, crafts), and the materials must be available. Those inexperienced in the various media must be given supported experience in them but also the freedom and inspiration and provocation to go beyond whatever kind of experience any leader can devise. Information relating to the chosen areas must be available, whether it be through books, visiting experts, trips, or on-the-spot teachers. Finally, there needs to be a calm but expectant patience, a willingness to let those "students" arrive at their depths in a variety of ways and at a variety of paces.

Those general aspects describe more than what happened this summer; they describe a style of education that we worked in for a month and then took back with us to our classrooms. Over the bridge.

Chapter V

Beginning Teacher Centers: The Supporting Work of the British Schools Council

Introduction

The British Schools Council was a kind of miracle performed by Sir David Eccles, Minister of Education, in 1964. Thornbury has related a chairman's memorable early account of it:

> ... I remember standing in an unlighted village call box on a wet night ... ringing up my wife to tell her what I proposed to do. Her first question was one that was to become all too familiar in the next two years: "but what is the Schools Council?" Her comment when I told her put my own feelings in a single sentence: "it's not what it is, it's what it might become!"[1]

Certainly the teacher center movement in England owes much to the School Council's view of the importance of the role of the teacher in the total picture of education. Teachers control the Schools Council—45 of 80 members on the governing council are teachers—and its executive staff are on short-term contracts of three years, thus ensuring a constant flow of new and vital ideas.[2] Very early (1967) in the history of the Council its "little red booklet," Working Paper No. 10, "Curriculum Development: Teachers' Groups and Centers," was published. Walton credits this small publication with the spectacular rise in the numbers of teacher centers: "According to the *Times Educational Supplement* local education authorities were positively responding to the suggestion in the Working Paper in the very week it appeared."[3] The little booklet was a kind of emancipation proclamation for teachers:

> The essence of curricular review and development is new thinking by the teachers· themselves, as well as their appraisal of the thinking of others.[4]

> The most important function (of local groups and centers) is undoubtedly to focus local interest and to give teachers a setting within which new objectives can be discussed and defined, and new ideas, on content and methods in a variety of subjects, can be aired. The comment and criticism of local teachers can show very clearly whether an idea which works well in one school can succeed in another.[5]

> Effective local leadership is essential and this must come from among serving teachers.[6]

> The vitality of a center will itself determine the range of topics to be discussed and investigated. The centre's first task will always be to stimulate and draw together local initiatives.[7]

Thus Working Paper No. 10 is a manifesto for local initiative to be brought about by the local teacher center. This booklet is of inestimable importance to teachers and should be in the hands of every teacher center group.[8]

Since 1967, the national projects of the Schools Council have more and more emphasized "grass roots development," a corollary of local initiative as the *Times Educational Supplement* described it in the summer of 1973:[9]

> Nearly all the Schools Council's early projects followed the anglicized version of a pattern established by the Americans, who—so the story goes—were so appalled by the Russian Sputnik triumph in 1957, that they summoned their brightest university scientists to produce packs of "teacher-proof" updated science curricula. The Nuffield Foundation introduced the idea of a central curriculum development team producing materials here with one big difference: its team included teachers. In the Nuffield view the best recipe was to give the good practitioners the time they could not get during school time to develop their ideas. The ideas were developed and modified by experience in trial schools. Teachers' centres, which Nuffield primary maths project claims to have invented, provided local training on a project's aims and methods.
> The Schools Council initially adopted the same approach. But a growing reaction among teachers here, and international disillusion about the effectiveness of "research, development and diffusion" or "top-down" models of curriculum development, has led to support for grass roots development or at least grass roots involvement. This is known in the trade as "periphery-periphery" or "bottom-up."

Some of that grass roots development is documented in this chapter. A few years from now we may have rich documentation of teacher initiative and involvement as American teacher centers take shape. For now the most helpful materials on teacher initiative in beginning teacher centers are from the Schools Council, all but one of the documents included here (Working Paper No. 10) now out of print. For those in this country who are beginning teacher centers, however, this material will offer good counsel.

Notes

1. R. E. Thornbury (ed.), *Teachers' Centres* (London: Darton, Longman and Todd, 1973; New York: Agathon Press, 1974), p. 13.

2. Anne Corbett, "The Secret Garden of the Curriculum—Who Should Hold the Key to the Door?," *Times Educational Supplement,* July 13, 1973, pp. 4-5.

3. J. Walton, "Teachers' Centres: Their Role and Function," *Forum,* Autumn 1972, p. 15.

4. Schools Council, "Curriculum Development: Teachers' Groups and Centres" (London: Her Majesty's Stationery Office, 1967), p. 5.

5. *Ibid.,* p. 6.

6. *Ibid.,* p. 7.

7. *Ibid.,* p. 15.

8. Available for 10 pence plus postage from H. M. S. O., 49 High Holborn St., London W. C. 1.

9. Corbett, *op. cit.,* p. 4.

AN EARLY MANIFESTO ON TEACHER CENTERS: WORKING PAPER NO. 10, CURRICULUM DEVELOPMENT: TEACHERS' GROUPS AND CENTRES (in part)

The British Schools Council

Research and Development: The Broad Aims

1. The Council's main concern is with curriculum development. It looks to other agencies, particularly the National Foundation for Educational Research, the universities, and the research councils, to further the growth of fundamental knowledge relevant to educational problems. The Council exists, in other words, to promote a process of which the essential elements are as follows:

(*a*) The careful examination, drawing on all available sources of knowledge and informed judgment, of the *objectives* of teaching, whether in particular subject courses or over the curriculum as a whole. The object is to help as many teachers as possible to define, cooperatively and from personal conviction, these objectives. They will probably reflect, so far as is humanly possible, the contemporary needs both of the pupils themselves and of the community as a whole.

(*b*) The development, and trial use in schools, of those *methods and materials* which are judged most likely to achieve the objectives which teachers agree upon.

(*c*) The *assessment* of the extent to which the development work has in fact achieved its objectives. This part of the process may also be expected to provoke new thought about the objectives themselves.

(*d*) The final element is therefore *feedback* of all the experience gained, to provide a starting point for further study.

2. Nothing in education is ever entirely new and this is as true of curriculum development as of anything else. Teachers working on their own or in groups have always been setting themselves new objectives, devising new procedures and improving their methods in the light of experience. Training courses and conferences of many kinds organised by local education authorities, H.M. Inspectors, institutes of education, and teachers' and subject associations have always provided opportunities for teachers to re-examine their work.

3. The Council's most important role is to help to promote and guide this cooperative process of curriculum development. Experience in the U. K. and abroad has shown that organised development work can accelerate the process of continuous improvement. Moreover, the pace of intellectual, social, and economic change calls for determined action by all concerned with the educational system to ensure that the schools shall keep pace with the rate of change outside.

4. In addition to encouraging and helping local activity the Council has been associated with or initiated a limited number of development projects on a national scale, but these should be viewed as no more than one amongst a number of forms of support for local effort, and it should be remembered that national development projects, such as the Nuffield work in science, have not been based upon ideas thought out by people remote from the schools but upon ideas which have been almost entirely drawn from teachers themselves.

5. The object of such national projects is not to provide authoritative national answers to current problems but to provide a means of collating and feeding back knowledge, ideas, and materials drawn from the country as a whole and from overseas. The ideas and information which have been given to teachers are intended to be used by them in the classroom and, where they are found wholly or partially acceptable, used by them as a basis for further development work.

6. A standard national pattern is neither desirable nor necessary. The first basis on which development must rest is a keen interest on the part of teachers in curricular progress. The Council's hope is that teachers will, more and more, meet in groups to discuss curriculum problems and that local education authorities will do all that is practicable to encourage such groups, and in particular help them with the use of accommodation, apparatus, and secretarial assistance as may be necessary.

7. Secondly, the Council hopes that in as many areas as possible local education authorities, whether singly or in collaboration with neighbouring authorities, should consider ways of responding to the expressed wish of teachers to come together to conduct for themselves curriculum development in order to help them to sharpen their judgments on objectives, improve their experimental procedures, and play a full part in assessing the results of development work. It is clear that decisions by local education authorities and others on how best to make the response to teachers' needs can only be realistic if genuine consultation occurs at the earliest opportunity.

8. Thirdly, the Council hopes that the universities and colleges of education will consider how best they can increase their support for the work of the teachers and the local education authorities. It could also be of benefit to both the staff and the students of colleges of education if some participation were possible in the work of local teachers' groups. But what universities and colleges can do in support will depend upon what the local education authorities and the teachers say that they most need. In particular they should be able to place at the disposal of local groups any relevant knowledge about the particular problems with which they are concerned and to offer training facilities to teachers, particularly those who are acting as leaders of groups or centres, or they can undertake studies to provide starting points for local work.

9. At certain universities the Council will commission national projects. Work of this kind would not be permanently allocated to any one university: it would be a matter of enlarging, for the duration of any particular commission, the normal staffing and other resources. It is not, however, envisaged that work of this kind should be commissioned exclusively from universities. National projects might also be undertaken by colleges of education, local education authorities, teachers' associations, examining boards, or, in the fields of research and assessment, by the National Foundation for Educational Research.

10. When such bodies become responsible for a national project, they will need to work in close liaison with local centres for curriculum development and these latter cannot help but benefit from such cooperation. Local centres, however, may not wish to be limited in their work to the subject of any specific national project. Their structure and programmes should be devised by the cooperative decisions of the teachers and local education authorities on a local basis.

*   *   *   *   *   *   *

Coordination

26. No local centre can expect to be self-sufficient over the whole field of curriculum development. It will need to draw support from many different sources, but particularly from the local education authorities and the universities. And this support will need to be supplied in a coordinated way, often across administrative boundaries. Arrangements for such coordination are of course a matter for local discussion and decision. Some large local education authorities will no doubt be able to supply all that is needed, making use of long-established traditions of cooperation with the universities and the colleges of education. Others, and particularly the smaller local authority areas, are already sharing, or planning to share, their resources with their neighbours and with the colleges and universities in their part of the country. And in

some cases, a university is being invited to play the part of coordinator. But whatever arrangements best suit local circumstances and traditions, the need for some measure of coordination is clear and urgent; what is important is that the arrangements made should be acceptable to all the main partners in the operation.

Conclusion

27. There are two basic principles on which, in the Council's view, progress on curriculum development should be built: first, that the motive power should come primarily from local groups of teachers accessible one to another; second, that there should be effective and close collaboration between teachers and all those who are able to offer cooperation. There is no hierarchy of initiative or control. The cooperative effort of each interest needs to be involved in equal partnership, and all parties should be ready to give or to seek support.

A FIELD STUDY FROM A BEGINNING TEACHER CENTRE: FIRST YEAR, 1969

The British Schools Council

> The Centre's first task will always be to be able to stimulate and draw together local initiative.[1]

It was in 1966 that the city education authority was accepted as a trial area for the second phase of the Nuffield Primary Mathematics Project. One of the conditions for acceptance was that it should provide premises for local courses, so two rooms were found for a study group in a primary school on a new housing estate. The deputy headmaster, a mathematician, provided "crash" courses for teachers from both primary and secondary schools. The idea was to get as many teachers, as well as representatives from the local college of education, involved as quickly as possible. The interesting point about these crash courses was that part took place in school-time and part after school. Neither the local education authority nor the teachers seemed to feel that this was making unusual demands, and this happy cooperation enabled 80 teachers to complete the course in one term.

Such was the success that the local education committee, at the instigation of the chief education officer, agreed to release the leader of the project from part of his normal duties to hold two further courses in school-time. When these were completed, the teachers concerned felt that they would like to continue with a follow-up in their own time, some asking the leader if he could arrange for general meetings on mathematical subjects, some for an infant teacher "study" group. The leader agreed that he would do this as secretary of a committee of elected teachers, and each school was asked to nominate members. The membership was four from infant and junior, three from secondary modern, and one from secondary grammar. The chief education officer, whose cooperation was sought, sent a representative from his staff.

It was clear that the local teachers felt a need to come together to widen their experience and share ideas, not only in "in-service" training, but also in the wider area of curriculum reform. It was clear also that, such was the interest, they would be prepared to spend some of their own time on this. This initiative, and the interest and cooperation of the chief education officer, were the most important factors in influencing the education committee to take two major steps. The first was to consider the appointment of an adviser to schools, which it had not had before, part of whose duties would be to organise in-service training, to help the new teacher committee with its projects, and to develop curriculum study within the city. In May 1967, the advisor took up his post, not as a teacher-warden, but as an "Education Office" man, truly advisory, and in no way a director of policy, which remained firmly in the hands of the teacher committee.

The second major step was the finding of new premises in the centre of the city. The policy of slum clearance and the trek to the new housing estates left empty an old primary school. It looks Victorian, grimy, and rather grim from the outside, but inside it is imaginatively furnished, and the atmosphere is relaxed and friendly. The education authority allocated £750 for improvements, and the accommodation consists of a maths/science workshop, a lounge, and a small hall and stage. There is also a kitchen and a small office, which houses the small library and the beginnings of a film library. There is room for expansion, as more of the rest of the building could be taken over from its present occupant, a college of further education. A part-time assistant was appointed, and she acts as booking officer and is generally in charge of the building.

Long before its "Grand Opening" in November 1967, the Education Centre, as it is now called, had begun to function as an important factor in the life of the city's schools.

> The whole concept of a teacher's job is getting more and more complex . . . and the more complex it gets, it will be more and more necessary to mobilise the expertise of the teachers.[2]

The job of trying to bring into circulation the expertise of the teachers in the city has been marked by very close cooperation between the local authority and the Teachers' Committee. The policy is very practical and aims at getting as many people interested as possible. Each term every teacher in the authority's area is given a booklet which gives a fairly full account of "what's on," and the chief education officer operates a series of reminders in his own bulletin to schools.

Perhaps more important than this policy of communication is the policy of consultation. There are two points of interest here. First, the teachers are asked to suggest the programme of activities.

> The Committee is anxious to know the type of course you desire.
> Suggestions should be forwarded to the Secretary . . .

says the booklet, and the Committee do all they can to give the teachers what they feel they need.

The second point is that the Committee have taken the trouble to find out, by means of a questionnaire, the most suitable times of meetings for the majority of teachers. Often the question of meeting times seems to present problems in teacher centres. In this case the difficulty seems to have resolved itself in an emerging pattern of in-service training and other meetings quite late in the evening. The important point here would seem to be the initial consultation. Nor is it necessary to be part of an organised "course" or "meeting" to use the Centre. In the same booklet we read:

> Any group of teachers may use the building in and out of school-
> time, for projects and meetings.

All you have to do is book ahead . . .

* * * * * * *

The Centre Committee elected for one year is hoping to extend its work still more in the future, and it has already met this June to plan a year ahead instead of one term ahead as this year. This move is part of a deliberate policy to make sure that headteachers can plan timetables, and their own school organisation, to fit easily into the work of the centre. This, of course, means the more formal timetable, but it is made clear that there will always be time and space for the ad-hoc groups and working parties which come together naturally to meet the needs of the teachers.

Besides the regular in-service training, the exhibition, and the local curriculum development, the centre is linked with one of the Schools Council's Humanities Projects through two of the city's secondary schools. There is also the prospect of it being used as a local resource centre for the same project.

Next session will see an even stronger link with the local college of education, when groups of students will use classes in all the local secondary schools for six afternoons over six weeks in a team-teaching experiment. This should provide a new and interesting basis for discussion between the college of education and the teachers.

In the near future the secondary teachers can attend a series of weekly discussion groups concerned with the city's plan for reorganisation of secondary education, led by guest headteachers from a wide variety of reorganised schools.

There will also be two changes in the organisation and management. Firstly, the Committee has widened its membership to include a teacher from the local college of further education, so that every kind of educational force is now joined and has an interest in the Centre, which, incidentally, is used by teachers from local private schools as well.

Secondly, the local education authority has recognised that the volume of work has increased and will be increasing. A teacher/warden dividing her time between a secondary school as an assistant mistress and the Education Centre, and acting as secretary to the Committee and Warden of the premises and equipment, has been appointed. There is no doubt that she will be expected to include the fostering of curriculum development as part of her duties.

The former secretary took over as chairman of the management committee, and said:

> We would like it to remain a teachers' centre. If the spirit of the early pioneering work continues, the city's teachers will have a programme in the Education Centre which gives them what they think they need.

Notes

1. Schools Council Working Paper No. 10, *Curriculum Development: Teachers' Groups and Centres* (London: Her Majesty's Stationery Office, 1967).

2. Edward Britton, in an interview reported in the *Times Educational Supplement.*

GRASSROOTS DEVELOPMENT

The British Schools Council (*Foundation Stones, 1966–1968*)

The following is an example of work being encouraged by the local curriculum development committees in working groups meeting during and after school hours.

The teachers are responsible for compiling a report on their work. This, together with work produced by the pupils, is then considered by all the teachers in the schools and at meetings of the local committee. The accounts are pieced together from the reports and from conversations with the teachers and pupils.

An Experiment in a Local Survey

During 1966-67, a curriculum study group was formed, attended by teachers from the seven secondary schools in the area. As a result of the discussions it was decided to set up a subcommittee to carry out some experimental work: seven teachers, one from each of the schools, met together each Wednesday afternoon during the autumn term of 1967.

The subcommittee was given three instructions: (1) study the teaching around one topic, "A Street"; (2) involve all subjects, but with emphasis on the humanities; (3) aim the work at the lowest ability group in the third year.

It was left to make its own decisions with regard to the organisation and material to be used but was requested to examine in particular: methods of presentation; organisation of groups; contributions of staff; methods of study; and sources of information.

It was intended that the members of the subcommittee would try out the material with pupils in their own schools, only meeting together to decide upon material and to discuss results. Early on, however, they decided to work as a team and to teach together in one of the schools.

The school selected was a small church school in an industrial township which is the centre of the area. The 42 pupils were in the lower end of the third year grading. Of the pupils, 22 travelled by coach to school each day from an overspill estate of a nearby city and 15 were living "in care" at a local children's home. They were friendly, anxious to help, but not inclined to work of an academic nature.

It was anticipated that three weeks would be spent preparing the work, three weeks trying it out, and the rest of the term compiling a report. In fact six weeks were spent in planning the work, four working with the pupils, and four preparing an exhibition of work and the first draft of the report.

Six planning meetings were held:

September 6   Chairman and secretary elected. General discussion on the topic resulted in (a) listing of the various subjects for study in the topic and compiling a cross-reference grid to illustrate the different aspects from which they could be examined; (b) a decision to teach as a team; and (c) the selection of the school.

September 13   Main aims discussed and laid down. Two overall points would arise for evaluation at the end of the work: (a) the topic (local environment) and (b) the method (teaching as a team) in organising integrated courses which will have the maximum interest for and impact upon the pupils.

The north end of the High Street was selected for study.

September 20   Discussion on availability of material from different sources, after which the group went into the High Street to study what was actually there and to find out what information was most likely to be required. On return the best method of approach was discussed. It was decided to divide the street into four physical divisions and also to look at three other general aspects—traffic, services, and shops. Each member would be responsible for work in one of the seven topics and for the group of pupils which would work on that topic.

For recording purposes each group should have a board to display the results of its work with the intention of transporting them for exhibition in other schools.

September 27   Sources of reference were brought and discussed, and a further look was taken at the High Street, this time with each member's own topic mainly in view. Discussion later took place on necessary maps and other equipment, and on the method to be used in forming the groups. A letter was written to local residents.

October 4
Acting on a suggestion offered by the Curriculum Study Group, an article was written for local newspapers. Final form of introductory talk to pupils was settled.

October 11
This was a working session for individual members to prepare material and methods for their own groups. The subcommittee was finally able to confirm that equipment ordered was available and that the work with the pupils could begin on October 18.

For the next four Wednesday afternoons the team worked with the 42 pupils on the topic.

From the beginning the pupils were made to feel that they were "the experts" who could advise the teachers on what should be found out about the street and suggest how it could be done. Apart from the introductory "lesson," the stimulus came from visits and discussion. Actually a better word than "discussion" would be "talk." The pupils talked about what they saw and heard; they talked about what it meant, the problems revealed, and how this could be presented.

The materials and methods encouraged talk in the groups. Slides, photographs, and maps were used to pinpoint details of the street; observation prompted comments. Questionnaires were framed to guide the actual visits. Portable tape recorders (half a dozen of these were provided by the authority) were used for interviews with the residents and officials. Pupils took photographs or made sketches. These provided the basis for the discussion out of which came the written reports, graphs, maps, models, and the panoramic photograph that make up the exhibition.

The teachers were very critical of what had been achieved. The two main weaknesses they reported were that they had been too ambitious in what was attempted, and that they did not pay sufficient attention to the attitudes, skills and background of the pupils. They started from what *they thought* were the needs of the pupils, instead of from where the pupils actually were in standard of skill.

There were some other anxieties, in particular the reluctance of the pupils to record in a written form, "which was perhaps a recognition, based on their own experience, that this was something on which they could be too easily criticised." Some were worried that the group organisation produced too much fragmentation: the pupils saw only part and not the whole of the enquiry. But all these weaknesses were related to the lack of time: only four afternoons were spent on the topic and there was "so much more to be done."

Nevertheless the team was encouraged by the results of the work. All who saw the pupils at work during the four afternoons were impressed with their keenness. There was a degree of mental activity and an eagerness in discussion that had not been shown before. Along with this went a growth in self-confidence and the beginning of independent judgment. On the whole, the teachers were impressed with the quality of the work produced: "it was very noticeable that the pupils wanted to improve the quality of the work where they recognised that they could, a very significant feature." This increased interest in work, a recognition that it is possible to have a friendly working relationship with "sir," and greater involvement in the work (these are features commented on by the headmaster of the school). They are revealed in the comments of the teacher and the pupils:

> Children complained of haste at this point.

> On return to the school, these questions were discussed and many of the pupils' ideas seemed suitable answers, and it was agreed to adopt these.

> Quantity and quality of work was lower than expected but children were more critical than I.

> Finished fourth afternoon with none of the work completed properly (their opinion) and they volunteered to come along at a later time to finish off and help prepare for exhibition.

The pupils' evaluation was very favourable:

> More was learnt than would have been done in an *ordinary* classroom lesson because of contact with people who gave explanations and reasons. Books only contain facts and are sometimes difficult to read, but it is very much easier to remember what you have asked and found out yourself.

> Meeting people was very interesting and they were more helpful than expected. People in the street now seem to be different than as formerly viewed. It is easier to remember manners and politeness when realising how they helped us.

> Tried to work neater, because of exhibition. Teachers not using red pencil made us realise our best was needed.

And a final suggestion:

To have more of this kind of work in school time for lots of
different lessons.

The subcommittee also recommended that this line of approach was worth
pursuing further; the teachers had gained by working as a team. They felt that
it would be possible to achieve good results with a less favourable staff-pupil
ratio.

Another group of teachers has now been set up to take the work a stage
further, and to prepare a topic to be tackled by a team of teachers working
with a more normal staff-pupil ratio.

Potential and Problems

Within the best of the development committees, two features are common:
the first, an almost fierce sense of independence—assistance is welcome, but
the committee *will* decide what is to be done; the second, the enthusiasm of
the active members. There is a realistic appreciation of difficulties—shortage
of staff, money, and facilities—but also a feeling that the activities begun are
professionally worthwhile.

Involvement of teachers. The report of one of the humanities groups
reveals *what teachers see* of value in the work.

They welcomed the experience of working together on a teaching approach
which they tried out in the classroom. Their task was not to consider "important, high-level problems not closely related to us; we started from an isolated
action arising from *our* needs." This was why they felt so involved.

They appreciated that such cooperation broke down barriers. A young
geography teacher was "amazed at the fantastic interchange of ideas between
myself and this ability level of pupils" and that the teacher could become so
approachable to the pupils. A mathematics teacher was grateful for the opportunity to think "about teaching children and not teaching a subject." A headmaster was impressed with the cooperation which broke the barriers between
the seven schools—not only did they pool teachers and equipment, but they
also shared the experience of the work.

In all the groups there is a recognition of a breaking down of barriers:
between teacher and pupil, between schools, and between teachers.

For one headmaster the greatest value of the work was that it "brought to
my conscious notice teachers not noticed before in my 16 years of service in
the area."

A teacher in another group echoed this, welcoming: "This opportunity to meet staff from other secondary schools, non-selective and grammar, and the chance to liaise with the primary schools."

A colleague emphasised the value to him, personally: "The value to me is purely selfish: it is associated with the change in my own attitude as a result of committee meetings."

"Met people never met before . . . not afraid to discuss problems," such a comment pinpoints the factors aiding change. Out of such meetings comes the realisation that difficulties thought to be unique, or a particular weakness of the individual teacher, are faced by many colleagues. This breeds the confidence to identify and to tackle the problems standing in the way of a more relevant curriculum for our pupils—and such a result can hardly be called "purely selfish."

Few in the local committees would claim that what is being done is new, either in the experimental courses or in the surveys; they recognise that most have been attempted many times before and in many schools. What is significantly new is the attempt through the local committees to systematise the experience at both school and area level, and as a result to identify what must and what can be changed. To do this, the teachers must deal with many problems to make the work more efficient.

What are the administrative and organisational measures needed to create effective experimental courses? How are they to record and assess what has been done? How can the active minority best communicate ideas and results to the majority? The programmes arranged by local development committees constantly raise these problems, but they must also answer the needs of the teachers in the schools *as the teachers see them.* Many examples were quoted, such as a modern languages group. A handful of eight or nine teachers met to discuss general objectives, but when work began on a syllabus to meet a suggested middle school reorganisation, attendance shot up to 40.

This is not to argue that teachers are not interested in fundamental educational aims, but that they believe such consideration is more fruitful when it is based on conclusions drawn from an attempt to answer a practical problem. Such an insistence means that theory must relate to practice and not become empty speculation; it certainly produces discussion and argument amongst teachers who feel involved in the work.

Involvement of schools. "These ideas whilst they are very good must be fitted into the framework of school. I can understand why heads can be dubious about them." This remark by a grammar school teacher expresses the legitimate concern of schools, and the biggest organisational problem facing the committees. To do the work, teachers need time and energy; this means that a commitment to the local committees must be written into the time-table. In the most active development committees, schools are timetabling staff to be released for the working groups, albeit on a limited scale and at a great expense of ingenuity. The gain in staffroom atmosphere is enormous; the work is an integral part of a professional responsibility, not done at the expense of colleagues "covering" classes.

If development work is to be concerned with pupils of the whole range of age and ability, and not just the least able (who are thought suitable for "experiment" because there are no examination demands on their timetable), then schools must be prepared to pay a price in terms of added demands. The programmes of some committees are making greater demands on schools, particularly to enable wider contacts to be made.

Inter-school visits, secondary and primary, are seen as potentially the biggest breakthrough, for they provide the experience that is most productive of change. Contact with primary schools is valued by the secondary teachers who realise that they cannot fashion a five-year secondary course without basing it upon the six years of education that have gone before. Two major difficulties are seen: firstly, the traditional reluctance of teachers to share problems in the classroom situation; secondly, resentment in staffrooms unless the visits can be timetabled as an integral part of the work.

As the work of the local development committees increases, so links will be forged that will inevitably make more demands on the teachers, and therefore on the schools. Two committees already have representatives on the committees from colleges of education and welcome "a more positive dialogue with the college." The proposal for a piece of research recognised and supervised by the university, but carried out as a cooperative venture by the local committee, is a significant and encouraging development. Other committees have representatives from the careers advisory and youth services; one committee has invited training officers to help in a study of careers teaching.

The composition and work of the committees are extending, and in so doing teachers are taking on more responsibilities. Nevertheless it is the work and its needs that determine the organisational form of the local curriculum development group, not the desire to impress with an important looking committee on paper. Where this is recognised, then the involvement not just of individual teachers but also of the schools can be asked for and obtained.

Conditions of growth. An active interest by the head teachers is the prime requirement if committee talk is to be translated into classroom experiments. Without this, the groups can very easily become frustrated and moribund.

Two other conditions appear necessary if development committees are not to degenerate into dwindling talking shops. After the initial lead by head-teachers the committee must have a balance of heads, senior and experienced staff, and younger teachers. The second is for the committee to keep its "ear to the ground," so that its programme is allowing teachers to work on prob-lems they see as relevant.

One committee sponsored a working group in mathematics and science. It laid down terms of reference, which is a welcome procedure—working groups appreciate some guidance and opportunities to report on the stages of the work—an attitude of "we've given you the opportunity, now you do some-thing" can be inhibiting. However this group became composed of mathematics teachers who found the terms of reference leading them away from their main concern. The working group nearly foundered before the committee became aware of the situation and altered the terms of reference.

Local committees must guard against a bureaucratic organisation. It is a good thing for committee members to be closely involved in development work, either as members of working groups or attending meetings when the work is reviewed. The local development committees exist to promote work that helps the teacher, not the other way about.

Such close contact helps to solve the problem of deciding which young teachers can make the best contribution on the committees. They practically select themselves by their enthusiastic involvement in the development work.

Role of the headteacher. All that has been said so far on the work of the local committees underlines the role of the headteacher. For curriculum de-velopment at local level to become part of the professional work of the teacher means it must have a fairly rapid effect upon what goes on in the classroom. Within each school it will be the headteacher more than anyone else who will determine whether there is a favourable climate of opinion; cer-tainly it will be the headteacher who will determine whether the organisa-tional arrangements encourage or discourage participation in the work by members of staff.

To build up a fund of experience, both of our successes and our failures, requires schools (and this means teachers) with the opportunity to work to-gether. Headteachers are only too aware of the many demands on staff time and the constant juggling to cover staff unavoidably away. Nevertheless, ade-quate time has to be found so that teachers can recognise the professional importance of the work and be able to take part in experiments.

Ingenuity and a deal of hard work is called for to make curriculum development a built-in feature of the school organisation. Above all, it requires from headteachers a commitment to local curriculum development, seen as a necessary and inescapable part of their professional responsibilities. This is essential if local committees are to flourish and if their centres are to be workshops for creative responses—not the monuments of an experiment that failed.

A REPORT ON THREE NATIONAL CONFERENCES, 1970
The British Schools Council

Foreword

One of the more significant movements in education in recent years has been the development of teacher centres. As with most important movements, the origins can be traced back a long way. Some teacher centres came into existence soon after the passing of the 1944 Education Act. A little research would almost certainly reveal activities as far back as the early 1920's that had some of the characteristics of teacher centres today.

But although the origins of teacher centres go back a long way, the recent development started in 1965 with the publication of Schools Council Working Paper 2, *Raising the School Leaving Age: A Co-operative Programme of Research and Development* (H.M.S.O.). The subsequent growth has been rapid. At the time of the conferences described in this pamphlet the Schools Council listed no fewer than 308 centres, and the list was known to be incomplete.

Such rapid growth indicates that the centres are meeting a widely felt need. It is difficult, however, to define that need exactly. Working Paper 2 argued that teacher centres should be set up to make the Council's working papers, projects, and other activities the focal points for local discussion and local curriculum development. This was undoubtedly a valid proposal, but it would be idle to pretend that the discussion of Schools Council activities constitutes a significant proportion of the work of the majority of the centres. The need they are meeting is clearly more fundamental.

As yet the development is too recent for anyone to know in detail what the centres are doing or exactly what is the motivation for their growth. They vary from area to area, and it is right that they should, for different areas have differing needs, and different organizations evolve to meet those differing needs. Nevertheless a large element in the motivation has been a growing consciousness of the rapid changes that have been taking place inside the schools. There is growing realization that the old method of allowing new ideas to percolate slowly through the education system is no longer adequate. The process has often taken a long time, and it no longer meets present needs.

It is a truism that we live in an age of change. The vast and far-reaching

131

changes in modern technology are obvious to everyone. But changes are taking place in the schools, which, though less obvious, are no less far-reaching. Teacher centres are a response to these changes.

The Schools Council decided that it would be helpful at the present stage of development to find out what is happening, and to this end they arranged three short residential conferences for teachers, administrators, and others connected with the teacher centre movement. There was no attempt to provide tightly structured conferences, nor any special attempt to provide a series of lectures to tell the members of the conferences what they ought to be doing. Teacher centres have not yet reached the stage where anyone can be dogmatic about them. The method was to bring the members of the conferences together and encourage them to talk about what they were doing. As a result of their talking a much clearer picture emerged.

By publishing an account of these conferences the Schools Council hopes that knowledge of some of the things that were said will be made more widely available and will prove helpful to those who are themselves engaged in the task of creating or running a centre in their own area. Teacher centres have the potential to become an important influence in the education of the future. The publication of this pamphlet is a further step towards the realization of this potential. —*E. L. Britton*

I. A Note on Background

Introduction. This is a report of three conferences, or nine days of talk and argument by 300 people. It is not a verbatim but a selective account that concentrates on the major points of agreement and disagreement.

Many of those who participated in the conferences may strongly disagree with much that is written; the aim has been to capture the clash of opinion that took place, in the hope that readers will want to continue the arguments. The report is not intended as an authoritative statement of what should be done; it contains few, if any, answers. If it is of use as a basis for discussion in local centres, then it will have more than served its purpose.

The position in 1968. Between July and September 1968, local education authorities replied to a Schools Council questionnaire on teacher centres. Two points must be made. Firstly there are considerably more local development groups than shown by a list of centres; they are by no means all covered in the authorities' returns. Secondly the picture is constantly changing; there are by now considerably more centres in existence than were revealed in the

1968 return. However, the return did give a picture of the situation shortly before the three conferences were held and also some indication of the pace of development in this field.

A total of 308 local centres was listed. Of these, 113 were based in school buildings but had the use of at least one room put aside for centre work; the vast majority of these were attached to or part of primary schools. Eighty-nine of the centres were exclusively or almost exclusively concerned with work in Nuffield or Schools Council projects in mathematics, science, and modern languages; most of this work was in the primary field.

Few centres had been purpose-built: only five such were listed. The majority, 175, were in accommodations that had been adapted and were now specifically allocated for no other function than that of a local centre. Such accommodations included old schools that had been taken over completely, parts of buildings set aside as a centre, and prefabricated annexes set up on school sites; a few authorities had also adapted very comfortable and spacious houses. There were 31 centres sharing accommodations, most of these being in further education establishments and a few in colleges of education.

Hardly any centres had fewer than two rooms allocated—a comfortable lounge or discussion room and a workshop, with some facilities for making tea. The lounge and the workshop made up the core of the centre: other accommodation was an extra. Thirty-eight centres had a science laboratory as well as a workshop, but only 19 had an audiovisual aids room, and of these 11 were in the London area. Catering arrangements varied greatly: 71 had kitchens (one of which was described as a cafeteria to cater for upwards of 70), the rest had tea-making facilities that ranged from a small tea-bar in the lounge to the use of an electric kettle. Only 57 mentioned the provision of an office, which must mean that some wardens had to be content with a briefcase and the dining-room table at home.

Control of the centres was, in the main, firmly in the hands of teachers. On management committees they outnumbered local education authority officials and education committee representatives in the ratio of five to two. In 45 centres there were no management committees, but most of these were single-subject centres which came directly under the control of local education authority advisers.

Apart from the 89 subject centres already referred to, the others had developed a wide range of activities. The usual programme was a combination of work related to national projects, courses arranged by local education authority advisers, and curriculum study-groups established by teachers. Only in a minority of centres was it clear from the returns that study-groups had developed to the stage of systematic local curriculum development. The activities involved primary and secondary teachers, with many centres encouraging overlapping programmes.

The majority of the centres relied upon the voluntary leadership of teachers with some part-time paid assistance: there were 101 part-time appointments either as secretary, warden, leader or coordinator. However, there were already 63 full-time wardens, and many local education authorities indicated that an appointment was either pending or being seriously considered. Three-quarters of the staff at centres were either practising or former teachers; 41 came from outside the teaching profession, but only one of these was a full-time appointment—the rest of the 41 were clearly part-time clerical appointments to assist teachers in the role of honorary secretaries.

What was clear from the returns was that the suggestions in the working papers corresponded to the reality of the situation. The principle of school-based work organized through local groups had been found to be feasible, but the manner in which such work was carried out displayed the variety of local circumstances.

The purpose of the conferences. This then was the background to the three conferences held in 1969. They brought together close on 300 people, all concerned with teacher centres throughout England and Wales but with very different kinds and length of experience. For three days at each conference members worked together in study-groups, listened to speakers with some relevant experience, and discussed the factors that helped or hindered local curriculum development.

As was to be expected, a number of practical difficulties received a good airing: the ever-present problem of money and the demands on teachers' time. But so, too, did some of the key issues raised in the working papers: the organization of work in the centres and their role in relation to curriculum change.

The conferences were a pooling of experience in the first stages of local curriculum development. From it teachers and authorities can draw assistance for future plans. The Council sought help in planning the ways in which it could give most effective support to those engaged in the work of local centres.

II. Variety and Agreement

Kinds and amounts of experience. Not all members of the conference came with the same amount of experience or for the same purpose. Some were from authorities or centres with a number of years of experience of the work of teacher groups; some were from areas anxious to discover the best ways of setting up centres that were still only a twinkle in the eyes of their chief education officer. There were those—not many, it is true—who came with what they felt were all the answers: it is hoped they returned sadder but wiser men. There were others who came more humbly, looking for *the* answers to all their questions: it is hoped they too returned disillusioned yet happier men. Whatever they did or did not gain they owed to their fellow conference members. It was the collective experience that shaped and informed the proceedings.

Representatives were chosen by the local education authorities from those who had definite responsibilities connected with teacher centres. They were administrators (including a small number of chief education officers and members of education committees), local inspectors and advisers, centre wardens, and teachers—in the main headteachers. The teachers who attended were either chairmen or secretaries of development groups or management committees. The teachers and wardens were outnumbered by the LEA's' administrators and advisers in the ratio of three to five. The reason for this was that authorities still considering the establishment of centres, or where the formation of local groups was lagging, sent administrative officers or advisers who had been given responsibility to frame proposals for development work. They came to listen and to learn from the experience of others.

The composition of study-groups reflected this variety in stages of development and forms of organization. An example of one group of 13 members will illustrate this. The chairman was a chief inspector from a city with three large centres, one acting as a focal point of an ambitious regional curriculum development project. There was a leader from a centre engaged in that project and an organizer from a small borough associated with the project but as yet with no centre. A centre leader and an education officer came from two counties with centres having full-time wardens. A teacher-leader and an education officer represented two counties whose centres have part-time leaders. There were three primary school headmasters from three small counties with centres run by the voluntary work of teachers. The group was completed by three education officers from two counties and a county borough proposing or hoping to establish centres. The groups were deliberately "unstreamed," in the hope that variation in circumstances and experience would contribute a more balanced picture of the situation.

Those participants who came looking for a Schools Council book of rules on centres and local development groups were quickly disillusioned. The view of the majority was rapidly established that the form taken by groups and centres and the activity developed were very much the product of local conditions and needs. Centres took root and grew where attention was given to the local circumstances. To ignore these circumstances, to seek to impose a model based upon theory unrelated to what local people saw as their needs, carried the danger of inhibiting a natural process of development. There was also felt to be a positive danger in attempting to force the pace of a development that should take its start and momentum from its own educational environment.

Therefore, underlying all conference discussions was a fear of attempts to find a rigid pattern either of organization or of work. Certainly any attempt to find a pattern in the experience represented at the conference would be a formidable task. As has already been indicated, centres ranged from one room in a building to large resources centres with up to £30,000 spent on their adaptation. A small number served as few as 22 teachers, whilst others as many as 8,000; some served only 20 schools, others as many as 50 secondary and 120 primary schools. The terminology of leadership indicated the full variety: directors of educational development centres, wardens, centre leaders, teachers-in-charge, coordinators, teacher-advisers, consultant teachers, administrative officers, development assistants—or simply secretaries.

From a diversity of backgrounds members talked and argued out of their own particular experience, successes, failures, frustrations, and downright prejudices. Yet, surprisingly, out of it all came agreement on certain common factors in local development work.

The basic principle. What was stressed above all, over and over again, has already been mentioned: that the main concern of centres was with development work that was local. This was their primary function: to make possible a review of existing curricula by groups of teachers and to encourage attempts by them to bring about changes. The other functions mentioned in the working papers—those of acting as a base for national projects and as a centre for the steadily increasing amount of in-service training required—were also important, but they did not of themselves constitute a reason for the establishment of a teacher centre for curriculum development.

Many speakers stressed that too many areas and too many schools were, alas, still waiting for the answers to curriculum problems to come from on high. National development projects aroused unreasonable hopes, despite all the efforts of project directors to explain the limitations of what was being attempted. When materials and approaches failed to answer all the problems in the subject area of a particular school or group of pupils, then "they" were criticized as being out of touch with reality.

Speakers argued that all teachers, including headteachers, must become more expert in achieving curriculum change in the schools. This meant that they must build up a stock of experience, for only in that way would they be able to make informed judgments on suggestions from national projects or higher education establishments. Only centres that were helping in this process were playing an adequate role.

This then was the basic principle on which agreement was reached—that the rationale of a teacher centre was local curriculum development work. Yet it was from discussion of how to implement this basic principle that most of the arguments and disagreements stemmed, and these will be recounted later.

Establishment and accommodation. The procedure adopted to establish centres varied according to the differing arrangements for local education authority/teacher consultation. Where some formal arrangement had obtained for some time, the official consultative committee, largely composed of representatives of teacher organizations, took a major part in the first steps to set up a centre. Where centres had been successfully established in this way it was agreed that the local education authorities' role had been largely one of giving tactful, sympathetic advice.

As money had to be obtained from education committees, it was obviously necessary that the local education authority should be very closely involved in the early stages of planning. An education officer or adviser was often the person best equipped to prepare the case to go before the education committee. Yet it needed to be made clear that the dominant role in the running of the centre would be that of the teachers.

Those with experience of fairly successful centres were most insistent that from the beginning it was essential to involve teachers and to see that they were in a majority upon any steering committee. Teacher organizations had much to offer at this stage, both in terms of people with wide experience of committee work and in well-established lines of communication with members; but it was also worthwhile inviting the views of subject associations and school staffs and informing schools directly through letters and bulletins to staff-rooms. It was essential for teachers to get the feeling that this was a centre for them and that its organization would reflect their views.

Arrangements for administering the centres again varied widely, but a general pattern did seem to be appearing, although with a wide degree of local modification. Generally it was felt that the day-to-day running of the centre needed a small management committee to advise or direct the warden. In size of membership this might range from six to eighteen; where it was bigger, some form of executive committee had already been set up or was taking shape. At least one representative of the local education authority was on the committee; his advice, particularly on requests for financial assistance, was invaluable and saved precious time. Subcommittees were appointed to look after particular aspects of the work, but the consensus was that they should not be set up until demands and needs clearly made them necessary.

Apart from the need for the management committee, the experience of many centres indicated the need for two other organizational procedures. The first was a larger meeting of all those interested in the work of the centre, partly to spread news of developments but even more to ensure the widest participation and degree of democratic control. Some centres had representative councils that met about once a term, membership being drawn directly from schools and other educational institutions. Other centres achieved the same ends less formally, preferring to hold open meetings to which the reports of the management committee and the various working groups were presented. The second procedure was to ensure that the various study or working groups were represented in central discussions. With some centres this had been achieved by forming curriculum development committees, divided into areas such as primary or secondary, and these were directly concerned with the programme of development work. Others had chosen to co-opt group leaders on to the management or subcommittees or, less formally, simply to ensure that the management committee held regular review sessions with study-groups.

Experienced members of management committees realized that it was important to avoid a proliferation of committee work; but at the same time they believed that teachers, and especially users of the centre, must feel that the management was an open, democratic system and not the preserve of any clique.

The same pragmatic approach was recommended to the question of accommodation and equipment. There were three basic demands upon accommodation: comfortable surroundings for discussion; a workshop with room enough to leave work or to store it easily; and facilities to provide a cup of tea. More was desirable, but this depended upon what could be provided and even more upon what could be of use at a particular stage of development. There was evidence of some ambitiously large establishments that had had to justify themselves in terms of activity; the extent of the consequent demands made upon teachers' time produced an antagonism which had made the growth of development work more difficult.

Certain items of equipment must clearly be provided by the local education authorities and the management committee. There must be enough comfortable chairs for reasonably large discussion groups, work tables, shelving and storage racks in the workroom, along with facilities to display work and books. Centres should have their own supply of crockery; vending machines and paper cups had not proved a worthwhile investment in promoting the right social atmosphere. Centres would require the use of a typewriter, a duplicator, projectors, and a tape recorder; whether these would be stored at the centre or easily accessible nearby depended on how much they would be used.

Advice was given not to order beyond the obvious minimum of equipment; it was easy for the individual enthusiast to recommend a piece of equipment which then lay unused. Much the best policy was for a local education authority to make available to the centre committee a sum of money that could be used to buy the things needed as demand arose. This step in itself reinforced teacher involvement in, and control of, the affairs of the centre. There could be no independence without the financial means to implement decisions.

Attracting the customers. Once again, in discussing how teachers were to be made aware of the centre and how their support had been won, those with experience stressed that this was largely a matter of local circumstances. From the outset it must be made clear that the centre aimed to provide what teachers in the area wanted, and this meant that their opinion had to be canvassed. It was often a slow business and at times disappointing to the enthusiasts involved, but it was an essential preliminary stage.

Naturally, the committee or the warden needed to show as early as possible that the centre was a going concern. The early programmes would be likely to rely heavily on what some members called "the bread and butter" of courses. Work in connexion with national projects, such as primary mathematics, provided an introduction to the centre for many teachers and a source of interest to many not actually involved in the project itself. The local inspectors and advisers, from their knowledge of local needs, could suggest and organize programmes of courses, those of a workshop variety being preferable to straight lectures.

Activities of this kind could stimulate interest and increase the use of the centre by teachers. Nevertheless, the aim was for more of the activity to take the form of local study-groups and working parties pursuing work determined by the teachers themselves. This stage, once reached, affected the rest of the programme: the courses were arranged to satisfy particular needs for information or training encountered by the teachers in their groups. One lesson had already been learnt by centres. When launching study or working groups, it was essential to limit the aim and demands on time. What was attempted had to be capable of producing a tangible result, be it a report or some teaching material, within a definite period of time; if this were not so then the group was in danger of becoming a dwindling talking-shop.

This growth in activities placed greater and greater demands on communication. Centres used a variety of means: a regular newsletter to schools, items in local bulletins, invitations to individual teachers, displays at the centre, travelling exhibitions. The most efficient method was personal contact. The more successful centres all reported that their wardens and leaders spent a great deal of their time visiting teachers in the schools. At first this was in order to introduce themselves and to listen to what teachers hoped for from the centre. Later, it could involve working alongside groups of teachers trying out centre-devised materials and approaches. What this led to was the development in the schools of a core of activists who identified themselves with the work of the centre and were its best publicists.

Heads were a decisive group in ensuring the success of the centre. It was essential that some of the most influential of them should have not just a benevolent sympathy towards the work of the centre but an active commitment to it. Some must be leading members of the committee. As a group, it was they who could give the greatest practical support to the centre leader and most encouragement to teachers in their work. Their willingness to be ingenious in arranging the release of teachers for work at the centre might be the key to making a good start; without it, the frustrations of warden and committee might multiply to the point of resigned desperation.

The definition of a centre. Most members of the conferences were agreed that it was desirable for a centre to be housed in separate accommodation; if this were not possible, then at least it should be housed in a section of a building set aside for its exclusive use. The facilities offered by other institutions, particularly colleges of education or further education, were recognized; nevertheless, independence in accommodation was accepted as the desirable aim. There was in fact a fear that institutions of higher education could too easily dominate centres housed either within their buildings or relying too much on their facilities. The collaboration desired with such institutions could best be fostered by approaches from independent teacher centres.

However, a centre was not just a building—it was the hub of a wheel of activities. An analogy used was that the congregation not the building made up the church: so too with teacher centres. Many of the activities stimulated by the development groups took place outside the centre.

This belief was given practical expression when the differing needs of primary and secondary schools were considered. For the primary schools partly because of size, the most pressing need was for workshop development courses, including those associated with national projects. The teachers looked for a venue and for the special facilities required. The larger secondary schools, however, had many of the facilities needed, and sometimes it was far more convenient for meetings and development work to take place in a school. Teachers in these schools looked far more for the assistance of a centre leader than for the facilities of a particular place.

Naturally, as the scale of the work increased, so these two objectives came together in the centre, especially where the common problems of transition from primary to secondary education were considered; but the programme of work would never be wholly contained within the centre.

As the needs of teachers became known and found expression in the programme of work, so the centre developed a multipurpose use. There was a continuing programme concerned with national project work and workshop courses, but the heart of the activities became the increasing number of curriculum study-groups. These steadily pumped forth demands for opportunities for working groups and for relevant training courses. And it was this form of activity that made the greatest demands on the staff of a centre.

Clerical assistance was essential; this was emphasized over and over again. It was not possible to rely upon the leader or the voluntary help of teachers to cope with the clerical work once the scale of activities passed beyond a limited range of in-service training. Most centres had part-time clerical help for from three to five half-days; few had a full-time secretary.

There was general agreement that a full-time warden or leader was necessary, but not on when he should be appointed. Some argued strongly that the success of a centre depended upon having the right person appointed as warden from the start. Others argued equally strongly from their experience that the move from voluntary to part-time to full-time leadership must be determined by the pace of development. All agreed that it was vitally important in every case to choose the right person.

The salary inducement ranged between a Grade C and Grade E school head-of-department allowance, with a few "directors of development centres" placed on the headteachers' scale.

Such then was the area of general agreement reached by the conferences out of their collective experience. Within it there was ample room for disagreement, and arguments took place in plenty.

III. Argument and Disagreements

The role of a centre. Half-way through each conference the members were asked a question: Is a teacher centre an optional extra or an indispensable instrument of curriculum change? For a number of fairly obvious reasons everyone was prepared to agree with the second assertion; the problem was that not all interpreted the word "instrument" in the same way. The questions that should have followed were: An instrument to do what? To be used in what ways? And in whose hands? Too often these questions were either not posed or posed only in very general terms, so that not surprisingly the arguments in the groups, though often heated, tended to be muffled. Nevertheless, contentious issues did emerge—from so many discussion groups as to be clearly key issues facing local development groups and their centres. Usually they arose in the course of seeking some agreement on the lessons learnt from experience; inevitably, therefore, in this section we shall return to some of the issues considered earlier.

A mixed bag. Many of the arguments arose out of apparently minor points. They make up a very mixed bag bearing on the purpose of a centre and its relationship with schools and other bodies.

The choice of title for a centre was discussed. Many felt that the name "teacher centre" was too restrictive, both in terms of role and of those who would naturally form part of the membership—people such as advisers, college lecturers, and youth and community workers. They urged a name such as "development centre." Really what was at issue in this argument was the divergence of views on the role and functions of a centre between those who emphasized the "organized" activities and those who believed in "grass roots" development.

It was a matter of emphasis, but nevertheless in many study-groups there were two quite clear and sharply differing points of view. The "grass roots" camp saw the initiative as resting in the hands of the teacher groups: the thinking, work, and demands of these groups were of first importance, and the centre existed to encourage and facilitate this process. Therefore it was correct to lay emphasis on the "teachers" in the name. The other camp agreed, but felt (if it was not always said in so many words) that this was at best a naive and at worst a romantic view. Development by teacher groups required the support of a programme of activities, making full use of the stimulus of national projects and of proven courses of training. This meant that the assistance of advisory and college staff was an integral and indispensable part of the centre; and this should be recognized in the title.

This role of the "experts," it was argued, would become of great importance as the increasing scale of work demanded an extension of the resources offered by the centre. Some large urban local education authorities were able to provide impressive evidence of provision of, or proposals for, large, well-equipped centres. The words "resources centre" and "educational technology" dominated a large part of the discussion in some groups. There were speakers who urged the claims of colleges of further education as the homes of teacher centres in the smaller authorities, because such establishments could provide the facilities required by a resources centre.

The strongest warning of the danger of being swept off course by over-stressing the aim of a resources centre came, very fittingly, from one of our largest urban authorities. A centre could not and should not aim at providing a total advisory service, was the warning given. An over-concern with the problem of defining what was meant by a resources centre, and an even greater concern with the manifold difficulties of the equipment to be used (whether software or hardware, to use the current jargon) could make excessive and wasteful demands on the time and energy of centre wardens and leaders.

Such a concern could lead wardens away from their prime task of helping teachers to think about the curriculum. The discussion paper on educational technology added a relevant piece of advice, when it stated:

> Teachers' centres should be places in which teachers can familiarize themselves with new equipment, evaluate it, and indicate their needs.
>
> Conversely, it is equally important that educational technology, in so far as it concerns schools, should be *developed by teachers who are involved in curriculum development.* In the past audio-visual aids have tended to be ancillary pieces of equipment added on to a scheme or method of work already established. Too much attention has been given to equipment as a thing in itself. It is an essential part of curriculum thinking and of the thinking behind educational technology that the content, the method and the teaching materials should be planned and developed as one, in pursuance of the objectives which have been defined.

The centre must exist for the teachers and their schools; the teachers are not there to serve the hardware installed in the centre.

There were some conference members who, after arguing that the place for curriculum development was in the schools, went on to claim that centres were making so much demand on teachers' time as actually to weaken development work in the schools. It was agreed this might happen where the programme of activity at the centre was not determined by the needs of the teachers and schools in the locality, but it was hard to imagine centres in such a situation surviving for long. As some members pointed out, centres could do more than organize work arising out of local demands. In particular, they could protect those very schools that were most active in development work.

Such schools faced two difficulties. One was that they might be "over-visited" by the many people, including teachers from other schools, anxious to see new ideas in practice. The other could follow: a reaction and rejection of innovation if the pressure to produce evidence of success too quickly led to disappointment and failure. Centres could help by presenting evidence of innovation at the centre itself; some already did this through exhibitions and displays. Often it was found that the atmosphere of the centre could promote a more relaxed and helpful exchange of views between the teachers concerned and their colleagues examining the evidence.

Members raised problems of who should use the centres. Some were very much in favour of groups of pupils using them. One authority proposed that the centre should also be used by pupils as a homework centre, although in this case the major reason was the saving of money—an added attraction for members of the education committee. What they had in mind here was the kind of experimental activities developed by such pupil centres as Childwall, which of course exists to carry through an experiment and not as a teacher centre. The general feeling was that however valuable such experiments were with groups of pupils taken out of the normal school environment, there was a greater value to the teachers in the atmosphere created when the centres were separated from school pressures. For this reason, therefore, pupils should not use the centres.

Other members envisaged centres being places where parents were informed of and shown developments in teaching, and that this would be a piece of valuable liaison work. But, again, the majority feeling was that such liaison was performed better by individual schools. Centres were seen by some advisers as places that could give valuable support to one particular section of the teaching profession, the probationary teachers. Once again, the feeling was that whilst probationary teachers would find much of assistance and interest in centre activities, the responsibility for their supervision belonged to the schools and the local advisers and that this was not the work of the centres. In all these matters, as with the question of resources, the warning was given that centres must beware of allowing peripheral concerns to overshadow or distort their prime function.

A major problem for many centres was how to attract secondary teachers to their activities. Many reported that the vast majority of habitués were from primary schools and that this determined the emphasis in the programme of activities. Some speakers drew a distinction between the nature and needs of the two stages of education. The very nature of class teaching in primary schools forced the teacher to consider the implications of new developments for the total curriculum. The appeal of the centre, both for its retraining courses and as a place to discuss developments with colleagues, was strong. The secondary teacher, however, was more likely to be a subject specialist and therefore to have a strong tendency to think along narrower subject lines. One speaker asserted that the average secondary teacher had a guilt feeling about the total curriculum. Whatever the reason, the secondary teacher, in the opinion of many, did not recognize so easily the useful role of the centre.

A distinction was also seen between the roles of primary and secondary headteachers. In the smaller primary schools the heads exercised a direct influence upon what and how their staff taught. Therefore it was natural that they should play an active and key role in the leadership of centres. In secondary schools, steadily growing in size, heads were finding more and more of their time taken up with managerial functions. The key people in influencing what and how staff taught were the heads of departments. Some advisers and secondary headteachers argued that the heads of departments were the people to be most closely involved in centre work; what was asked from secondary heads was sympathetic support.

Where this argument was put forward in group discussions it tended to be accepted as a valid explanation, even though in later arguments on the influence of heads and the needs of teachers it was implicitly attacked. This was even more surprising in view of the aim within centres of promoting greater unity between the primary and secondary stages. It deserved closer examination, particularly for the implications it carried for the nature and organization of development work in what is assumed to be the two separate spheres of primary and secondary education.

Release of teachers. The greatest problem seen by all members was the demands of development work on the time and energy of teachers. They found it impossible to envisage any large-scale increase in such work based purely and simply on activities carried on in the centres after four o'clock. At the same time they realized there was a limit to the release of teachers for centre work, given the present resources, the demands of other commitments such as work with CSE boards, the need to cover absences of staff through illness, and school journeys and visits. Difficulty in releasing teachers was seen as the biggest barrier at present to more rapid curriculum development work.

Many suggestions were floated to improve current ad-hoc arrangements, which made a tremendous demand on the sympathy of heads and the good-will of staffs. They fell into three categories: timetable arrangements; use of replacement staff; contractual obligations.

Some members felt that new methods of learning would allow for a more efficient use of teachers' time. The method most commonly quoted was team teaching, but there was also mention of a greater part of pupils' time being spent on private learning instead of class or group teaching. If these developments were reflected in a more scientific organization of the timetable, then more teachers could be released for development work. It was claimed, not that this would solve the problem, but that some advance in the numbers being released could be made along these lines.

A more effective contribution was seen in the use of replacements for teachers released. Suggestions fell into three broad groups of expedients, although the proposers did not see them as such but as arrangements to be built into our educational system. The first was the greater and more imaginative use of peripatetic or supply teachers. The second was the more efficient use of students in training, through the planning of their teaching practice by colleges and schools to free teachers for the centres. The third was the development of the "three-session day" in secondary schools, which, involving perhaps youth service and further education personnel, might make redeployment of teachers possible.

Linked to these suggestions was the idea of a contractual period of time for retraining and development work at the centre for all teachers. Naturally there was argument as to whether one or two weeks in a block was the best way to organize such work and whether centres and support facilities could meet the demand.

But more fundamental was the argument about the implications of a contractual arrangement for regular retraining and development work. All were agreed on the need for such regular periods for all teachers, but many violently disagreed with the means suggested. For these latter, the need for schools and the profession to undertake curriculum development as a normal part of work meant that the staffing ratio must be maintained. Attempts to dodge this issue in talk of redeployment of teachers' time smacked to them of the time-honoured attempt to get education on the cheap.

Some posed a further question: a contractual arrangement for what? The administrative arrangements to release groups of teachers for courses of in-service training appeared to them to be both straightforward and desirable. But they thought this quite different from teachers being involved in the process of curriculum development, which made different demands on time, with group meetings and work spread throughout the year. Even stronger was their feeling that such work was the free response of teachers who recognized it as a function of their profession. Mass retraining by compulsory contractual agreement they saw as something different.

Indeed, underlying this discussion and constantly breaking into it were three basic arguments. These were about the nature of the centre, the relationship of in-service training to curriculum development, and the role of the warden.

What kind of a centre? Throughout the conferences, punctuating the discussions almost as reminders of the hard world outside, there were constant references to the small numbers of teachers already using the centres and to how the majority might be brought into the centres, in particular those regarded as being the most apathetic and yet most in need of assistance. The estimated proportion included in this last section varied from an alarming 50 percent to an optimistic 10 percent.

In considering this problem it was assumed that the way to attract and hold the majority of teachers was by providing courses on very practical and useful techniques, with an obvious relevance to immediate teaching problems. For some, teacher centres therefore bore a resemblance to a Venus fly-trap: the colour and scent of courses were to draw the teachers forward on to the sticky surface of curriculum development!

Against this, however, some members urged the claims of the teacher-innovators, the minority who worked on what one member called "the frontiers of curriculum practice." These were the pathfinders who, it could be argued, had greater need of support than the inefficient members of the profession. Precisely because they experimented they were most likely to be under the greatest pressure. From the centre they required support in the form of practical assistance in organizing the work, in arranging consultation with expert advice, or in the supply of relevant information. The need and the function were accepted by most members, but along with a proviso which was more in the nature of a dark suspicion—that the centre should not become an exclusive and in-growing club.

For most it was obvious that the centre was for every and any teacher, and its programme must cater to the needs of teachers. Equally obviously it was not just a place for training teachers to understand and apply the ideas of others; it took its being from the attempt to provide a framework within which teachers could exercise their own thinking on the curriculum.

It was striking a balance between the two demands that proved so difficult.

In-service training or curriculum development? More time was spent on discussing the differences between in-service training and curriculum development than on any other theme. Much less was spent on the similarities between them. In some groups, the argument was so fierce that battle-lines were drawn; the opponents appeared seized with a religious fervour in their debate on the niceties of curriculum theology.

On one side there was the "sweet reason and commonsense" party of those who saw teacher centres as a logical step in the development from the tradition of in-service training courses. As one background paper put it, "the centre is as much an educational tool in the advisers' hands as it is a medium through which teachers can shape their own educational development."

Opposed to this viewpoint were those, at times iconoclastic, who saw the process of local curriculum development as introducing something distinctively new, which made in-service training its servant. So strongly was this expressed in some groups that several centre leaders became quite apologetic about their programmes of courses; one diffidently apologized for "mentioning the unmentionable" of in-service courses.

However, agreement was reached on a definition of the two processes. For a given area of learning, curriculum development was the process of defining the aims and the objectives of their teaching, the construction of methods and materials to achieve the objectives, an assessment of their effectiveness, and finally a feedback of these results to form a new starting-point for further study.[1] In-service training was essentially the imparting of the results of successful curriculum development and the reinforcement of that success. That relationship had always existed, even if it had not been recognized so explicitly. Perhaps it was the scale of the involvement of teachers working in a cooperative fashion that had made it necessary to spell out the relationship more clearly.

Disagreement was expressed on two points. The first was how fast and how far teachers and schools could be involved in development that demanded yet more change in traditional methods and organization. The second was over how precisely the difference between in-service training and curriculum development worked in practice.

The first point was put very forcibly in one group by a headmaster who is the chairman of a local centre steering committee. He complained of the tendency to equate curriculum development with change: wasn't far more of it concerned with making the traditional more efficient and more relevant to pupils' needs and the society the schools served? The continuation of this process into the work of centres had been described by a warden in one of the background papers to the conference:

> At this moment in time we must not underestimate the effects of the enormous volume of new ideas, methods and materials that is flooding our schools. Teachers find themselves bombarded with them and very often good and conscientious teachers become uncertain as to their own objective. It is essential that we maintain a balance between encouragement of new aspects of education and maintenance of the old (where desirable) through in-service education. The service provided by teachers to the children in our schools can only suffer if teachers find themselves lacking in security and confidence in the work that they are doing. Teachers' centres can do much to develop and maintain this security and confidence.

The question posed was how much in the way of demands for new thinking and change the schools could absorb.

But indeed what was in-service training without the challenge of new thinking? There were those who argued that the view of in-service courses as "tips for teachers" was sadly out of date. There was always the need for a means of spreading "Charlie Jones's good ideas"—often the germ of successful innovation. However, most in-service work now consisted of active investigation by workshop groups, powerfully stimulated by national projects, rather than lectures to passive audiences with the odd enthusiast pouncing on the latest scrap of educational fashion. The term "in-service training" was perhaps too restrictive a description of what went on.

Speakers on a number of occasion referred to the advice of Sir Ronald Gould: no teacher could afford to spend a working lifetime relying only on the capital he had acquired in the years of initial training. The scale of re-equipping members of the profession with new knowledge during their working life was so formidable as to demand an enormous expansion of in-service education. Within that, there was a complex interaction between in-service training and curriculum development; workshop techniques in particular did not just transmit results of successful practice, but often were the means of opening up possibilities of innovation.

Nevertheless there remained those who, whilst agreeing with much of the above formulation, remained sceptical as to the actual impact at present of most in-service courses. They felt that too often they took the form of the experts telling the teachers what they ought to do. There was recognition, too, of the dangers and difficulties of local curriculum development—that sometimes teachers conscious of practical classroom problems were repelled by what they saw as abstruse discussions of aims; of the even more serious damage when groups were frustrated by their inability to try out ideas in their schools.

This, these members argued, meant that more emphasis must be placed upon the local centre as the place which encouraged and facilitated development work, characterized by its origin in teachers' exchanges of views on aims, and on its expression in classroom work designed by the teachers. How far and how fast this process could go was not just an argument about the balance of activities within in-service education; it was also about the roles of those who served the teachers in the centres, and in particular about the role of the warden or centre leader.

The role of the centre warden. The very variation in title, especially between the words "warden" and "leader," indicated the first question: What was he appointed as? Three answers were given in most of the groups. The most unsatisfactory role, perhaps reflecting in choice of language the disappointments of at least some wardens, was as a general "dogsbody" with duties ranging from summarizing Schools Council working papers to washing up the cups and saucers. A step-up was achieved when his functions were seen to be mainly administrative; the ideal warden was described by one chairman of a management committee as the person who set up everything for the teachers and then faded into the background.

A more widely held view was that the warden must be someone who above all could provide leadership because he was a good teacher with the kind of qualifications and experience needed in some crucial area of work being fostered by the centre. The danger here, as some saw it, was that really the person appointed would inevitably be forced into the position of a subadviser. As one contributor put it:

> Working in the company of advisers and organizers, and having no other example to follow, we tried to emulate them. We could not resist the temptation of offering advice on what was good education.

The pressures to take on such a role could be greater in a small authority, where the temptation to employ wardens to provide an advisory service otherwise lacking could be very strong. Yet the wardens at the conference felt that their relationship with teachers was less formal than that of the advisers, however friendly.

The alternative to a junior adviser's role was not seen as necessarily an administrator's, however high-powered. Some wardens advanced the argument that as catalysts for change they had a role which was defined by the particular needs of teachers who came together in local development groups:

> Briefly, we have to establish ourselves in the role of a consultant in local curriculum development. This means that teachers must ask for our help and not have it forced on them by various forms of blackmail. In order to achieve this we must be seen to be offering something of value. This "something of value" has to be more than an interesting discussion and a cup of tea. If the centre leader is to be more than a warden he must offer skills which go beyond a statement to the effect that curriculum development is a matter of stating objectives, selecting content and evaluating the outcome. If we cannot offer a system which enables a teacher to take his *own* educational aims through the complexities of this process and emerge with a piece of curriculum that has some chance of working in his school, then we have no role, and the centre has no function.

There was little time at the conferences to expand on what the particular skills were, but some were suggested: a greater expertise in group discussion work; a sound understanding of behavioural psychology, of the work done on curriculum planning, and of related fields of sociology; and a working knowledge of resources and information needed by teachers. But this is a very sketchy outline of the skills required for this role.

It was enough to alarm some members. Already the point had been made that the title "warden" was to be preferred to that of "centre leader," because the latter had connotations of teachers being controlled by an expert in curriculum development. Now came the suggestion of a mystique of curriculum studies. It was felt that a movement based upon teacher control might result, in practice, in yet another level in the educational hierarchy.

The reply to this anxiety was that the knowledge demanded was capable of being understood by all teachers. The more this spread amongst teachers, the greater the demand by teachers themselves for the "consultants," as some saw the role of centre wardens; it was the teacher's need for time and energy in these particular skills that defined the warden's role. To some members, however, particularly experienced chief local inspectors, this was too simple a view of the demands of local centres. These were likely to be so wide ranging in terms of particular kinds of expertise as to be impossible for one man to provide, no matter how high a status he might be given. In practice, teachers with particular skills in some areas of the curriculum must be released to staff the centre.

Here of course the relationship of centre leaders with local advisers and with H. M. Inspectors, was touched upon. There was some suspicion and some dissatisfaction, but also evidence of willing and fruitful collaboration. The relationship could only be defined against the practical necessities of local conditions. There was one measure of agreement: centre wardens could never carry out the inspectorial and policy-recommendation functions of advisers; to do so would impair the particular quality of their relationship with teachers.

This whole question of role, and of training in the skills required, was bound up with the status of wardens. Where did they fit into the educational pattern? What career prospects did their experience fit them for—in or out of the schools? Clearly some of the most experienced wardens from areas differing widely in educational and social structure felt that the answers to these questions were crucial in the development of local groups and centres.

There was general agreement that there was some separate and definitive role for centre wardens, although not on its precise nature. Not all had the same sense of urgency for answers as the wardens mentioned, who felt that when the centres were established, when the courses were running, when the study-groups were defining aims and encountering only partial success, then the anxious personal questioning came—what should I be doing to help the work forward and to show the way?

The conference agreed that the local centre was an indispensable instrument of curriculum change; but much more argument and questioning will be required to clarify its use and probable future within the educational system.

IV. Questions for the Future

Changing roles. The conferences were friendly occasions. People came to contribute and to learn; they came as partners in a joint undertaking, with different contributions and roles. Nevertheless, it was not surprising that at times the arguments were intense and disagreements were strongly voiced. If we are serious about the part to be played by local groups and centres in producing curriculum change, then it must be accepted that this calls into question traditional roles and relationships within our educational hierarchy. Talk about the changing role of the teacher and headteacher is now commonplace. Is not the role of the local adviser, of the college lecturer, of the H. M. I., of the professor of education, of the chief education officer, also in question? May not the local centre function as a catalyst in raising these questions as the inevitable concomitant of change in education?

Contributors at the conferences stressed that the significance of teacher centres did not lie in the buildings and their equipment. Their importance lay in what they represented: a movement to promote change in the curriculum which drew its strength from school-based developments and the widespread participation of teachers who gave the lead in the whole process. If this is to be more than a pretty piece of mythology, then the consequence of change must be accepted. Participation is the popular solution for many political and social problems. The logic must be followed through; in a democratic society greater participation by people may offer more possibilities of solving some problems, but equally it will raise other problems. This is true of a strategy of curriculum development that seeks to give a dominant role to teachers in the schools. And it is why at the heart of so many of the areas of possible future development lie the human problems of adaptation to new attitudes and relationships.

Staffing the centres. One demand that was clearly voiced at the three conferences was for more assistance to centre wardens, in particular with courses or conferences that would help them to gain a greater understanding of their role and a greater mastery of the skills that the work at centres would demand. This was a request that must be listened to by Schools Council, local education authorities, and other educational bodies. The job of centre warden was attracting able teachers, people with enthusiasm and a deal of good experience to draw upon. To confine them to a mass of routine administration or to do nothing to help them to think their way through the many disappointments encountered in development work would not frustrate only them but the whole future of local groups and centres. Wardens at the conferences reported that they had organized full programmes of courses, study-groups, and development groups; what they wanted to know was what they could do to break through the deadlocks that so many development groups encountered. It was relatively easy to begin the process of rethinking aims and objectives; the difficulties lay in knowing what kinds of skills and resources could be marshalled to enable groups to overcome the problems implicit in new approaches to learning and teaching.

No one was in a position to outline the training courses required. Some institutes of education were conducting courses for centre leaders and much undoubtedly would be learnt from them. It was felt, however, that at the present time it would be the height of folly, and indeed arrogance, to attempt to devise a definitive course to satisfy the needs of centre wardens. Probably it was not courses that were required, but rather series of conferences for groups of wardens; some of these might be intensive and longer in time, others just occasional days when a group could review current problems as well as the conclusions from the more formal sessions. The major contribution at the longer meetings could come from the wardens themselves, using the experience of work in centres and schools to fashion discussion sessions and workshops in simulated situations.

There were two other sources of assistance. One was institutes and colleges, in making available the findings of relevant research and the contributions of psychology, sociology, and philosophy. The other was people experienced in the development and techniques of educational retraining—local advisers and H. M. I.'s; some of the problems of centre wardens might appear in a completely fresh light when viewed within the historical context of the development of in-service training.

One thing was most important—such courses or conferences must not appear to be the training of a curriculum development elite. If such an impression were given, then it could only increase the problem of centres by leading teachers to think that such work demanded a level of academic thinking which was beyond the capacity of "mere teachers." It must be made clear in the centres that such courses were adding to the collective expertise of teachers by seeking ways of making useful knowledge and skills more freely available to them all, and not by producing a breed of consultants whose diagnoses were received with awe largely because they were in unintelligible language.

As the work in a centre increased, so one full-time warden might prove insufficient. The first and most immediate requirement was for an improvement in the amount of clerical and secretarial assistance at most of the centres. It was uneconomic to release a well-qualified teacher to do a highly professional job as a centre leader, and then force him to spend a large part of his time doing perhaps inefficiently the work of a clerical assistant.

A further development could be along the lines of a suggestion in Working Paper 10: that as a multipurpose centre developed, so groups might require the services of part-time leaders. Possibly these could be teachers already freed for the in-service requirements of national projects. The work they would have done with the projects could be a valuable preparation for the further demands of development groups. The scale of this would depend, among other considerations, upon the relationship of the centre with the local advisory staff.

A similar point had to be borne in mind when considering the likely response to a further staffing demand—for technical ancillaries at the centre. Where an authority had well-established and well-staffed advisory services in the field of audiovisual aids, then much of the required assistance in servicing and maintenance might be met by an improvement in liaison between the centre and the other services. However, where the centre becomes a base for such services, then it is essential to provide the technician in order to prevent misuse of the warden's time and energy.

As the last two points have indicated, a further development must be more collaboration at the centres between teachers and all concerned with the educational system, particularly the local advisory staff. Enough was said at the conferences to make it clear that centres cannot, and would be foolish to try to provide a total advisory service. A centre was essentially a place where teachers were encouraged to think about the curriculum, and where the facilities required to translate thought into deeds were provided. Therefore, as the work of centres grew, so would the demands upon the advisory services. These would require strengthening rather than be replaced by the centre.

Up to now most centres, possibly very wisely, had concentrated upon the organization of work by groups of teachers. As this developed in the future so centres would need to improve collaboration with other bodies important to schoolteachers, particularly colleges of further education, technical colleges, and colleges of education. How far centres could make a distinctive contribution to the initial training of teachers was problematic. Certainly, some training establishments were anxious to see whether a working relationship could have some impact upon training courses. If it only introduced student-teachers to the existence of local centres it would remedy what at the moment was a sad gap in the knowledge of most of them.

Growth-points in accommodation and equipment. Two specialist areas appeared to have priority on the list of most centres: one was separate provision for audiovisual equipment; the other was for a working library.

For audiovisual aids there were two distinct demands. The first was for opportunities for familiarization with, and evaluation of, equipment, with loan arrangements for items not available in the schools. This might mean that centres would require a stock of tape recorders, cameras, projectors, and so forth, particularly for the use of smaller schools. The second demand was for opportunities to produce materials needed in curriculum work. Above all in this connexion experience was proving the need for reprographic facilities: copying machines, dark rooms, and sound-proof booths.

There was a strong feeling that centres should have a library, but that this should be essentially a workroom and not an alternative to a reference library or to the excellent teachers' libraries maintained by some local education authorities. Rather it should be a place where books, magazines, documents, and photographic and recorded material were kept, which had a direct bearing upon the current programme of work. Therefore, it presupposed the concurrent development of an efficient loan service from a wide range of bodies: the library and museum services, archives of various types, and the local education authority's own resources.

There was much nebulous talk of resources centres. There might later be a widespread need for extra assistance with two functions of the centres: the first the production of more sophisticated teaching materials; and the second the recording of curriculum experience to enable it to be stored for communication to other groups or for evaluation over a long period. In connexion with both these activities closed-circuit television and attendant videotape recording facilities were frequently mentioned.

The real question to be answered by future developments would be whether the local centre was the right place for such expensive and sophisticated equipment. The experience of the few large centres moving in this direction would show whether such provision furthered the work or distorted the essential nature of a centre, making it a high-powered institution with a less direct relationship with the classroom. For the majority of centres, future growth would probably lie in improving links with bodies already possessing the facilities and expertise required, especially institutions of higher education and the specialized services of local education authorities.

The criterion for deciding whether a centre should aim at owning a particular piece of equipment—apart from the limiting factor of money—was whether or not it was easily accessible elsewhere. Indeed, in terms of resources the logical and sensible development could be for teacher centres to further develop their function as organizing centres, the place where local teachers could find out what was available and how it could be obtained.

Regional links. In some areas there already existed arrangements for the leaders of local centres to meet and to engage in some common programmes of action. It was likely that there would be a natural tendency for this to happen on a regional basis. Indeed, the strengthening of ties with institutes of education might well be initiated at this level. There could also be sound financial reasons behind such moves. It was inevitable that centres would make more and more demands upon local education authorities' purses, especially to make available specialized equipment and services, and this might be more easily available through forms of cooperation on a regional basis.

Such cooperation could not be imposed from above, but would develop as centres, in their search for relevant information, recognized common problems. This was the best guarantee against an over-organized and parochial regionalization, which could restrict the experience and help available. Many of the problems were national in scope, and demanded a national interchange of ideas and experience.

There were two geographical problems that emerged most sharply at the conferences and which clearly demanded further consideration. In very scattered rural areas and in a conurbation, teachers, curiously enough, faced similar difficulties in travelling to the centre. Traffic congestion could be as big a barrier as long distances along minor roads.

Teachers in the centres. No prediction of future developments would be valid unless it assumed a policy that facilitated the release of more teachers to work in the centres. Present circumstances might not appear the most propitious in which to urge more generous staffing to allow for this, yet a longer view is needed, and it was well to draw upon the experience of those whose service enabled them to appreciate the improvement in staffing ratios that had taken place over a period of 40 years.

It was hoped that when further improvements took place, due attention would be paid to demands for release to take part in centre activities. In particular, part-time secondment to a centre could be one way of providing opportunity for retraining as a normal feature of teacher service, a first step towards the sabbatical year arrangement that has always been a cherished hope of the teaching profession.

In many centres the transition from the primary to the secondary stage was perhaps the most profitable area for development work, and certainly one that was attracting the interest of many teachers. The most obvious way of tackling this was through an extension of joint primary-secondary teacher study and development groups. Where these had already been formed, even on a limited scale, there had been mutual benefit from sharing insight into the learning difficulties of the various age groups.

No doubt there were significant differences in teaching and organizational problems between the two stages of education; but equally significant was the fact that joint study was the best means of establishing the nature of those differences and the evolution of the educational process throughout the years of formal education.

Problems of communication. Growth in development work was also seen as heavily dependent upon a rapid spread of ideas. Centres and wardens were badly in need of two kinds of information. The first was to know what was going on in other centres and other areas; the second was what knowledge and research already existed relevant to their immediate tasks and difficulties. The adequate provision of this information would require the fashioning of a national information network.

The first kind of information was essentially a drawing upon the experience of local centres and groups themselves. In the first place, centres must not be afraid of recording what had been done, either by teachers writing about it or using audiovisual techniques. They should get rid of the idea that local experiments were too fumbling and simple; what teachers wanted at the moment was as much evidence as possible of classroom efforts to solve teaching and learning difficulties. The second stage in this process was to have some kind of clearinghouse for local information, a place that centres wanting certain types of evidence could refer to.

The second kind of information wanted concerned work done for centres—making available to them in the most convenient form the results of research and of national development projects. Centres must be able to have at their disposal a picture of curriculum developments over as wide a geographical and academic area as possible. Some of this work might be done by local education authorities, by regional groups or by institutes. The Schools Council itself, it was agreed, should do more to provide a service in the field of information, and investigations are now proceeding as to how this might best be done.

Notes

1. See Schools Council Working Paper No. 10, *Curriculum Development: Teachers' Groups and Centers* (London: Her Majesty's Stationery Office, 1967).

Chapter VI

British Teacher Centers: Continuing Development

Introduction

Since the publication of the Schools Council Working Paper No. 10 and the Plowden Report, *Children and Their Primary Schools,* both in 1967, teacher centers in England have multiplied at an amazing rate. They are estimated today to number over 600.[1] The Plowden Report stated their value in its usual direct way:

> We hope that . . . teachers' centres will encourage initiative in teachers and will certainly not be used to draw up school syllabuses, though examples of the materials which can be handled by children at various ages, and of the ways in which investigation has developed in individual instances, can be useful. They should provide opportunities for teachers to extend their own . . . knowledge by practical work, and by study courses and lectures given by experts. *The new methods demand more knowledge in teachers.* There ought also to be opportunities for them to make apparatus to use in school and to discuss with their colleagues the innovations they are trying out, and opportunities for them to see each other's work in classroom.[2] (Editor's italics.)

The British centers vary widely in organization and views about their purposes, as will be seen in these pages, particularly in the thoughtful article by Audrey Griggs, a Schools Council field officer. How does the teacher center foster educational change in the individual teacher? In many ways, the new methods do demand more knowledge in teachers, and the simple confidence born of knowing more can help a teacher change. Being a learner oneself in a teacher workshop can help. And being asked to contribute ideas to a national curriculum effort like the Nuffield projects gives a teacher a chance to influence the educational system. Above all, the opportunity, directly in line with Piaget's recommendations, of doing research and contributing it in some form to other teachers, is a great step forward in personal growth for a teacher. E. M. Millington, who is warden of the London teacher center described by Arnold in this chapter, tells of the center's practice of having students present the work of a project to a teacher audience. They tape record their presentation and replay it, giving both teachers and students an opportunity to re-think and evaluate the work.[3]

It is in the crucial areas of personal and professional development, how-ever, that Colin Richards, in this chapter, sees the centers as, in fact, failing. He believes that centers have made the greatest contributions in support of the national curriculum efforts but are lacking in local initiative. He cites the fact that many teachers are apathetic and are unwilling to give their own time to the centers. They see teaching as a job which ends at 3:30, a problem Ameri-can centers will undoubtedly face. One solution, which the James Report in England has recently advocated, is more released time for teachers. Others have argued that the chance for creative action and thought with colleagues will encourage teachers to give of their free time willingly, as Ellison so ably describes in her article in this chapter on Shropshire workshops.

Not all teacher centers will survive as Owen points out here, and his article goes on to analyze the qualities of some of those likely to be successful.

Notes

1. R. E. Thornbury (ed.), *Teachers' Centres* (London: Darton, Longman & Todd, 1973; New York: Agathon Press, 1974), p. 3.

2. Central Advisory Council for Education (England), *Children and Their Primary Schools* (London: Her Majesty's Stationery Office, 1967), p. 244.

3. E. M. Millington, "Teachers' Centre . . . Organization and Function," *Ideas*, June 1968, pp. 21-22.

A CENTRE IN BRITAIN
Ronald Arnold

In Newham the centre's layout and resources were determined by what it inherited, the top floor of a three-decker school, built in 1897. The hall became a concourse and display area, the classrooms centres of activity. The LEA inspectors and advisers, with the full-time "teacher-in-charge" of the centre, are committed to working out new ideas to meet present and projected needs. They have worked in partnership with the teachers of the borough to make the centre an effective instrument of development work, in-service education, and professional renewal. In fact, the process is almost that of a chain reaction. There is nothing haphazard about it; the objectives are identified, the courses provided, the study groups formed. Each activity suggests another and the pattern of linked activities that emerges is related to the set of central objectives, which are developed in their turn.

Teacher Working Parties

Perhaps the best starting example is that of a working party which generated an unexpectedly large number of possibilities. The secondary inspectors invited heads to form a small working party to consider aspects of reorganisation and their implications for in-service training. In due course, this group suggested that it should be paralleled by subject panels, which would work on certain topics in relation to their own fields of interest. These were: (1) curriculum content for the first two years of the comprehensive school and links with the primary school; (2) the raising of the school leaving age; (3) teaching the full ability range; (4) integration with other subjects; and (5) equipment, facilities, and resources.

The secondary inspectors and advisers formed these subject panels by open invitation and launched each one with a talk by a visiting speaker, usually an H. M. I. Most areas of the curriculum are now represented, and some of the panels have developed into subject associations, to add to those that already existed in the borough. One of the first panels to be formed was English, which began with a talk on developments in the teaching of the subject. This meeting was arranged jointly by the primary and secondary inspectors, and it was attended by very nearly a fifth of the teaching force of the borough. It gave rise to a good deal of teacher activity in the shape of secondary working parties, whose discussions included but went beyond the original brief to the subject panel. For their part, the primary inspectors followed up the meeting by inviting to the centre the "Children Talking" team of Staffordshire NATE. Six groups of primary teachers now meet to discuss transcripts of tapes they have made of children's talk, and they are joined by a lecturer from London University Institute of Education. They are at present engaged in making up a master-tape of their material.

Thus, the in-service courses are seen not as once for all efforts, but as an element organic with the teacher activity. How well teachers respond to need is illustrated by the fact that a recent course on the teaching of reading was attended by 305 of the 875 Newham primary school teachers. This course was linked with a project on the *Breakthrough to Literacy* programme, which the authority financed in pilot schools. Heads of certain of these schools spoke on the course, along with outside speakers who have been involved in research into reading. The contribution of the heads was itself the product not only of their practical work on the project but of their regular study-group meetings with other interested teachers. In short, then, the courses and the development work are seen as mutually nourishing activities; together they accounted for no fewer than 4,000 teacher attendances at the centre in the recent term.

The number and range of the working parties and similar groups illustrate how such a degree of teacher involvement is made possible. One working party set itself the task of creating an infant classroom in the centre, principally to show probationers and young teachers what might be achieved. The result was a stimulating source of ideas and encouragement which prompted a second group to follow it up with a junior classroom. Another working party, composed of junior, infant and nursery school heads, was formed by one of the primary inspectors to make recommendations on the education of young children in multiracial schools. It has organised courses for welfare assistants covering such topics as language, social training, and play and has produced a useful booklet which has been issued to teachers throughout the borough. This, by the way, is also an example of the centre's support for inexperienced teachers, who are encouraged to see it as a teaching resource. There are frequent talks and discussion sessions for probationer teachers, and at one series of meetings young teachers of longer experience played an equal part with the primary inspectors in running tutorial groups. It is also an example of the inclination of the working parties to produce material which can be used in the schools. The party considering integrated social studies in the first year of the secondary school has devised an outline of work which it has since offered to schools in the borough. Similarly, the one involved with humanities in the upper forms of the secondary school is producing resource material, and it has organised conferences for fourth and fifth year pupils on a variety of themes. There is also a group working on a Mode III interdisciplinary CSE syllabus issuing in a multiple certificate. It has already produced a British studies syllabus which qualifies candidates for three passes. Another is proposed for a five-subject syllabus based on the literature and history of social change from the repeal of the Corn Laws to the present day. The teacher centre serves as a focal point for CSE development, notably in the display facilities it offers for course work and similar material.

The Arts

The Centre has a specialised counterpart in the form of the drama/arts centre. The two do not operate in isolation, but the drama and art advisers have found that the latter gives them better scope for their activities. Here again it has been a question of adapting part of an old school and here again handicap has been turned into asset. It provides for a teachers' drama group and a youth theatre and for various creative activities for children. Some of these take place after school, when the peripatetic drama teachers and art teachers organise open sessions. Others are on a "block release" basis, with the intention of reproducing as nearly as possible the atmosphere of a residential course. A class spends every day of a week at the centre and works on drama-based projects with one of its own teachers and the peripatetic drama teachers.

Another activity that has been particularly successful has been a programme of children's theatre visits to infant schools, a scheme which allows the class teacher and the visiting drama teachers to work in close cooperation. Each sequence opens with a meeting at the teacher centre between a group of infant school heads and a primary inspector and the drama adviser. This is followed by a three-session course for class teachers from the schools involved in the project. Working with the peripatetic drama teachers they evolve a play or a piece of dramatic activity which they then take back into the schools to develop with the children elaborating it into art and writing. The next stage is for the peripatetic drama teachers to come to the school and join with the two teachers in developing another dramatic experience, which gives rise to more work by the children. Among the interesting forms this has taken has been a link in one school with the work in the *Breakthrough to Literacy* programme.

A Resources Centre

All this teacher activity needs resources, and the centre tries not only to meet but to anticipate demand. It is common for a study group to ask for the extensive reproduction of material it has produced for use in schools. It is also common for a teacher to ask for anything up to 200 copies of material for classroom use—for example, diagrams, pictures, cut-outs, and so on, and the centre now has an electronic scanner to meet all these needs. There is also a collection of over 3,000 coloured slides which was built up by public appeal. In the first instance the Association of Science Teachers was invited to make recommendations on the level at which each slide would be useful. After this there was an open viewing which produced interesting ideas from teachers of various subjects. At the moment the teacher-in-charge at the centre is building up packs of slides for infant schools, with information sheets and a tape recording to accompany each. Finally, there is the library, which among the more usual reference material contains an exceptionally good collection of contemporary poetry. This too is an example of the will to let no promising line of development peter out. A weekend poetry course aroused an enthusiasm which resulted in groups of teachers forming to discuss poetry in general and read modern poetry in particular. The authority promptly bought this large collection for the library and it will be a particularly valuable resource.

The Newham Teacher Centre, to use the term in its collective sense, would not yet claim to be fully developed. In fact it is doubtful whether it would accept the concept. The moment its role could be codified it would feel itself circumscribed. The only statute is not to miss an opportunity, for that might mean missing a dozen that could grow from it. This kind of situation can develop only from a real partnership and that in its turn from understanding and reciprocal respect.

JUNIOR WORKSHOP IN SHROPSHIRE
Mary Ellison

In 1956 I was appointed Adviser for Primary Education in Shropshire. My main interests lay in the fields of curriculum development and in-service training. After some four years of getting to know the county four major problems had come to the surface: (1) the isolation of heads in two- and three-teacher village schools in this rural county; (2) the lack of continuity and development in the teachers' courses which were largely run as weekend courses at Attingham Park, the adult college near Shrewsbury; (3) the narrowness of much of the work in schools; and (4) the need to increase the amount and quality of the discussion concerned with educational ideas.

A partial answer to these problems might be the establishment of a permanent study-group of junior school teachers to discuss common problems, new developments, and current educational ideas. Seventy to eighty teachers turned up one evening at Attingham Park to discuss the idea. At the end of the evening the following points had been made: (1) there should be ample opportunity for discussion so that people could get to know each other well; (2) heads of village schools should have an opportunity to meet and discuss on their own; (3) some meetings should be held in different parts of the county; and (4) special attention should be given to mathematics and natural history.

Much has happened since that early meeting when the germ of the idea of Junior Workshop was looked at. It was launched on an evening in November 1962 at Attingham Park when Mr. K. Gardner came from the Walsall remedial centre to talk about the Augmented Roman Alphabet, now known as the initial teaching alphabet. After his talk the 70 teachers present broke up into groups for discussion, the village school heads forming one group in the library. This pattern of a talk followed by group discussions has remained the basic Junior Workshop pattern ever since. Usually group discussions are followed by a short time before coffee when leaders report back briefly or put questions to the speaker. Such a Junior Workshop meeting is held each half term. When the number of teachers attending passed 100 we had to move out of Attingham Park to Radbrook College and from there, two years ago, to the Council Chamber at the new Shirehall where up to 200 teachers can be most comfortably, indeed luxuriously, seated and where committee rooms are available for the six or seven discussion groups. It has been most rewarding over the years to find a steady rise in the level of discussion, in the skill shown in handling a group, and in reporting back to the main body. Visitors never fail to comment on this. Shropshire Junior teachers support these meetings in large numbers with loyalty and enthusiasm. They welcome the opportunity to hear Sir Alec Clegg, or Lady Plowden or Mr. J. Burrows H. M. I. or a head from Oxfordshire or a member of the university staff, but they also appreciate an opportunity to hear from their own colleagues. Now in preparation is an evening on children writing, when a head and a deputy head will talk about their work and their own growth in sensitivity towards the use of words.

For a time the heads of village schools formed one of the discussion groups at Junior Workshop meetings until it was suggested they might meet on a separate occasion. And so the group known as Heads of Small Schools was formed. This meets for one afternoon each term, perhaps to discuss a main Junior Workshop lecture further or to hear about an interesting piece of work, as for example this term when the head of a two-teacher school showed and talked about the work his children did following a four-day environmental-study visit to Borth. Because of the difficulties heads experience in working in cramped, inadequate buildings special attention has been given to ways of improving the classroom environment. With the help of charts, diagrams, and examples, the design of light mobile furniture to replace desks and tall cupboards has been discussed; the layout of classrooms to create work areas for small groups; the storage of materials and equipment, so that it is easily accessible to children; and the display of children's work so that it is esthetically pleasing. Over the years members of the group have got to know each other very well indeed and look forward to these termly meetings attended by 40 to 50 colleagues dealing with similar problems. New heads, including newcomers to the county, are readily made to feel at home.

It seemed only right that heads of large junior schools should also have their own forum. They too meet for one afternoon each term. Very often a member of the group will have prepared a paper which is circulated before the meeting. This forms the starting point of discussion, perhaps on some aspect of the curriculum, of relations with the community, or a matter of school organisation. The topic this term is Team Teaching and discussion will be based on the experiences of a Shrewsbury school as described by the headmaster. These meetings are an opportunity to learn what others think and do, to consider possibilities, to test and refine arguments. The small school in a rural county can seem isolated but the head of a large town school is isolated in his own office.

At a meeting called to consider further the initial request for the establishment of a group to be concerned with Natural History it was decided that this should essentially be an active group. Lectures, film evenings, and talks were ruled out. Members agreed to concern themselves with getting to know the county and to developing their work with children. They further agreed to meet for one full Saturday each term and this is the pattern which has been maintained since.

From 30 to 50 teachers meet, usually in a village school, and spend the morning seeing and hearing of the environmental-study work of the school and preparing for the afternoon's expedition. Very often the group is joined by experts with detailed knowledge of the locality, geology, and history. There have been many memorable days: the morning the children from the Stiperstones portrayed in drama how their forbears lived as miners; the view from the top of Brown Clee; the afternoon by the Shropshire meres; the walk through the Wye Forest in the rain. Such shared experiences have enabled and encouraged members to widen and enrich their work in integrated studies. They have formed a spearhead in the county which has led the way in environmental studies and pressed the need for Field Centres for primary children and the need for transport to make it possible for small groups of children to study at depth. The film *An Environmental Study* shows the work of one class of fourth-year juniors in a Shrewsbury school and indicates what can be achieved.

Work based on first-hand experiences outside the school highlighted the juniors' need to tell of what they had seen, heard, touched, and felt in a wide variety of ways. Many teachers spoke of their lack of confidence in dealing with paint, collage, wood, scraper board, lino tools, clay, plaster, wire, and other materials. To meet this need members of Junior Workshop come to Attingham Park for one day each term to work with materials under the guidance of a head teacher. As numbers grew two Creative Activities Groups were formed. To begin with they were essentially concerned with the exploratory use of materials but gradually the emphasis shifted to communication. Over the years the scope of the work has widened to include not only the use of art and craft materials but also experience in movement, sound, drama, and writing. Usually the day begins with a common experience shared by 40 teachers. There might be listening to music or poetry, going out and looking at something, handling objects in the room, or exploring an idea. Sometimes there is little preparation, sometimes much time and thought is given to it, as for example when a group of teachers prepared a tape on the Bible, which included readings, music and singing.

One day each term may not sound much, but this regular commitment over the years has given many teachers confidence in their own ability to create and insight into the value of creative activities in the education of the whole child. The film made last summer entitled *The Creative Spirit* shows something of what is being attempted by children and teachers in the county.

Within the past three years, two further groups have been established by Junior Workshop—the Poetry Group and the First Seven Years' Group—largely for young teachers. The Poetry Group meets on four evenings a term. It has a core of 20 or 30 very keen members and a larger number who come occasionally to meetings—which although relaxed and informal, are yet serious and purposeful. The emphasis is on reading and sharing interest and enjoyment in poetry, but since all present are teachers there is also discussion of children's response to poetry and consideration of their writing. Very often members bring to meetings poems they wish to read, occasionally a poet is invited to read and talk of his work, sometimes a programme of readings is prepared by a member or a small group, at times a local poetry reading is attended or an evening is devoted to reading children's work. Last January when Junior Workshop held their yearly social evening they were most royally entertained by members of the poetry group with verse, prose, and sound.

When a young teacher said she found it difficult to come to Junior Workshop meetings at Shirehall because there were so many people and so many imposing looking headmasters, it was clearly time to launch the group for young teachers.

Members of Junior Workshop who had been teaching for less than seven years were invited to meet and discuss the kind of group they would like to have. Ideas ranged from discussion of present social and educational problems to visits to the theatre and social evenings. The group began by discussing aims and purposes and went on to consider the role of the head and the deputy head and relations between school and home. In spite of the initial insistence that they wanted simply to talk together, the most popular meetings have been those where distinguished class teachers have talked about their work. This term an infant teacher with a small group of children in a village school described their investigations of seeds, plants, and small garden creatures. Each child's voyage of discovery was so described that the fifty or so teachers present were able to appreciate more fully the meaning behind such phrases as "learning by experience," "integration," "use of the senses," "the development of language," "individual differences," "formation of concepts," and "the importance of teacher-child relationships."

It would seem that the quality of work in the schools is closely related to the dialogue going on between teachers. Junior Workshop exists simply to put teachers in the county in touch with each other and in touch with current thinking and developments in the country as a whole. Members not only discuss at meetings, more and more they visit each other's schools, they share their expertise, and joint projects are undertaken. These include neighbouring schools gathering together for an afternoon of informal music making, or meeting regularly over a period of time to carry out some local study or project, or offering hospitality and a base to children and teachers who wish to do environmental work in the area.

To enrich the dialogue, three years ago *News and Views* was launched. This is published yearly and includes brief accounts of Junior Workshop activities and articles contributed by teachers. These are largely descriptive of particularly good and interesting work being done in a classroom or school, together with some discussion of underlying principles. *News and Views* can challenge a teacher to think out what he is doing and can open eyes to new possibilities. The present issue includes articles on religious education, mathematics, and changing from secondary teaching to primary teaching.

The success of Junior Workshop reflects the enthusiasm and determination of Shropshire junior school teachers to do the best for their children.

TEACHER CENTRES: THE BRITISH MODEL
Audrey Griggs

The first thing I feel I must say about the British model is that there isn't one. At least, not structurally. There are now approximately 500 set up, over half of them during the last two years or so and they are many and varied in kind and organisation. Insofar as they all have an underlying unity, it is in that they are mostly patterned, for curriculum development, on the simple model expounded in Schools Council Working Paper 10,[1] that of a coming together of teachers and others drawing on all available sources of knowledge and informed judgment to define their curriculum objectives; preparation and trial in schools of methods and materials to carry these out; evaluation of what they are doing; feedback to start new development.

The origins of teacher centres lie partly in the Science and Mathematics Curriculum development projects, funded and set up by the Nuffield Foundation in the early 1960's. The essence of these was that practising teachers should play the major part in them. This was ensured by the setting up of regional development centres where groups of teachers could meet to review what they were doing in the light of recent advances in knowledge, current views of the nature of knowledge, and emphasis on the pupil playing an active part in the learning process, the whole thing aiming to be essentially non-hierarchical and cooperative.

The Schools Council for the Curriculum and Examinations was set up in 1964, a national body representative of all educational interests, but with a majority of teachers on its governing council and main committees, funded since 1970 half by the Treasury and half by local education authorities. In its concern with what to teach and how to teach it, particularly in view of the raising of the school age, it has continued to encourage the setting up of local centres, some directly developed from the original Nuffield maths and science centres, where teachers may meet and work together.[2]

It is impossible to generalise about the centres. More usefully, a brief description of something of what has been set up to date in the southeast of England might give some idea of what has been tried so far.

One local education authority (LEA) with a population of over 1.25 million has set up nine centres. These are either in small, no-longer-used schools, colleges of further education, youth centres, or wherever suitable rooms have been available in schools themselves. In most cases, there is a comfortable lounge, workroom, small library, and audiovisual resource area. Sometimes reprographic facilities are available. Eight of the nine centres have a part-time warden, a practising teacher who spends half of his or her day in a school with a specific teaching commitment, the other half both visiting other schools in his area finding out what teachers want him to provide and in the centre arranging programmes, organising courses, and possibly leading discussion and development groups. The ninth centre has not yet got a warden. This is because in this authority the general policy has been to leave a committee of local teachers to start things off (usually in temporary accommodation) and if the need has been seen to be there, to then step in and provide more permanent premises and staff.

The second LEA, with a population of approximately one-half million, has five centres, one of which is newly purpose-built on the campus of a large (over 2,000 pupils) secondary school, the others again in premises conveniently vacant and adaptable. Here, the wardens are full-time appointments to the centres and have considerable status and freedom to do what they assess the teachers want and need.

A third, with a population of just over one million, has a much more coordinated organisation in one sense, in that the 11 centres they started are a combination of specialist (for example, educational technology) and general centres. The wardens, often head teachers of primary schools or heads of departments in secondary schools, are full-time teachers and run their centres after school, for which they are paid extra. This authority has a schools council of its own modelled on the national Schools Council and makes available to all its schools the termly programmes of what is happening in every centre in the county.

Though there are differences in structure, and these could be replicated throughout the rest of the country, I think it is true to say that most centre leaders I know have tried to promote as they interpret them the two concepts Geoffrey Caston, previously Joint Secretary to the Schools Council, described in his paper "The Schools Council in Context."[3] That is *pluralism,* dispersal of power in education, and *professionalism,* the exercise of choice and judgement in the interests not of ourselves or our employers, but of our clients, the students. The fact that the council has no authority over teachers and does not want it, but rather engages to stimulate and encourage local development, is a crucial factor, particularly in the way the governance of centres is envisaged.

Most Centres have either steering or management committees which consist primarily of teachers representing a cross-section of the schools they serve with possibly additional members from colleges of further education, teacher training, and the advisory staff of the local authority. The warden usually needs and has the confidence of this committee and relies upon it to some extent to feed back the reactions of the people it represents and to support his own actions. The relationship between the local advisers and the teacher centres is ambiguous and interesting. Traditionally the advisory service, consisting of specialist and general advisers of an LEA, is responsible for, amongst other things, in-service training. Provision for this is made nationally by Department of Education courses, regionally by the Institute of Education and University Departments, and locally often in a local authority's own residential in-service training centre. Now that teacher centres are providing a variety of courses in both in-service training and curriculum development,(and not everyone agrees that there is any valid distinction or division between the two things) it is likely that duplication of effort can become a wasteful possibility. It also means that there can be considerable role ambiguity for both advisers and teacher centre leaders, particularly where there is little central coordination and/or poor internal communications.

This can be ameliorated, and attempts are being made to do this in the second and third of the two authorities I was describing earlier. In one case there is an overall coordinating committee, consisting of all the five wardens, representatives of head teachers, the University Education Department, College of Education, advisers, H. M. I., and the education officer meeting twice a year. In the other there is a staff inspector responsible for curriculum development and in-service training who also acts as secretary of the local schools council and holds meetings with T/C wardens halfway through the term previous to the one being planned. From these, synopses of programmes are sent in, summaries fed back, clashes picked up and sorted out, and resources organised.

In some ways these overall arrangements do avoid piecemeal training and overlap of development provision. However, if it is accepted that courses should arise out of ongoing activities on a smaller local scale, then the immediacy of the response to teachers by the centres is lost. The corollary to this may well be that the teachers cease to feel that their needs are being considered in any real sense and lose interest.

The financing of the centres is another aspect about which it is impossible to generalise because it depends so much on how the LEA sees the expenditure in relation to its total commitment. Some authorities make available to their wardens up to £1,000 ($2,500) or more per annum, to be spent as they think fit; others require that even petty cash should be channelled through the central administration. The financial considerations may need to include the payment of teachers' travel expenses to and from the centres, payment of teachers for leading courses or discussions, maintenance of buildings, conversions of perhaps old schools, setting up of staffing both ancilliary and caretaking, cost of consumable materials used for making classroom-type apparatus, and provision for library, audiovisual, and reprographic equipment. The question of release of teachers during teaching time impinges upon this too.

In trying to identify the aspects which are peculiar to English education, that teachers generally do not acquire any credits for undertaking in-service training or development (with one or two exceptions) is notable. But it may well be that because they are often working with advisers, they amass credit which could stand them in good stead if they wish to apply for promotion, for the advisers are often influential in this area. Here there is a clear distinction, for the teacher centre leader is seen to have no influence in this way and for many teachers this means the centre is a place in which they feel free to discuss developments and experiments that have failed. The onus to be seen or heard to be successful, which they may feel necessary in the presence of advisers, is off them.

Historically, too, the head of an English school has had complete autonomy to decide upon the curriculum and how the school shall be run. Therefore, his consent or in large schools the consent of a head of department is at least necessary. His active support might be the key factor. This lack of central direction is jealously guarded, though in fact the public examination system from the eleven plus examination onwards does determine the curriculum to a great extent. However, the introduction of new modes of examining, in which teachers in schools work out their own assessment systems internally and moderate between groups of schools, is now permitting much more flexibility and freedom.

Bearing in mind these considerations it might be interesting to examine what was provided between January and March this year in one teacher centre in a small country town in Sussex:

1. French—twice weekly, 4:00 p.m.
2. Raising of the School Leaving Age—weekly, 5:00-9:00 p.m. (continuation of a course held at Sussex University the previous term).

3. Home Economics Curriculum Development Group—1 meeting, 5:00-9:00 p.m.
4. Seminars for Probationary Teachers—3 meetings, Wednesdays, 4:30 p.m.
5. Preschool Play Group Tutors—weekly, 10:00-3:00 p.m.
6. Team Teaching in the Primary School—2 meetings, 4:30 p.m.
7. The Middle Years of Schooling, Discussion Groups—3 meetings, 7:00-9:00 p.m.
8. ROSLA and After, B.B.C. Discussion Programmes—3 meetings, 6:15 p.m.
9. School Assemblies—2 meetings, 4:45-6:15 p.m.
10. Childrens' Literature—weekly, 7:00-9:00 p.m.
11. Science in the Primary School—3 meetings, 4:15 p.m.
12. Teachers of English Group—2 meetings, 7:00-9:00 p.m.
13. Drama in Education, All Ages—1 meeting, 4:30 p.m.
14. A.G.M. of the Teacher Centre—7:00 p.m.
15. Infant Education, Reception Classes—1 meeting, 4:15 p.m.
16. Primary Fieldwork—1 meeting, 4:15 p.m.
17. National Bureau for Cooperation in Child Care—weekly, 7:00-9:00 p.m.

This is probably a reasonably typical programme of a centre. There are different emphases according to locality, interests of the leader, and shifts in county policy. The times vary because wardens find there is no one best time to put on a course. In some authorities, teachers will be able to get release for day courses; in others they will be able to attend only in their own time.

One of the problems of the leader is how to assess the best conditions for his own teachers most easily to have access to all the centre's resources. Another is to define his own status and role. If he is attempting to provide what the teachers want it may be straight in-service training courses to increase teaching skills and the warden may find difficulty in reconciling this with how he sees his role as a curriculum innovator. The fact that many other people—administrators, advisers—neither differentiate between these nor see the need to, adds to the conflict: is he one of "them," the hierarchy, or one of "us," the teachers? Most wardens I know agree their unique strength lies in the second concept, yet that can bring difficulties when working, for example, with some administrators. Can a warden himself be an innovator or can he only act as an organiser of resources to help others innovate? How far should he promote or indeed can he promote development of curriculum which might not meet with the approval of the powers that be, whether at school, community, or county level? How can he evaluate what his centre is doing?

The question of evaluation is very difficult. All that it seems possible to say at the moment is that certain projects (for example, the primary mathematics written up in Schools Council Curriculum Bulletin No. 1)[4] have definitely changed the way teachers have gone about organising their maths programme in the schools. How to assess whether the change is only apparent rather than a change in whole attitudes is another problem. Wardens will agree that, for instance, a course on handicrafts in primary schools will mean that teachers who did not use clay, wood, and chalk for sculpture before will after then do so. But real curriculum development groups are slower to show results. Some wardens argue that the real innovators do not use the centres anyway—they do not need them. Where much support is needed is for the next layer down.

This is a very simplified account of how I see centres at the moment and does not do justice to all the subtleties of the interactions of all the enormous number of variables there are. Where are the centres going? Since the publication earlier this year of the James Report on Teacher Education and Training[5] with its recommendations for Professional Centres to which teachers in the second year of the proposed second cycle and the third cycle of training should have easy access, many centres have seen this as a natural development of what they are already trying to do. It seems to me that in England it is fairly easy to have an idea of what is wrong and react against it in all sorts of directions, on a kind of trial and error basis, with not much control over which ways or how much. I believe that changes already worked out and accepted in schools by the innovator and then passed on at teacher centres do not in themselves change the attitudes of the individual teacher. In this case the teacher will engage in an innovatory practice because it has already been proven, and this attitude is basically no different from the traditional one. The change I think the teacher centre is aiming to bring about is to make the teachers feel professionally strong enough to look at their own positions and discuss with colleagues, parents, and pupils the direction in which they should go, to work out together what is needed to make this possible and then feel free and able to act on it.

Notes

1. Schools Council Working Paper No. 10, *Curriculum Development: Teachers' Groups and Centres* (London: Her Majesty's Stationery Office, 1967).

2. Schools Council Working Paper No. 2, *Raising the School Leaving Age* (London: Her Majesty's Stationery Office, 1965).

3. Geoffrey Caston, "The Schools Council in Context," *Journal of Curriculum Studies,* May 1971.

4. Schools Council Curriculum Bulletin No. 1, *Primary Mathematics* (London: Her Majesty's Stationery Office, 1965).

5. Department of Education and Science, *Teacher Education and Training* (London: Her Majesty's Stationery Office, 1972).

TEACHER CENTRES: A PRIMARY SCHOOL VIEW
Colin Richards

Some of the statements made about teacher centres may be deceptive in the picture they give of what is actually happening. It is said, for example, that the centres are places where local groups provide "the motive power"[1] for progress in curriculum development; they are centres for the dissemination of knowledge about research and development; that "in all of them teachers study curriculum development and new approaches to teaching through the child's own discovery."[2] Are teacher centres the physical manifestation of teachers' professional responsibility for curriculum development or does a closer examination of the centres' participants and activities disclose the fragmentary nature of this claim? This articles seeks to examine centres from a primary school viewpoint. The shortcomings outlined here may or may not apply to secondary curriculum development work: that is for others to say.

Many teacher centres have three main functions. They are used for inservice training; they provide a social centre for teachers; and they support curriculum development work. Schools Council Working Paper No. 10 confines its attention to the third aspect, as will this article.

In that paper three main bases for curriculum development were outlined. There were national development projects with feedback from local groups, there was participation of universities and colleges of education in the work of teacher centres, and lastly there was "the expressed wish of teachers to come together to conduct for themselves curriculum development, in order to help them to sharpen their judgements on objectives, improve their experimental procedures and play a full part in assessing the results of development work." Centres were to be the physical means whereby these three bases were to be developed in a local area.

My personal experience of such centres, reinforced by discussion with a number of other people (some involved in national development projects) leads me to the conclusion that such centres have only really been successful as far as the support of national work is concerned. Groups of teachers have met to work through and discuss Schools Council material with varying degrees of objectivity and precision, but these discussions have been structured along more or less definite lines, and a specific time-limit has been placed on teachers' involvement. Participation by universities and colleges has been fruitful as far as national work (and in-service training) has been concerned, but in general teachers have not gone far with defining new objectives of their own, devising their own experimental procedures or developing their own mini-curricula.

To acknowledge that this is the case is not to blame teachers, wardens, the Schools Council, or any other body of people. It was perhaps inevitable in view of the embryonic nature of the curriculum development enterprise in Britain. Basically though, Working Paper No. 10 underestimates the complexities of local curriculum development, especially the definition of objectives and the procedures for evaluation. A lot of good teaching does go on in any local area, but this is largely "intuitive." Teasing out the underlying rationale of good practice, formulating it for others to try out, and then evaluating it in a wider setting are very difficult procedures, calling for much expert help and entailing far more time and effort than the vast majority of teachers can reasonably expend. Many interested teachers have been misled into thinking that local curriculum development work was comparatively easy and able to provide plentiful results in the short term. The diffuseness of many meetings, the lack of definite terms of reference, and the inability of many group leaders to see where they were going may have all contributed to a fall-off of teacher interest.

The majority of teachers have not been involved at all in the discussion of new objectives and methods, except in so far as these are discussed over coffee at breaktime—not the most effective time for curriculum development. To the interested but overpressed primary school teacher, curriculum development work in a local centre is another burden to bear and he can scarcely be blamed for considering it of secondary importance when balancing the competing interests of home school and class. In addition to this, a good many teachers are only interested in teaching as a means of earning a living. These resent any intrusion into their "own time" after the bell rings at 4 p.m. How typical or atypical these are is open to question, but that large numbers exist must be borne in mind when discussing the widespread "primary school revolution" or the role of teacher centres in *nationwide* curriculum innovation.

Curriculum planning is not yet fully recognized as part of every teacher's professional responsibility. Some heads still covet it as their preserve; many teachers shy away from it anyway, preferring the curriculum planning of the text book or the autocratic "boss." Only if time is allocated to this planning on a school basis will some teachers begin to realize their responsibility, and by this is meant more than the occasional half hour at lunchtime, constantly interrupted by children with bleeding knees or messages from Mum. In a sense teacher centres are trapped in a vicious circle. Teachers need to realize their responsibility for curriculum planning before they will fully participate in local development work (all other things being favourable), but how can they be made to assume this responsibility if they are not stimulated to thought and discussion by some of their colleagues at such a centre?

As a result of factors such as these, teacher centres as a whole are far from being the dynamic sources of "motive power" for curricular progress in local areas. Because their major contribution to development has been in support of national projects, they are in danger of becoming mere outposts for the dissemination of Schools Council orthodoxy, an orthodoxy all the more dangerous and insidious for being unrecognized by the recipients and unsought by the Schools Council itself. In the light of this two viewpoints are possible. Some people would maintain that a measure of central influence over curricula is to be welcomed at a time when educational changes are occurring thick and fast and when the population is increasingly mobile, so as to ensure some degree of continuity, progression, and stability in schools. Others, however, proclaim the traditional autonomy of the English primary school teacher to decide his own curriculum and see any diminution in this as the first step leading to rigid centralized control.

If the present process continues, teacher centres will tend to reinforce this central influence, but local autonomy as far as curriculum development is concerned *can* be promoted at a cost. This promotion of local initiative would require some radical changes. LEA's would have to provide their own research personnel to back up development work (or employ educational consultants); change-agents would have to be employed to get innovation moving in schools; changes in teachers' conditions of service would have to be effected so as to ensure that teachers spent a considerable time on curriculum planning either on the school premises or at the local centre. Local advisory staff would have to be expanded in numbers, and much more use would have to be made of personnel in colleges and universities. In this way effective local projects could be developed to complement and sometimes replace national ones. The latter, too, would benefit from closer, more critical scrutiny at a local level.

Such a course may appear unlikely at present, but to me it seems the only credible alternative to increasing central influence over primary school curricula. Certainly the latter will not be combatted simply by LEA's providing buildings and expecting primary school teachers to have the time, energy, initiative, and expertise to develop new curricula for themselves.

The dissemination of Schools Council orthodoxy is increasing month by month and will continue to increase unless steps are taken . . . But perhaps the complete autonomy of English primary school teachers has always been illusory after all?

Notes

1. Schools Council Working Paper No. 10, *Curriculum Development: Teachers' Groups and Centres* (London: Her Majesty's Stationery Office, 1967), p. 8.

2. Alex Evans, "Teachers, Trainers and Development Centres," *Dialogue,* No. 6, 1970, p. 3. (Republished this volume, Chapter IX.)

DEVELOPING TEACHER CENTRES
J.G. Owen

The ways differ in which a teacher centre can bring into use facilities, personnel, and aid. If a local education authority chooses to be prescriptive, it can attempt by itself to arrange most of what goes on in a local centre. This is unusual, since the teacher unions made it clear in the mid-sixties that teacher centres should be what their name implied: teachers were to organise their own training to meet their own needs. To accede to this idea has been difficult for some authorities. For others it was, early on, difficult to do other than leave the total organisation of the affairs of teacher centres to the teachers. Neither policy, as an overall way of doing things, worked successfully. A too tight control by an LEA led to the idea of compulsion and consequent unwillingness by teachers to attend what were seen simply as traditional training courses; too much autonomy for teachers led to a wallowing about. Teachers in England and Wales were, after all, neither accustomed nor trained to manage their own re-education. Devon's policy was to allow teacher centres, first, to find their own level and then to support them with part-time and, later, with an increasing number of full-time leaders and wardens. To find their own level it was necessary that there should be ample experiment with a number of differing modes of professional self-renewal. Straight courses of instruction in new materials and teaching methods are still arranged; but the idea of seminars, workshops, groups in which the practical trial of ideas can be mingled with discussion and review—each of these represents some type of fresh attempt to allow teachers to relearn in a way which suits their own needs.

Two types of centre had come into being by 1967—one functioning as a disseminatory base for specific national projects, the other with a broader, exhortatory, and inspirational background of total curriculum renewal. Not surprisingly, teachers in areas where a disseminatory centre had been set up took more naturally to the idea of broadening the scope of their efforts. There were arguments about whether there should be in any one area of the country a series of single-purpose centres or a string of generalised curriculum centres. The arguments were not, however, crucial; local education authorities, teachers' associations, and teachers themselves seized on the ideas outlined in Schools Council Working Paper No. 10.* A rapid expansion in the number of centres followed; between 200 and 300 were calculated to have come into being by 1968. By 1972 the figure is estimated to be more than 400.

There has to be some element of guesswork in calculating how many centres there are in England and Wales at any one moment; this is because some centres are physically identifiable, with specially designed (or redesigned) buildings, while others are centres only in the sense that there are agglomerations of teachers who come together in schools within a narrowly defined geographical area. Some centres have full-time organisers (sometimes called leaders, at other times called wardens); others depend on the part-time work of an enthusiastic teacher to map out, with his local committee, the centre's events term by term. Some centres quickly flourish and stay that way; others crawl into life, die, or seem at any moment ready to disappear. And success and failure, in terms of survival or disappearance, depend on several factors.

Conditions of Success

The more tightly bound a centre is to one national project (or more) the better are its chances of survival. If it is a local focus for national work in the humanities, or moral education, or technology, or a new reading method, it can virtually guarantee itself a caucus of interested, committed teachers. But it may also have evolved its own variant in some one aspect of the curriculum—quite independently of national schemes. For example, centres which have consistently produced their own local cooperative schemes for new mathematics teaching find that the vitality of reappraisal and curriculum renewal spreads elsewhere—to art, to language, or to environmental studies.

Other centres will succeed because their leadership is strong; their secretary or their committee may demand of teachers in the area a positive commitment to at least one local scheme of curriculum development. Others, yet again, will succeed because their local authority adviser is respected, supportive, noncondescending, and enthusiastic. Or the local institute of education, or the local college of education, may lend staff and resources to centres. All these are marks of strength.[1]

*In part this could be attributed to the development of the Certificate of Secondary Education in the mid-1960's: as an examination based on regional boards and as an examination whose syllabuses were ostensibly teacher-controlled, many small syllabus-making groups of teachers had already come into being—highly localised and concerned with subject content and examinability. The fact that the idea of professional, self-directed teachers' groups already existed clearly had some significance; but the transfer of interest from separate subjects to the larger concept of curriculum did not prove easy—nor did it have any effect on what happened in *primary* schools.

Marks of weakness can be seen where those who attempt locally to organise a centre's programme aim at a teacher consensus of what is wanted in the way either of regular discussions or of courses—and then fail to gain that consensus. Or the sheer teaching problems of an area whose whole environment is anti-educational may be too great to leave the teacher with the energy to give yet more time and effort to the task of professional self-renewal which a teacher centre may demand of him. This is likely to be the problem of some decayed urban areas; by contrast, in an idyllic country district the teacher may be so accustomed to isolation in a small school that the chance to meet other teachers in the examination of professional problems will be welcome but strange—and the distance (even if it is only 20 minutes in a car) may be enough to discourage even the ardent teacher when there is ice on the roads or when, in summer, a large lawn needs to be mowed. And, in justice to the teaching profession, quite apart from off-the-job satisfaction and compensations, many of its members are already deeply involved in the work of their own subject associations.

There is no better way of giving the flavour of local variations than by quoting the experiences of full-time wardens at a handful of centres in Devon.[2]

First, at the longest established centre, which not only provides very attractive residential facilities but also forms an enclave in one of England's very few colleges specialising in music, drama, and the arts, the number of in-service training courses, conferences, seminars, and workshops has doubled in five years. What is particularly significant is that while work which is a separate concern of teachers in primary and secondary schools has increased gradually and steadily, the combination of primary and secondary work has increased very dramatically. This does not reflect a movement in the reorganisation of middle schools in Devon at the same pace as in other parts of the country, but it does reflect a growing (and national) preoccupation with the period which is now commonly described as "the middle years of schooling." The establishment of comprehensive schools in greater numbers, the abolition of selection tests and of other procedures for separating children according to their abilities at the age of 11—these movements have led to a clearer realisation of the continuous nature of education. One of the strongest forces for continuity is interconnection within the curriculum. The development of stronger lines of continuity is arduous but interesting for teachers who come new to the idea of their dependence upon each other. It is, however, helpful that many national development projects still offer a model of work which, in common with the earliest work which was launched by the Nuffield Foundation, covers the needs of pupils in the age range of 8 to 13 years.

Another noticeable aspect of growth has been the increase in the number of courses and conferences which teachers have attended. In five years, there are twice as many topics covered in the field of primary education; twice as many, too, in secondary education. The increase in the number of topics covered by both primary and secondary teachers together, however, shows a six-fold increase. The growth has, in each case, stemmed from the addition of courses which cover broad topics as well as single subjects. This again illustrates the gradual breakdown of separatism in British education. Not only are the stages of education coming to be more clearly seen to be linked but so also are the subject-matters and disciplines of education.

In a part of the county where, because of topography and tradition, teachers have been accustomed to isolation, another centre shows a comparable increase in the generalised type of course. Here, the centre although it has the longest-serving full-time warden is still only three years old. In that time, however, the teacher centre has passed through three phases: first, what was provided was the instructional type of course which teachers asked for simply to reduce their ignorance. The effects of metrication on British life and the changeover to metric measures at school was a clear example of this kind. New developments in the teaching of reading, new approaches to the humanities, the improvement of careers and counselling services, how best to use various new types of audiovisual aids—each of these found, in the early days, a strong following. Gradually, however, teachers came to feel that there were too many instructional courses. Two strains became apparent: first, an adult has only a limited capacity or patience for being taught rather than for devising something for himself; second, the repetitious demand for attendance week by week created an increasing lethargy.

Group Work

At this point the description was invented of teachers being "overcoursed." A demand developed for more semi-autonomous study groups. The focus of effort moved from the extrinsic to the intrinsic domain. Teachers still ask for information and for (some) instruction; for the rest, however, they prefer to learn for themselves, under good guidance with good support.

But what does guidance or support amount to? Successful groups (to quote the warden of this centre) are characterised by "having (1) a clear purpose or common interest (e.g., to identify the functions of the careers teachers or the characteristics of various reading schemes); (2) an energetic and knowledgeable leader/secretary; and (3) administrative support when needed—in that order of importance."

The same warden goes on to describe how these factors differently affect primary and secondary school teachers, how they differ in their intensity in work which has a continuous thread (for example, the development of methods of team teaching) as against efforts which are short lived or have one straightforward purpose:

> The first two characteristics are seldom found in ad hoc groups of primary teachers. The success of this term's team teaching seminars seems attributable to (i) Heads being concerned about how to make effective use of staff when limitations of space have prevented their using the traditional class/teacher type of organisation; (ii) a very able Head who seemed to the group to have workable solutions to a wide range of detailed problems; and (iii) my being able to attend all meetings, work with the Heads involved and produce detailed minutes of meetings for subsequent study.

And again:

> We have held a substantial proportion of one-off meetings. Most have no obvious follow-up in terms of subsequent meetings but are intended to enable ideas, information and examples of work to be presented which one hopes may be taken up by a small group or in individual schools or classrooms. This does happen. Such meetings are the staple of 'local' centre work where limited numbers inhibit courses or specialised group work for which teachers come to the main centre.

This comment on the effect of single meetings which lead to a proliferation of smaller scale and more localised efforts of teacher-initiated work is in itself interesting. The Warden covers a region of the county; but within that region there are in addition to the centre from which he principally works, smaller country towns, with their own population of teachers who find it easier and possibly more congenial to work together on the basis of a small cell or family of professionals.

In commenting on the changes in attitude and acceptability which he has noticed in his time at this centre, the same warden points out that:

> . . . the relative success of these approaches is only quantifiable in terms of teacher attendances which have been as follows (since accurate records have been kept):

> | | | |
> |---|---|---|
> | Autumn Term 1970 | 28 meetings | 325 attendances |
> | Spring Term 1971 | 22 " | 447 " |
> | Summer Term 1971 | 23 " | 500 " |
> | Autumn Term 1971 | 40 " | 741 " |

These figures must be set against a total "catchment" of some 150 primary school teachers in the major area. Approximately one third of attendances are made by teachers from three neighbouring areas. Secondary teachers' involvement this term, owing to reorganisation, has been negligible.

The latter point that the reorganisation of schools is taking the time and energy of teachers in secondary schools is itself a useful sign of the benefit which the admittedly brief tradition of teacher centres has brought to the profession. Large-scale changes in secondary and post-secondary education in the area have affected four schools and a college of further education (post-16 years). This reorganisation in itself calls for a considerable degree of curriculum replanning. If teachers had not been used to the *idea*—even if they had previously done nothing about it—of being responsible for their own development work, for their own schools' curricula, and for their own subjects' syllabuses, reorganisation would be unlikely to have been accompanied by the same degree of professional self-awareness.

In another area of the same county, rather nearer to the centre of things in that it is geographically nearer to the principal county town, to the local authority headquarters, to the university, the institute of education, and to professional libraries, the same pattern is visible of movement away from specific and instructional courses to more generalised teacher-group enquiries. The warden (again full-time) here suggests that the reasons lie partly in his own increasing awareness of what his job is, growth of experience on the part of the executive committee, of teachers with and through whom he works, a growing and general awareness that what teachers themselves want is important (rather, perhaps, than what others think they need) and the growing acceptance of what teacher centres can achieve—an awareness on the part of teachers and their employers and of other agents in the process of retraining.

The warden suggests, too, that teacher centres have to pass through a process of development which cannot be artifically shortened.

The first stage is that of catering for rudimentary needs ('tips for teachers') and attempting inappropriate in-service techniques (copying existing provisions). Then the Centre begins to develop an identity and its role becomes clearer. Teachers become more actively involved as they learn to dispense with authoritarian leadership. As the surface needs of teachers become gratified, they become more aware of deeper needs—the need to examine critically what and why they are teaching. From this stage, I would prophesy that they will go on to want to examine critically the curriculum as a whole, and from that point to a critical look at the education system.

Three other comments by the same warden have their own interest; he feels, for instance, that:

> ... changes of attitude have taken place in the minds of all the parties involved in Devon with the in-service education of teachers. These changes have come about partly through experience, and partly through deliberate attempts to study and explain the role of teachers' centres in the County. The full-time wardens, who are professionally oriented towards the aims and ideals of in-service education at teachers' centre level have consciously addressed themselves to the task of self-education. It is not recognised clearly enough that at present there is no organised (or even unorganised) form of training for wardens, nor is there very much relevant literature.

Again:

> ... teachers are coming to accept the teachers' centre as part of the educational system, and are becoming more aware of the need for them to play an active as opposed to passive role in their own professional education. This is not to deny that there is still a considerable body of teachers who have not so far found any relevance in the teachers' centre. I suggest that the onus is on the Centre to make itself relevant to teachers. It must not expect an automatic loyalty.

And finally, a comment which has appropriateness for a rural area:

> ... the teachers' centre has become popular with teachers working in small village schools because for the first time in their careers they no longer feel isolated. The opportunities provided by teachers' centre meetings for a conversational exchange of professional ideas, problems, etc. has been of inestimable advantage to such teachers.

Eleven factors are identified by the same warden as being likely to have had particular importance in bringing about changes of attitude towards teachers' centres. Most of these have been mentioned briefly: two which should, however, be noted are that:

> ... many of the changes which have happened are due to more mundane things. The provision of a building has had a big influence on the development of this centre. If nothing else, it has at least given it a physical identity. Again, the provision of generous clerical assistance and good office facilities has been another potent influence. This has enabled the centre to develop better communications, and communications are vital to success—particularly in a rural area.

Teacher centres in any loose structure of curriculum reform such as that of Britain will form a nodal point at which pressures will meet. Prestigious trial projects, the whimsies of those who lead local educational opinion, the strategies (or stratagems) by which change will come about or by which development will be planned—these can clash whenever teachers gather to examine their professionalism. The significance of the clash, whether it destroys cooperation or creates new impetuses will vary from area to area and from subject to subject.

In a recent American commentary it has been suggested that together with child-centered infant education and open-plan primary schools, the British invention of local teacher-based reform of the curriculum may have a very far reaching and significant effect on the educational practices of other developed countries. But the invention is barely seven years old. At present it is enough to say that it seems to be the beginning of a strategy which will succeed.

Notes

1. For an Australian view see G. W. Bassett. *Innovation in Primary Education* (New York: Wiley-Interscience, 1970), pp. 129–130.

2. For these comments I am indebted to Mr. T. A. Q. Griffiths, Mr. J. M. Batten, and Mr. J. le F. Dumpleton.

Chapter VII

American Teacher Centers

Introduction

The chief function of an American teacher center should be to foster the self-education and self-reliance of the teacher. Ironically, the chief initial obstacle to its success is likely to be the attitude of many teachers toward themselves as learners. Too many are inclined to say, "Tell us what you want us to do." Self-respect in teachers is lacking. It needs to be nurtured.

For most teachers the idea that valid knowledge can be gained from their own experience is something new. After a year of running a program for eight experienced Chicago English teachers, R. Parker concluded: "These people suffered, not only as students in schools, but also as teachers, from having been taught that their own personal experiences were not valid data for making inferences about themselves, the world, about teaching, about whatever they are involved in."[1] This attitude is difficult to overcome because the active learning advocated by modern learning theory is best understood actively. Truly to believe it, teachers must themselves experience its superiority to the old passive way. Yet, as Amity Buxton of the San Francisco Teachers' Active Learning Center says, "At first active participation is shocking to teachers because many of them have forgotten what it is like to be a learner."[2] Studied actively, as seemingly frivolous a subject as kites can have immense appeal for teachers as well as children. Bruce Raskin explains:

> As it is done at TALC (Teachers' Active Learning Center) kite-making is academically sound. More than simply cutting, hammering and gluing, it calls for mathematical measurements, scientific balancing, reading instructions, writing down procedures and studying history.[3]

It is a wise commonplace that the education of children must begin "where the child is." It is no less true that the true education of teachers as learners must begin "where the teacher is"; and these beginnings are likely to be humble and slow. They must be respected as such. Objecting that "often the real questions of the teachers have been judged naive," Leonard Marsh quotes Jean-Paul Sartre:

189

... it's much easier for a philosopher to explain a new concept to another philosopher than to a child ... the child, with all its naiveté, asks real questions.[4]

In order to find answers to their real questions, teachers will need help, but it must come at their own request and at their own pace. Ernestine Rouse, former teacher and director of the Advisory Center in Philadelphia, tells of the teachers at the Philadelphia center (including herself) who requested one math workshop after another. A few years later they were asking for and getting a college course in mathematics. These teachers were able to ask for what they needed from their teacher center and were given time for growth. No other kind of teacher education can succeed.

Teachers must also learn to learn from one another. Regretting the "lack of shared experience at the basic professional level," Marsh points out that "a visit to a classroom to see another teacher at work is still a rare opportunity for probably the majority of teachers..."[5] Emily Richard, who directs the Learning Center in St. Louis, sees the center as a "supportive learning environment that brings teachers out of the isolation they may now face and removes the loneliness and uncertainty that so often surround us all."[6] But it is quite possible now to hear teachers say, "Who wants to go to a workshop led by another teacher?" If teachers learn to respect what they can learn from one another, teacher-run centers can quite naturally evolve. The Kennebunk, Maine, workshop on weaving run by three teachers who "wanted to do something," three years ago was a natural beginning point for a teacher center.

The ultimate results of such learning and questioning could be exciting indeed. Calling for educational research "which responds to the real needs of particular teachers and students in the classroom," Irving Spitzberg envisages a "cadre of practical scholars, an unknown breed in American education today": "By enabling teachers to become their own applied research workers, a national program of teachers' centers might do more to improve the quality of U. S. education than all of the NIE's present projects combined."[7]

Such a result, however, will take decades; the American educational establishment will not easily relinquish the right to guide and control teachers in the old ways. Milton Schwebel has stated, "One opportunity a teacher must have is free use of her intelligence. Lacking that she is no boon to any classroom of children no matter what other qualities she has."[8] The free use of intelligence, however, is exactly what is denied teachers by school boards, parents, administrators, college faculties of education. Each group wants to tell the teacher what to do, and even the finest teacher's professional judgment is rarely respected by those who have authority over her. Enlightened teachers need to fight hard for advanced ideas of learning. For the most part, even college of education faculties in this country teach as they themselves were taught, by telling, although most would readily admit that most of what they learned so passively has been lost and forgotten.

The most perilous problem that I can see for American education is that even in their teacher centers teachers will not be allowed to think for themselves. Independent American teacher centres have commonly existed on a shoestring, and funding from governmental or foundation sources is certain to come with built-in conditions. Can this situation change? A partial exception to current funding practices is the policy of the Oakland Unified District in its use of Office of Education funds for teacher centers. This district has announced that it wants "many of the big decisions made by teachers." As Raskin reports, the district "has the power to make grants directly to teachers to set up centers of their own, and at one point gave some of its money to TALC."[9]

Edith Biggs, who is one of the leaders of the teacher center movement in England, has said, "teachers must be in control. After all they're the ones who know best what they want and need."[10] This country needs people at the highest levels who believe this and act on it.

The work of some of the very able people working in American teacher centers appears in this section. The question is: Will they and others be supported, not just with money, but also with respect for their professional integrity and autonomy?

Notes

1. R. Parker, "Symposium: Problems, Issues, Questions, and Application of Piaget's Theory." Conference, Application of Piagetian Theory to Education: An Inquiry Beyond the Theory. (New Brunswick, N. J.: Rutgers University, Graduate School of Education, 1970). Quoted in Milton Schwebel and Jane Raph, *Piaget in the Classroom* (New York: Basic Books, 1973), p. 285.

2. Bruce Raskin, "Teachers Helping Teachers," *Learning*, September 1973, p. 30.

3. *Ibid.*, p. 30.

4. Leonard Marsh, *Being a Teacher* (London: A & C Black, 1973), p. 2.

5. *Ibid.*, p. 4.

6. Karen Branan, "Try a Teacher Center," *Scholastic Teacher*, September 1973, p.18.

7. Irving Spitzberg, "Teachers' Centers: A New Approach to Improving Education," *The New Leader*, June 11, 1973, p. 15.

8. Schwebel and Raph, *op. cit.*, p. 278.

9. Raskin, *op. cit.*, p. 31.

10. *Ibid.*, p. 30.

THE PHILADELPHIA TEACHER CENTER

Lore Rasmussen

The Philadelphia Teacher Center and its parent, the Learning Centers Project, are self-education endeavors for all who participate in them—teachers, administrators, parents, paraprofessionals, and future teachers.

Thinking of children's learning as the prime target, it is one attempt at reorganizing the resources of a school system and a community to facilitate simultaneous voluntary learning for all parties involved in a child's school experience. It is focused on creating stimulating environments, producing knowledgeable teacher-learners, strengthening healthy, honest, supportive relationships within and across peer groups.

The need and request for a Teacher Center grew organically and gradually out of local Philadelphia school history.

As early as 1963-1964, learning center laboratories were developed in several inner-city elementary schools so children could at least part of the day have activity-centered, informal learning experiences. Lab teachers were specially trained on the job. Classroom teachers accompanied their children to the labs and thus were simultaneously with their children exposed to the new environments and styles of teaching. These direct experiences of teachers were supplemented by after-school workshops in the labs where teachers worked with the children's materials. As a result some classroom teachers in some of the nine affiliated schools were gradually reshaping their own classrooms, assisted by a two-person traveling staff and the resident lab teacher whose labs became mini-resource centers of ideas and equipment for those teachers. Though started by small local funds, the success of the idea led to the creation of a Title I funded Learning Centers Project with a headquarters-advisory office in one of the schools. By 1967 the momentum for change and the request for help to reshape classrooms had become so vast and were coming from such geographically distant locations that a more efficient and more consolidated supportive staff development model had to be devised to supplement what the headquarters office could do.

It was at that time that our first approximation to our present Teacher Center emerged as the answer. In a small school with a receptive principal where we had both a children's lab and several changing classrooms, we extended one weekly school day into the evening, setting up a construction/ carpentry workshop in the gym. We held science and math lab sessions in the children's lab, while some teachers with the help of colleagues worked on their rooms. Not only did most of the teachers from that school participate voluntarily, but many other teachers who had heard about it by word of mouth came from their schools.

Dramatic change in teacher morale, teacher interaction, teaching styles, classroom appearance occurred as the year progressed. Not everyone was affected in the same way or to the same extent, but in no way was there any external pressure to change.

By 1968 the Teacher Center had so great a following that the school system responded by offering us our own quarters in the same building, where we were also allowed to gather together five of our most challenging teachers to establish a little mini-school. These teachers, who already had strong ties to the Learning Centers Project and the Teacher Center, continued to be nourished by the Teacher Center. They in turn became an extension learning opportunity for teachers who came to the Teacher Center and made visits as well to the mini-school. Since the mini-school had only the regular meager budget of any other school and no new equipment, their rooms became rich storehouses of Teacher Center-made equipment to be seen in use.

The third "tenant" in the building—also moving in at the same time—was the district superintendent, our patron, and his staff, who—luck would have it—this January became Philadelphia's Superintendent of Schools.

Not only did the Teacher Center for the first time now have permanent quarters but also its importance and acceptance in the eyes of the administration were nonverbally self-evident to every visiting teacher by this housing pattern. The teacher-run mini-school on the first floor, the superintendent on the second floor, the Teacher Center and a film-media center on the third floor, together presented a model for new patterns of linkages between children, administration, and teachers. Though privacy existed for each group, increasingly used opportunities for interacting in newly meaningful ways were built in from the start.

Teachers largely initiated both ventures, the mini-school and the Teacher Center, under the umbrella of the system's curriculum office. Expenses for the first part-time staffing and some of the materials were borne by the Early Childhood Education Study, O. E. O.

Beginning as an after-school voluntary program two days a week, it was soon extended through the cooperation of the administration into a "released time" day program for staff development, particularly kindergarten teachers. The facility was open not only for District Two, in which it was housed, but on a citywide basis. The school system also gradually increased its financial input to support the all-day program.

Emphasis continued to be on making equipment and learning aids of teacher choice for classrooms, on sharing ideas among teachers, engaging in learning mathematics and science by laboratory methods, using the mini-school to get some models for reorganizing the classroom physically, pedagogically, and content-wise.

When the following year a better building became available in a more central location which had a well-equipped shop, more space for the Teacher Center and the Learning Centers Project office, and more extended children's school, we moved to our present location, where we are finishing our third year.

The special and deliberate setting of the Philadelphia Teacher Center is now in the Durham Child Development Center, a first approximation of a "womb to tomb" public school, located in a 1909-built former elementary school in the center of Philadelphia on 16th and Lombard Streets.

The Teacher Center is one of the six special units of this neighborhood center although its service population has a citywide range. To understand the Teacher Center fully, we need to get acquainted with the other program features of Durham.

All components housed in the building interact in informal and organic ways though each has its own private housing, own target population, own staff.

The individual parts are: a continuous education program for junior high school age mothers who come during pregnancy and return soon after birth for a complete school year; an Infant Care Center for infants and toddlers, three weeks to three years of age, many of them the children of the young mothers; a Headstart unit for three and four year olds; a K-5 ungraded, informal Learning Center elementary school; and the headquarters-advisory office of the citywide Learning Centers Project.

The children come by parent choice from five neighborhood school populations. Preference is given in admissions to siblings, thus giving the school a strong bond with parents, who because of the teacher-parent center also have a school to come to. Many parents work in the building both in paid jobs and as volunteers.

Children come from all socioeconomic and educational backgrounds and are both black and white, although the majority are black, and poor.

Most of the conversion of facilities from their bleak look of old, typical inner-city elementary schools to their new imaginatively redesigned spaces was done by the staff and parents themselves, largely through assistance by or in the Teacher Center. The raw materials were bought, found, or donated, and little money was expended on commercial products. Thus the developing rehabilitation of the building and programs itself represents to all visitors from other schools and to the community the living proof of what a school can do on the grass roots level to change itself when it has an idea.

The building itself is a community for all ages of man. The rooms on the first floor are the "homes" of the young teenage mothers and the children under five years of age. The third floor is the private quarters of the five to eleven year olds and their staff.

A wing of the second floor houses the Teacher Center and the Learning Centers Project headquarters, while also on that floor are other special facilities such as the math lab, a library, a lounge, a dining room, and a kitchen.

This second floor becomes a shared community facilities floor where all age groups circulate as they use its facilities.

The hallways throughout the building are lively streets in a good climate community, reflecting in their "street life" the needs of the adjacent homes they serve. They are instructional, social, and work spaces.

The staff is continually newly exploring how to provide for every child the rich learning opportunities implied by such a wide age mix. Older children serve as assistants for toddlers and preschoolers. All children use the facilities of the Teacher Center and its shop. Teachers and parents who come to the Teacher Center mix there with the children or when numbers permit spend some of their time in the rooms of the children.

After school hours many a teacher from another school with a Teacher Center staff guide, tour the classrooms of the children—to find inspiration in the room arrangements, the evidences of children's work and curriculum content, or teacher-made equipment and learning aids. They then return to the Teacher Center to work out their own adaptation of something gleaned to apply it to their teaching. The power of that experience of direct access to teacher-children spaces in daily use is one of the strong assets in a Teacher Center built into a dynamic, ongoing school.

The mathematics lab, which is staffed by a math educator, and the Learning Centers Project headquarters office, which also houses a resident community designer, contribute by request to tailor-made planning or tutoring for teachers in these areas of specialization.

Through the wide range and long-standing activities of the Learning Centers Project, its headquarters and staff services attract large numbers of administrators for help in planning on the school and district level. These services are integrated with the Teacher Center. Similarly the Director of the building has become a focal point for advice from community groups, university groups, or school system groups interested in creating new services for young children. All of those visitors are exposed to the Teacher Center and see its essential function in both the creation of the rich resources of the building and as a continuous change agent.

This is dramatically demonstrated by the fact that several other districts are planning to build into under-utilized schools or phased-out schools infancy, preschool, *and* teacher-parent centers.

The benefits of this interrelationship of services and the natural richness of the in-service education possible are a matter of common sense.

The Durham Child Development Center itself in each of its parts has become a field training placement center for many kinds of paraprofessional, preservice, and in-service education. Child-care training programs both for infant-care givers and preschool trainees from Temple University place their students with us. Student teachers and graduate interns serve assistantships with us. The Antioch Urban Education Center has six undergraduates working with us for a year. For all of these people, as for the total building staff, the Teacher Center is a widely used resource on an individual and small-group basis.

The simple fact that the building is open every day until 5:30 p.m. because of our infant day care program and until 8:oo p.m. twice a week because of the Teacher Center allows adults working in the building to voluntarily extend their school day way beyond the 2:30 school closing time. That they actually do so most days is particularly attributable to the existence of the enticing self-help Teacher Center and other facilities on the second floor.

Many a 6:00 p.m. check on a Teacher Center day has shown that in addition to regular and special programs planned by its staff, combinations of trainees, Durham staff, and visiting teachers have filled every room on the floor with such self-organized activities as a singing or guitar group, a discussion group around a videotape of children, or a work-party in a classroom.

The core group of teachers who have been associated with the development of the Learning Centers Project, its first labs and lab classrooms, and the Teacher Center became teacher-writers at a time when few professional writers or publishing firms addressed themselves to the needs we had. These writings they exchanged as much as possible. They were sought out by newcomers who came to the Teacher Center.

The press of time and the lack of financial resources had kept us until now from making full use of these materials. A small grant from the Ford Foundation will make it possible this next half year to prepare for wider use by working teachers the store of experiences, curriculum sequences, and ideas which we as individuals have acquired. This will undoubtedly allow us to reach even more people than our personal interaction has been able to do, and the materials will become another program offering of the Teacher Center.

Gradually we are also assembling slide collections, videotapes, and design plans for sharing and are developing better techniques to give diversified workshops outside the building for large groups to acquaint them with our story.

Environmental studies, the use of community resources—people, places, and things—is probably one of the strongest emerging new themes.

Our experience has given us a new definition of "integration" for a school—namely *inter-age,* infancy to adult, in addition to the racial, economic, and educational ingredients. Thus the Teacher-Parent Center as the adult component of such a multiage center, is the core of the education of the young.

A VIEW FROM THE SHOP
Donald Rasmussen

The workshop of our Philadelphia Teacher Center (the part of the enterprise with which I work) was organized in 1967-68 in the basement of an inner-city elementary school. Our working area was in a gym-auditorium and we had the uses of an adjoining room for storage. Our tools consisted of a sabre saw, a power drill, and a few hand woodworking tools—most of which I brought from my workshop at home. Our materials were mainly scrap wood, bottles, and containers, with some lumber and wire that we purchased for animal cages. With these materials, a coworker and I advertised among the school staff that we would visit classrooms (only by invitation of the teacher) in order to suggest projects that might spark the program and otherwise be of help in whatever the teacher wanted to do. We were extremely careful not to challenge existing practices and programs and not to come as the representatives of a new approach with a superior philosophy with fresh slogans and jargon to meet the needs of a new day. Once a week for two or three hours after school teachers assembled with us in the basement to construct whatever they had decided was desirable for their classrooms.

I remember very well some of the projects. One second-floor third-grade classroom had a balcony outside one window and I suggested the construction of a bird-feeding station where children might study the birds that stay in the city during winter. The teacher liked the idea and we gathered branches, made feeders, and set up the station. The children observed the kinds of birds that came by, the numbers of each, the times they came, what the birds liked best to eat. They drew pictures, made graphs, and wrote essays. (Some children spent more time looking out the window than at their books.) Another class was studying Indians but through the facilities of the shop and a trip to the country to get some poles, the children were able to make a large tipi and a fireplace. The project created so much excitement, several parents came to school to check on the veracity of their children's reports. Another teacher made a classroom store, and the kindergarten teachers made some cages for the crop of Easter rabbits. It was not long before teachers from other schools asked if they could join in the use of the shop.

In this, our fifth year, five to six thousand teachers will visit our Center.

198

Thirteen to fifteen hundred will come to all-day workshops on released time from their jobs, and four to five thousand will come on a voluntary basis after school and on Saturdays. In addition to serving this number of teachers, we have tried to relieve the pressure on us by helping with the establishment of several more workshops in the city and two in the suburbs. (Helping with the establishment of centers in other parts of the city is consistent with our aim of becoming increasingly a local concern working with the parents and teachers of our district of the city.)

Our all-day workshops are scheduled affairs with the mathematics teachers of a particular district, the kindergarten teachers of another, the parents and teachers of a particular school, the Get-Set teachers of a supervisor, the Head-start teachers of a cluster, and so on. We schedule approximately 20 to 25 for a session. The voluntary after-school program attracts teachers of all age groups from all over the city and suburbs (even cities 75 miles away). Most of these teachers are from early-childhood programs and elementary public schools. Hardly a session does not now include a few nuns and lay teachers from the parochial schools. We are also getting more and more parents from our local area coming to make furniture and games for their children. And we have an increasing number of workers from day care centers, hospitals, and social agencies serving the children of the city.

The offerings of the Center have now expanded to include far more than a workshop for the construction of wood and tri-wall things. We have tools and materials for work in clay, weaving, painting, sewing, and other crafts. We announce through our *Teacher Center News* special workshops on weaving, macramé, needlework, cooking, potting, beading, science, photography, music, and many other topics. For the past several months we have had a regular series of games called "Interplay" attended each week by 20 to 40 people. And we have a mathematics laboratory—used by children during the day and teachers in the evenings. Here teachers come for informal sessions on announced topics or they come to confer on individual problems and participate in whatever activity evolves.

Although the workshop has grown over the years, the principles of our organization and our methods of working with teachers have remained essentially the same. From the beginning we have been committed to teachers who wish to help themselves—to change their style of teaching or their classrooms. Except for those who come to us on released time, teachers are not paid to attend the workshop. Those who do come on released time are introduced to the program by being offered as many choices for their personal development or for the making of things for their classrooms as we can provide. After being presented with alternatives, they are completely free to become involved as they wish. We therefore do not measure our success by the number of teachers who attend on released time. We begin to count them when they come to us on a voluntary basis.

Our methods of working with teachers are of necessity individualized because each one comes for a very specific purpose and from a different setting. We are, therefore, a kind of open classroom for adults—a demonstration of one of the alternatives teachers consider for themselves. Whenever we are asked we point out that we are organized as an open classroom out of necessity because no teacher would return (they would drop out) if we lined them up, kept them quiet, and dominated their activities.

We have found by experimenting with different formats that we are limited to 20 to 25 persons at a time in each of our shops and workshop activities. Beyond that number, people begin to line up for tools and materials and our help becomes mechanical instead of human and personal. We always have hot coffee or tea available at the workshop and explain to people that drinking a cup gives one permission to ask anyone else what he is making and why. It also requires a drinker to explain, when asked, what he is making and why. We try to facilitate as much conversation and exchange of ideas as possible because the best teachers of teachers are other teachers.

Our workshop began with a very simple objective—to help teachers get and make the things *they* wanted or felt *they* needed to work more effectively with *their* children. We entered *their* classroom with *their* consent to effect the changes *they* desired. This objective, supporting teachers no matter what they want, remains the same today as yesterday. It is not always easy to help different people with different objectives—perhaps going off in different directions—all at the same time! We ourselves are not devoid of an educational preference and think of many classrooms as little tombs and some schools as mausoleums. But to choose the path of promoting in our Center the support of a single educational program or a particular classroom arrangement or a certain type school would have turned away many teachers whose first step in transforming their classrooms could not possibly be described in terms of a particular philosophic view. Rarely have we found teachers unwilling to consider making some changes in their classrooms or in their methods. And most administrators in Philadelphia are generally supportive of many classroom changes teachers would make. Yet, it is difficult, oftentimes impossible, to take an initial step in any direction for lack of support within the system. For example, by the time many teachers can go through the procedures for acquiring a simple material like a few boards or sand or even paper, they have forgotten why they wanted it. A convenient teacher center is the means for a teacher to carry out an idea on Tuesday that occurred on a busy Monday.

Our Center would best be described by analysing each of the people attending it—what she came for, why she returned, what happened with what she made or learned. To do this is, of course, impossible. Descriptions of a few individuals might illustrate and make meaningful some of the general remarks made above.

I had oftentimes said that I would help a teacher make a paddle if he asked for that help. Fortunately we have not had that request, but one day a young man from a new junior high school came in to the workshop to make some hall passes. Little did he know what a complicated project that might become. I raised many questions. What is the best material to make a *durable* hall pass? What is the best size so that it will not be lost and yet is convenient? What color should it be? (We settled on day-glo.) What shape? Do we have to make them all alike—unattractive, dull, and uniform? What about the finish so they can be kept sanitary? We agreed on all the answers and proceeded with production—at a bench next to one of our best customers—whom we called the "knock-hockey teacher." He was busy making the fourth knock-hockey table for his classroom. Naturally as the two were working next to one another, they conversed. I did not question the advisability of making hall passes. That might happen in the conversation or it might happen in a future visit to the Center. On this occasion the young man did find out what children learn from playing knock-hockey in the classroom.

Our most frequent customer at the Center for the past three years came to us shortly after his school burned down. He with three other teachers and their classes were moved into a church basement. The teacher came to the Center to make some furniture which was very much needed. He liked making the display tables, room dividers, and easels so he continued on to the construction of some materials for science and mathematics. After a year of coming to the Center at least twice a week, he remarked one day, "You know—I don't teach like I used to. I used to have to yell and order kids around. Looking back, it seems that's all I did. Now I have an entirely different way of working with kids and my views on discipline are not what they were. If I have the furniture I want and put things around that capture the kids' interest, they start asking questions. They don't make trouble because they want to hear what I have to say. They discipline themselves and I don't have to yell at them all the time. For me I'd have to say I'm glad my old school burned." The teacher is now the science specialist in a large new elementary school. He comes to the Center at least once a week—no longer to make furniture but usually to make science equipment and to learn its uses.

We have had a large number of teachers from the parochial schools coming to the Center this year. They have been mainly interested in making tables, chairs, and bookcases. One evening some nuns brought five seminarians and together they made six round tables and 40 chairs. They used over a $100-worth of materials. Since it isn't my ambition to run a furniture factory, I was a little bothered and thought that next time they came, I would take them to the math lab to see what fine devices we had there. As it turned out, I didn't have to do that at all. On leaving with the tables and 40 chairs, one of the sisters expressed her gratitude—and explained that they didn't have in her school any tables where the children could sit around and see one another as they worked and talked. They didn't have the money to acquire the tables and therefore the Center was a blessing. They would return to make some other things. They had already seen the math lab without my noticing it.

A week ago a nun spent three days making a toy automobile out of a four-foot-long cardboard tube and some wheels. (The tube was scrap from a box manufacturer.) She brought it to her school located in a very poor ghetto area in north Philadelphia. Yesterday she told me that the kids wore the car out in three days but she succeeded in her objective—to start a car-building craze in her neighborhood. She said, "When the kids found out that I built the car, they said, 'Oh, if you can make that car Sister, we know we can do it.' Now they are looking for wheels and the junk to make their own cars." At the Center I can't yet decide whether she made the car for her own personal pleasure or to promote a serious educational program! She was back this week, covered with sawdust as she was making a desk for a child in his home.

We have seen the growth of our Center over the years but how about its influence? We have now worked with and observed more than 10,000 teachers as they have left the workshop with their shoe box labs, puppet theaters, chairs, tables, and a hundred thousand other things. Can we speak of the effect of all this on the lives of children in schools and classrooms? Did everything that was made even reach the children? For example, did the cubicle a teacher made become the isolation cell within a classroom prison or did it provide the privacy all children need from the active, busy people around them? Did the balance a teacher made for her kindergarten come to stand like a cross in the corner symbolizing her devotion to a personal ideal or did it become a tool for children to discover relationships in the physical world around them? Did the teacher in the workshop who cried, "I can't use that saw; I never did it before," and yet tried, recognize that children were echoing her every day with the same cry about math and spelling? We don't know the answer to these kinds of questions unless we are able to visit the classrooms of teachers who have been at the Center. Occasionally, all too infrequently, we have that opportunity and when we do, we are invariably impressed with the importance to a teacher of the least thing he or she had created at the workshop. Anything that has been constructed at the workshop is usually shown to us with pride and we in turn feel like parents looking at a child's first step.

On the occasion of our visits we also have been impressed with the need for a much closer relationship between our workshop staff and teachers. It is the most important objective in our next year. We feel we could multiply many-fold the benefits of the workshop to children. We could learn what services the Center should provide that it is not now giving. We could help teachers much more with the use of the things we have helped them make in the workshop. We have helped many teachers take a first step. Visiting classrooms would enable us to learn more and do more about the second and third and fourth. Some teachers get so enthusiastic about a giant first step they want to throw out all the desks on the second. Perhaps that should be the 99th step if it is to be done at all. At the Center as well as on the occasion of our visits, we get a barrage of questions—What do you think I should make now that I have the puppet theater? How do I use these geo-boards now that I have made them? (Teachers sometimes make the things other teachers are making and they find out what to do with them later!) My kids just loved the rabbits. What other animals do you think I can have? Do you think I could cook in my classroom? To answer these questions, to know what we are doing, to know our influence, to see what happens to children, to know how to help more effectively in the Center, the staff must get into more classrooms.

Two weeks ago I had the opportunity to visit the classroom of a teacher who had been coming to the Center rather regularly for the past two years. I found that she was the only teacher in a large old school trying to develop an activity-centered program for her fourth grade children. She had made many games, some looms, room dividers, book displays, and many other things at the workshop. She had not moved out any desks and now they were getting in the way of her program. Together we decided that we must build some storage facility to take care of the personal items of each child. Also we decided to put plywood sheets over clusters of four desks to make tables. In this way she would not have to answer that terrible charge (usually spread by an alarmed custodian), "My God, she's throwing out the desks. What's coming next?"

The principal of the school accompanied me to the classroom and I could comment to him how happy the children were, how all of them were occupied and how well behaved, how much self discipline they had as they shared materials and worked at a great variety of activities. It was very good that the principal was along because the teacher had transformed the classroom as much as she could without now involving other teachers and the principal. She was being observed by her colleagues and her program could very well become a threat to them. She had to have administrative support along with the support of our Center. In two weeks I have an appointment with the district superintendent to visit the classroom again. Knowing the superintendent, I am certain that the teacher will be able to continue developing her program and will continue to be able to come to the Center to get more ideas and to make more things for a long time to come. One day I am also certain that she will bring along a colleague or two.

THE TEACHERS' ACTIVE LEARNING CENTER:
AN AMERICAN ADAPTATION OF BRITISH TEACHER CENTERS

Amity P. Buxton, Florence Bradford, Sujenna Kofsky,
Amada Escosteguy Brown, Marilyn Burns, and Kazuhiro Tsuruta

Introduction

Three years ago, the Teachers' Active Learning Center was a vision in the minds of three teachers. It was a vision of how we could implement our perception of British teacher centers as we had seen them operating. Now the Teachers' Active Learning Center is a reality developed over the past three years: first, as a preservice mathematics curriculum in 1969-70; next, in 1971, as a one-night-a-week in-service program of mathematics open to all teachers in the San Francisco Bay Area; and, finally, this year, when we have refined the conceptual basis of the Center, designed a full-time program, and clarified the key operational components upon which we comment below.

The following is a description of its present concept, implementation, and process as one example of a teacher center—not a model or an instantaneous experiment with an imported model—but an example developed gradually from observations and experiences in England and adapted to the particulars of the participants, the locale, and the events of the San Francisco Bay Area.

Before proceeding, we state with pleasure our full recognition of the professional guidance, information, materials, cooperation, and encouragement that has been given us so generously by many educators in England—individual headmasters, local education authorities, the national inspectorate, the Schools Council, and the Nuffield Foundation. In particular we underscore our debt to the many individual teachers who unreservedly welcomed us and shared with us their knowledge, practice, and life of their classrooms.

The Center

What is the Teachers' Active Learning Center? What makes it a "center"? Why an "active learning center"?

Physically, the Teachers' Active Learning Center comprises the second floor of a building at the edge of the central city in a light industrial area. The space has a variety of learning areas which reflect and encompass the range of curriculum content but are used in conjunction with one another as a basis for making interdisciplinary connections.

The format is that it be open all day and three nights during the week, and other times, including weekends, for special events sponsored by the Center or requested by teachers. The staff, at present, includes six specialists with varied backgrounds at all levels and school settings but all with experience and familiarity with the English school system and local adaptations.

The Concept

Through our experience we have identified three major components of the concept of an active learning center for teachers: (1) a physical environment which is stimulating, flexible, but structured; (2) a personal climate which is supportive and collaborative; and (3) dependent upon these two factors, the direct interaction of the participants with the environment on a continuing basis through structured activities—namely, active learning.

Implementation

From the start, certain components seemed to be characteristic of the implementation of the concept of teacher centers as we had seen them operate in England—while we were highly cognizant of the fact that English teacher centers vary greatly in their operations according to local conditions.

From our particular experience, we have found five components to be essential conditions of implementation: (1) the centrality of teachers, (2) voluntary participation, (3) heterogeneity of participants, (4) focus on curriculum content, and (5) independence.

(1) The first essential component is the *centrality of teachers,* the central position of teachers in the work of learning and making of curriculum. The teacher center is teacher-centered—just as the major objective is that teachers begin to develop child-centered classrooms.

Here, teachers act; they do not just receive. At the heart of the educational process is the teacher who identifies his own needs. It is he who is responsible for his own learning and action necessary to change.

(2) The second essential component is the *voluntary participation* of the teachers and other teaching personnel. Because attendance is not mandatory, resistance—a primary obstacle to learning—is removed. Freed from resistance, a teacher is open to interact with the learning environment and structured

activities. He can focus on learning, on content, and on self-generated change in his own classroom.

Because of the voluntary nature of participation, it is a deliberate policy that communication or publicity be based on word-of-mouth, leading to teacher-to-teacher invitation based on their experience at the center.

The stress on voluntary participation has meant that the staff has to work continually to keep the quality of the content and process focused on needs of the teachers. When attendance waned, we knew that the quality of the program had waned.

(3) The third essential component is the *heterogeneity of participants.* In order to capitalize on teachers' individual and collaborative energy focused and freed to learn and to construct child-centered learning opportunities, the center has kept its doors open to all persons involved in teaching; from public/ private and inner-city/suburban schools at all levels. There has been no exclusion or subordination of any groups of teaching personnel to another. During the pilot year, for instance, the over-400 participants came from a variety of schools covering a radius of 30 miles, which included a range of community settings representative of the Bay Area population.

(4) The fourth essential component is the *focus on curriculum content.* The aim is that the activities and the environment of the center lead a teacher to become a learner and a maker of curriculum—not only of materials, or aids, or processes, although these are certainly important.

The focus on curriculum content is based on that holistic approach toward content that does away with subject-centered divisions of curriculum and instead promotes the perception of content as experienced in the environment. To this end, the staff strives to construct the center itself and the program to reflect the real environment of the world and to demonstrate the power of that environment to serve as a source and a means of learning. Thus, a teacher who interacts with the place and the people of the center finds himself interacting within a learning environment that allows for a new way of viewing curriculum content and thereby new ways of working with and developing traditional curriculum areas for his classroom.

While the focus is continually on content, the activities also relate to the ongoing classroom work and to the individual children who are there at that point in time. In turn, teachers bring feedback from their classes related to the ongoing experiences in the center. Through this two-fold active learning—in the center and in the classroom—a teacher begins to develop the viewpoint of curriculum content which is interdisciplinary and environmental and the competencies necessary to develop such a curriculum for his own classroom.

(5) The fifth essential component, at this time, is *independence* from the existing structure of educational institutions. As of now, the learning space of the center itself is on neutral ground, not housed in a school or college building. The activities offer no college or increment credits. It is a meeting place for teachers and all other educational resource people who contribute to the end product which is the quality of the educational experience in the classroom. At the moment, a physical separation from school and college is seen as necessary in order that the teacher center be perceived as different from the usual notion of in-service education.

Here a teacher dares to risk failures and to test alternative responses that are part of learning and by which learning can be stimulated, enhanced, and increased. From this experience, a teacher is better able to interpret the "mistakes" and alternative responses of the children in his classroom, to use them for increasing individual learning, and to develop a curriculum with extended content possibilities.

Distinctions in the Operation

Those are the major components of the Teachers' Active Learning Center as conceived and implemented. But as we commenced operation in 1970, three of these components began to assume more and more significance. The central position of teachers, voluntary participation, and independence became points of importance as we began to develop the program. It also became evident that these components were derived from a concept of teacher education in Britain which was different from that which most teachers have experienced in this country—a concept in which teachers have a central position, in which voluntary participation is practiced in most teacher centers, and in which most of the educational institutions support teacher-centered activity.

Therefore, in order to implement the concept locally, we found it necessary to clarify these three components and related characteristics during these beginning years.

The neutral position of the center, independent of other educational institutions is, in our viewpoint, a major difference in kind between this example and the British teacher centers in general. It has been only recently that there have been beginnings of an interlocking institutional context in this country for the support of teacher-initiated change, whereas in Britain there has been for some time a supportive institutional context of the local educational authorities, the inspectorate, and a number of national bodies such as the Schools Council and foundations like the Nuffield Foundation.

The remaining components and characteristics are, of course, similar to those found in the British teacher centers in general, but in the light of the different situation in this country at this particular time it has been important to clarify three related characteristics of the ongoing operation: the individual participant's *doing,* the nonjudgmental function of the staff, and the developmental nature of change.

First, we have found it has been necessary to stress the fact that it is through the teachers' *doing* and *becoming* that change can begin to occur.

Second, as a staff, we have found it important to be nonjudgmental in our own attitude and to act not as supervisors, rather as peers and resources in the continuing process of learning, each contributing with his own particular strength alongside the strengths of the teachers.

Third, we have found it ever so important to underscore the gradual developmental nature of change in teacher behavior and in the making of curriculum.

Process

From participation in and observation of the process of the teachers' active learning at the center, we have consistently noted that the above-mentioned components and characteristics were operating as constant factors whenever effective learning seemed to have occurred. These components then emerged as touchstones for gauging the quality of the educational experience.

But as we looked at what we were doing in the light of these factors we noticed, quite unexpectedly, that this continuous awareness and close scrutiny had become *per se* an additional factor in the process and that something different was happening in the way of evaluation—that is, the putting of words and actions together.

We found ourselves looking hard at what we were doing and demanding of ourselves what we were expecting of others, of the teachers in their classrooms. Moreover, it had to do with our taking immediate action to create conditions to re-energize any factors we found missing after close scrutiny. We found ourselves saying, for example, "Look, last night's session wasn't working because x, y, and z were missing; next Wednesday we must be sure that x, y, and z happen."

In other words, it is a different kind of evaluation that we foresee developing—not that of a final judgment passed, but rather that of looking, assessing, and reforming in a continual process—a three-fold dynamic of awareness, scrutiny, and action to maintain the quality of the learning experiences in the Teachers' Active Learning Center as it was first envisioned in our minds three years ago.

Chapter VIII

Teaching Resources Centers

Introduction

> There is much discussion among teachers, tutors and inspectors about more inter-play between the commissions of the Schools Council and the teachers' centres to spread new ideas and methods at all levels. The centres could also form part of a national system of resource banks, various types of which are now being explored. The University of London Institute of Education has employed an expert in computer filing systems to help design a flexible system which will classify and keep up to date numerous references, films, tapes, art slides, newspapers, etc., linking them to subject areas and themes. In another college in Kent a tutor and a group of 100 students are building up and using a system of this sort and are supplying the information it contains to local schools for teachers to use as a resource bank.[1]

What resources should a teacher center offer?

Environmental studies have played an increasingly important role in the development of the curriculum of the English primary school. Yet in a mobile society, knowledge about a particular area is difficult to come by for the individual teacher. Hubbard and Salt, writing in this chapter, cite the need for efficiently stored local educational archives. They see teacher centers as *teaching resources centers* and make a plea that centers reach out to become educational resources for the community at large. In this country, teacher centers would be optimally situated to make the needed liaison with community resources for learning: the museums, historical societies, libraries, local people, science centers, art galleries.

Walton's article in this chapter examines the growth of the University of Exeter Regional Resources Centre which he directs, and considers the difficulties of new methods of teaching which with their formidable demands on teachers make it unlikely that the teacher could provide all the unending resources she needs herself. Emmeline Garnett, who headed a pioneering Leicestershire experiment in resources centers, has spoken eloquently of just this need for a resources center from a teacher's point of view:

> Although books are still and no doubt always will be the most important single resource for learning, the traditional textbook, developing a subject linearly, and

211

carrying tram-lines in its very format, gives teachers increasing dissatisfaction. As they use traditional methods of instruction more sparingly, they want, instead of textbooks, printed information of a kind which will foster the techniques of research and evidence-sifting even among slow readers. They want prepared materials with a high visual content—film, slides, film strip, film loop, microfilm, photographs, videotape. They want materials which allow young students to seek evidence from original sources, or at least from facsimiles of originals: maps, documents, newspaper files, archives. They want materials with a direct impact on the ear—records, tapes, radio programmes. They want evidence of objects, people and places, and if these are not of a size and transportability to bring directly into schools, they want the evidence to lose as little as possible in transit—people on tape, for instance, rather than transferred to print. Alternatively, they want the information and know-how to allow them to take their young students direct to the mountain if the mountain cannot be brought in. And they want all this in duplication and diversity enough for students to work some part of the time as individuals and in small groups, with some element of choice and self-programming. . . . This is a sketch of what an Area Resource Centre might be and do. It is now the time for an Authority somewhere to establish the thing itself.[2]

Her own small staff, believing that they did not know, "and we have not found anybody else who knows, how to ensure that what the teacher wants is there when he wants it,"[3] decided against an effort to establish a massive library of abstract resource materials and instead concentrated on specific resources made by local teachers and students which could be shared through their center. Walton's center also has worked in close collaboration with teachers, providing resources for specific local needs.

One teacher, writing of resources practices in primary schools, contrasts teacher-developed resources or self-directed use of prepared resources with "ready-made assignment cards (that) 'tell' the children what to do . . . one has reduced the teacher's role to little more than a minding and correcting agent."[4] Clearly, the teacher's personal active role in resources development is not to be ignored. A high degree of involvement on the part of teachers in the center would be encouraged by storing, displaying and discussing their ideas and resources as Hubbard and Salt here suggest. Along with resources developed by teachers and focused on local needs, teacher centers could offer open-ended, flexible collections of materials which could be used in many different ways, on both the primary and secondary levels.

In this chapter Mitson indicates that his comprehensive school resources center for secondary teachers and students has been modestly successful in breaking down departmental barriers. He gives a vivid picture of a school working toward greater teacher and child initiative, which resources approaches encourage.

The secondary teacher in England is in the early stages of understanding a resources approach to learning, as both elementary and secondary teachers are in this country. As Douglas Holly has said of the English:

> Those intending to teach in secondary schools have hitherto perceived their job in terms of the conventional subjects: the needs of a "curriculum," which the pupil will "follow" . . . The sort of skills required of teachers using a resources approach . . . are not likely to be fully developed in such a context . . . Resources approaches do not, typically, set out to "teach history" or "sociology" or whatever: they seek to induce in the learner a growing awareness of historical, sociological or other modes of understanding. . . . The whole emphasis in the training of teachers for resources and independent learning approaches, therefore, must be upon the needs of the learner, just as it has always been in training primary teachers.[5]

Our country has years to go before even elementary teachers are being widely trained and supported in this way.

Notes

1. Lawrence Soule, "A Canadian View of Teacher Education in the U. K.," *Education Canada,* December 1969, p. 26.

2. Emmeline Garnett, "The Area Resource Centre," *Forum,* Winter 1971, p. 2.

3. *Ibid.,* p. 4.

4. Annabelle Dixon, "A Primary School Approach to Resources," *Forum,* Winter 1971, p. 13.

5. Douglas Holly, "Preparing Teachers for the Resource-based Learning Approaches," *Forum,* Winter 1971, p. 8.

RESOURCES, TEACHERS, AND DESIGNERS
Jack Walton

The style of teaching and the pattern of teacher organisation and management has been changing in English schools during the last 10 years in response to a variety of pressures—not least of which are the curriculum modifications and innovations that will now always be with us. Reorganisation has, of course, tended to give additional impulse to changes in the curriculum. Shipman compares curriculum change with transplant surgery; often it has the same results—tissue rejection. In the same paper he gives examples of this tissue rejection often caused by the teacher's disinclination or inability to change his style of teaching to fit in with the new demands of the curriculum project.[1]

If we look at the classroom organisation of both primary and secondary schools some 15 years ago I think that in most cases fairly normal teaching arrangements would be noticeable. All desks would face the teacher and the teacher would tend to depend on perceptual teaching using a blackboard and textbooks. Particularly in primary schools, but also in some secondary schools, this pattern is changing. Less preceptual teaching is taking place and various groups of children may be observed working on various topics. As a result of this the textbook recedes somewhat in importance and more flexible materials are required. In this more open situation the demands upon the teacher are far greater and it seems hardly likely that he, or she, is going to be able to provide for the children all the necessary resources that are required.

It was for this reason that the Exeter University Institute of Education applied for a grant developing on a regional basis a resources centre for a period of three years. Associated with the project are some 30 schools and four teacher centres. These are all able to draw upon the centre for information, advice and resources. In this centre the resources are interpreted as including all those materials which are required to enrich the learning process—materials rather than machines. Included within this definition are prepared tapes, films, slides, photographs, photostat copies, documents, illustrations, and models. The centre started, possessing none of these items. All existing stocks have been produced as a result of meeting the requests of teachers. A teacher in one of the associated schools formulates a request and the task of the centre is to attempt to meet this request in the terms of the appropriate resource. The centre is considerably helped in the design aspect of this work by art students in their final year who are attached to the centre as part of their course. Whenever possible these students are brought into contact with the teacher who makes the request; when this is not done the end product is never quite satisfactory. Also linked with a number of the associated schools are advisers whose role it is, not only to act as agents of the centre in the school, but to help the teachers to clarify the curriculum objectives for which the resources are required.

In the Easter of this year Exeter Resources Centre, in association with other people working in the same or similar fields, organised a national conference aiming to bring together both representatives from the projects' pilot schools and also other people concerned with resources in different parts of the country. The conference remit was as follows: to be concerned with an examination of the main problems which are associated with the organisation, production, and use of software for curriculum development; a consideration of providing organisations such as the schools resources centre and the regional resources centre; to provide opportunities for both producers and users of resources to meet to discuss common problems.

In the course of the conference a number of papers were read by teachers, administrators, librarians, and researchers. It is important, perhaps, to convey some sense of the involvement of the 120 people at the conference in this whole problem of resource provision. Librarians, art students, teachers, and administrators jostled with each other, threw ideas backwards and forwards, often disagreeing violently, but taken altogether as a conference, conveyed some sense of both urgency and excitement. The problems posed were not artificial or theoretical. They were all practically related either to the problems in the classroom or to the problems of administration within the center. Teachers wanted a quick reliable service that satisfied their immediate needs. They described the frustration of being unable to develop their work satisfactorily in schools as a result of the lack of materials. Artists or designers emphasised the importance of getting teachers to discuss their requirements rather than work in isolation. People from colleges and universities emphasised the importance of stating clearly the objectives of curriculum exercises. Librarians pressed the importance of developing satisfactory systems of classification and retrieval. Whilst there may have been disagreement on particulars there was no disagreement about the need for developing an appropriate resources service.

There was indeed a strong feeling that whenever possible teachers should be associated in some way with resource provision. The provision of resources was regarded first and foremost as a curriculum problem and those people who were concerned with the design and operation of a school curriculum were the most appropriate people to be involved in the policy discussions which decided the character of the resources to be created. Policy-making meetings of this kind, however, need not necessarily be totally composed of teachers. Other people—artists, photographers, university and college lecturers, if available—could give an added richness to such meetings. It was emphasised that if the artists and associated people were to be involved in the production side of the exercise, they must also be involved at an early stage in the policy discussion, otherwise they may incorrectly interpret the wishes of the teachers.

The implication of these suggestions was that there were two major roles in the creation of resources—policy making, involving decisions about methodology and curriculum objects, and design, which covers the "making" side. The former, it seems was mainly the teacher's responsibility and the latter that of the artist/photographer.

Two main problems emerged: (1) Did these suggestions imply that resource provision was all to be school-based? (2) Where was the ancillary help—artists, photographers—to be found?

Generally, as the conference progressed there developed a consensus relating to the first query—that the seventies would or should see a development of a network of resources centres. Some schools would—perhaps because of size or other special circumstances—be able to develop their own centres. Others may be less fortunate. Nevertheless no school is an island, and strong arguments were expressed in favour of area resources centres—directly associated with quite a large number of primary and rather fewer secondary schools. These would be the centres for local curriculum discussion and also for the manufacture of materials which could not be provided on a school basis. A large number of these area resource centres could be linked to regional centres which would undertake the most difficult tasks and possibly house a curriculum/resource unit. It may be that these regional centres could be based at University Schools of Education.

Staffing for resources was discussed at some length and it would perhaps be tedious to report too much detail on the suggestions for the different types of centres. There was general agreement, however, that as library skills were involved in some considerable degree a librarian would perhaps be the most appropriate person to be director of a resource centre in, for example, a large secondary school—the resources centre possibly being a natural development of the school library. In the case of other larger centres, a librarian's advice should certainly be sought and he should perhaps, as in the case of the Exeter Centre, serve as codirector. Additional help, dependent on the size of the centre, would need to be recruited from professionally trained artists and technicians. Courses such as that held at the Plymouth College of Art now produce men and women appropriately trained for this design aspect of the work. It should be noted that whilst there was considerable emphasis on the artists' contribution, skilled and inventive technicians were regarded as equally necessary. However, the volume of work will always be greater than can be undertaken by the paid staff which most centres will be able to afford to employ. The recent experience of the Exeter Resources Centre suggests that if final-year art students in Colleges of Art or College of Education students with Art as their main subject could work for short periods of time in a resource centre as a part of their training they would gain useful experience and the centres would gain extra and essential help.

Whatever emphasis was given to the practicalities of administering resource centres in schools, teacher centres, or schools of education, whatever time was spent on staffing or equipment discussion, time and time again the discussions returned to the curriculum in the school and acceptable ways of servicing it. It is appropriate that the National Council of Educational Technology gave its support to the conference. In the words of its Director, Geoffrey Hubbard, Educational Technology "springs from the new look at the changing situation which is being taken by teachers all over the country and from awkward questions they are asking about curriculum and the true objectives of education; its techniques aim at integrating the use of the whole range of available resources with an efficiently managed and controlled learning process." Looking back at the conference it would appear that most members were considering the development of resources in this controlled light. The growth of resources centres must not be yet another bandwagon, but a planned addition to the educational scene to enable teachers to act more efficiently in the ever-changing classroom.

Notes

1. J. Walton (ed.), *Curriculum Organization and Design* (London: Ward Lock Educational, 1971).

A VIEW OF RESOURCE CENTRES
Ron Mitson

Now that a large number of schools are eager to establish their own resource centres it may be worthwhile emphasising the point that a centre is not an end in itself; it can only be a means to an end. If you find, or have built, the necessary accommodation, install what used to be for education as opposed to industry, an unprecedented array of machinery, and stand back and rub your hands in gleeful anticipation, nothing will happen. You may even rub the machinery vigorously with a dry soft cloth, for long periods at a time, but you will find that this Aladdin's lamp will make not the slightest difference to the education you offer in your school. It is that education that must begin to gear itself to make demands upon the new facilities you have, and the staff and pupils who must be involved in different ways if your centre is going to be anything more than a well-set-up library-cum-mausoleum.

We have a resource centre at Codsall Comprehensive School because we needed one.

A number of years ago I began to bring teachers together to carry out a regular reappraisal of all we were offering our pupils in school, and to consider and plan new approaches where these were necessary. (See "Teaching from Strength," Worrall, Mitson, *et al.*, Hamish Hamilton, 1971.) We worked in teams so that the inadequacy of individual experience, awareness, and expertise might be overcome and so that the thinking and planning might not be ossified in paper syllabus or scheme of work, but might be translated into the regular rhythm of collaborative effort, action, and reappraisal.

It was then that the inadequacy of the normal educational services and facilities in our school became apparent.

Teachers who were concerned to involve pupils of all abilities in new courses which they felt were more directly relevant to their needs were having to rely almost entirely upon books and the printed word. They knew that some pupils would be more able to assimilate the information and approach the ideas, and more readily become involved in learning, if they could do so by using other media. These pupils found film, television, filmstrips, slide, tape, and record more acceptable, less frustrating, than the printed word, and very much part of their lives outside school in any case. If they tried to further their learning beyond complete reliance on the teacher at school, in

218

the large majority of areas of study the only resource available to them in the classroom or the library was the book or the printed word. Moreover, the meagre stock of other resources available was for special use in the hands of the teacher and scattered about the school in such a way that even an understanding group of teachers would have great difficulty in finding them and making them available at the appropriate times to the pupils who needed them.

Teachers who were planning and working out new courses in the curriculum became immediately aware of the fact that they could not rely upon textbooks or commercially produced material for support. Sets of textbooks, modeled perhaps on existing trends in courses, tend to dictate, even to perpetuate to some extent, a course that is no longer answering the changing needs of young people in a society that is changing so rapidly. Until recently, understandably, material was produced commercially when the demand was demonstrably there to be met. These teachers, who were trying to take a new look at the educational needs of young people, were placed in the position of having to create some of the material for themselves and forage extensively for the rest. Perhaps we must always be in this position if education is to evolve continuously alongside the continuous evolution of society and if we are to provide an adequate response to our pupils' present needs.

We found it difficult because, although for the first time we were being asked to rely upon our own professional skills and expertise rather than be the educational middleman, the secondhand purveyor of someone else's professional thinking and expertise, we were not equipped to produce our own materials easily or satisfactorily, we had no technical help or support, and many of the teachers involved, keen to do a professional job well, felt very much in need of additional advice and training.

The fact that we became a Trial School in the Schools Council's Integrated Studies Project meant little in terms of salvation. Our own planned and developing courses seemed more appropriate in our circumstances to the needs of our particular pupils and teachers. To be fair, there was no suggestion that we should accept the total package of any of the Project's Courses, but even where we tried to include much of one in the curriculum of one year, the readiness with which this, and many other, Schools Council Projects suggest that teachers may modify or supplement their packs as they wish, proved irrelevant in the event. We had neither the reprographic equipment nor the technical assistance that is available to the project teams, and without these, what little time we had enabled us to do only a fraction of what was needed.

All this was just as relevant when I moved to Codsall, determined from the outset to develop a school that would have the organisation, the facilities, and the supportive services that would to some extent answer the needs of teachers and pupils working in the school. The educational environment would be as much teacher centred as child centred. In concerning ourselves with the needs of our pupils, we may too long have ignored the need to give our teachers services and support and help them feel adequate to cope with the demands that education in the modern world is making upon them. At Codsall I was hoping we should link this to the achievement of a balance of teaching methods, from teacher presentation to a large group for inspirational or stimulative purposes, on the one hand, through a whole range of possibilities, to pupils being involved in good individual learning, working at their own pace and with the choice open to them of approaching their work through whichever media enabled them as individuals to learn with optimum efficiency.

Main Aim

The ultimate aim would be complete, self-contained courses in particular subjects in the upper part of school. Each course would map out for the pupil the information he would have to cover and what he would have to know by the end of the year—the ideas he would have to be able to understand, use in his thinking, and relate to the information by the end of the year; the skills he would have to have practised and gained some proficiency in by the end of the year; and a guide to further reading, investigation, and activities he could extend into during the year. Each course would be centred round a core or series of lessons, possibly more in modern languages and science, with the need to provide oral practice or laboratory work, than in some other subjects, but the teacher would be available as a guide or consultant and would act as a tutor, seeing each pupil once a week or fortnight to check on his progress.

You see, we pay lip service to the development of character and self-reliance in our pupils, but the teacher remains indispensable to his pupils' learning. We tether our charges to the syllabus we are riding and they stumble along step by step at the back, rarely knowing in any but the vaguest way what work they have to do today until we come into the classroom and say, "Now, today we are going to. . . ." The course remains our course that we have to get them through if they are willing; it rarely becomes their course that it is their responsibility to get through with our help, and so they rarely feel involved;

they are rarely given any real incentive that is not a push from behind rather than a call to achieve something that they too see as a goal ahead.

We have deceived ourselves time and time again with talk about motivation and incentive being related to the final goal of an insubstantial certificate or a career dimly perceived in the distance or as yet hidden beyond some horizon in the future. As adults much of our own motivation lies in the more immediate future, and the opportunity we have, or otherwise, to plan ahead a little, to order the development of our lives and have some control over our own destinies. Giving our pupils this in their work will not solve every problem, but it may at least make them feel less resentful of being dependent on our whims and the daily lifting of the blindfold or slackening of the chains.

One shudders to hear Newsom, sorry! Raising the School Leaving Age, solutions such as the few weeks' field study course here; or the purposeful building of something or other there; or activities that will take them out into the real world somewhere else, as if school were anything but the real world. There is nothing wrong with these as part of a total curriculum, and the implication is always that such peripheral activities will solve the problem for us, and give our pupils character, self-reliance, and maturity.

The real problem still has to be solved at classroom level, and the implications of what we do at that level belie our every intention of offering our pupils the opportunity to develop in maturity and self-reliance. In order to create the educational environment and learning opportunities that will change all this, Educational Authorities and schools have a great deal of reorganisation and redeployment to do in support of teachers, and teachers have an enormous amount of rethinking, retraining, and planning and working together to do. That is why we need a resource centre at Codsall.

Resource Centre

It was not purpose built; nor does it have to be. The Local Education Authority was persuaded to partition off part of the school foyer to create a new office for the secretaries, and the original secretaries' office became our reprographic room. It houses the electronic stenciller and ink duplicator, and it is here that the audiovisual ancillary records radio programmes and turns mocked-up teaching units, thought out and created by teachers, into their final printed form. Each item is given an accession number which links it to the card indexing system we use for storage and both staff and pupils use for retrieval in the resource centre. The skins are stored nearby in numerical order so that anyone wishing to reorder the following year need quote only the number of the item and the number of the copies required.

The staff workshop was originally the staff locker room, leading off the main corridor into one end of the staffroom. We built in the fittings ourselves at low cost and it is here that the heat copier, flat-bed copier, and spirit duplicator are kept, along with an available supply of all the small items like scissors, sellotape, water-colour and spirit-colour pens, letraset, glue, and so on, that staff may need in mocking up their own items. Most members of staff pass through this room on at least 50 percent of the occasions when they enter the staffroom, and a frequently changed display of new productions by teachers is maintained there so that other members of staff may see what developments are in progress. The audiovisual technician operates the equipment for staff in this room also, and recent new work has included an impressive range of overhead projector transparencies.

The resource centre itself was designed originally as a library. Comparatively few adaptations have been made; it is not the room and its furniture so much as the reorientation of what goes on in the room that is important.

Books are still stored here under the Dewey System.

Teaching units and items produced by staff are stored here.

The majority of slides, filmstrips, loop films, overhead projector transparencies, tapes, and records belonging to different departments in the school are stored here.

Collections of items such as pamphlets and recent newspaper cuttings are stored here under topic-headings.

All but the books are stored under the optical coincidence coordinate card indexing punch-card system. This enables items on particular topics, related to particular groups of people or to particular areas of the world, and of a particular degree of difficulty, and so forth to be traced and retrieved with ease by the permutation of a number of punch cards narrowing down the field to the specific type of item and topic.

Collaboration in the Use of Resources

The system supports collaboration in the use of resources amongst the various Departments and teachers in the school. All can contribute to the resources available, all can draw upon the resources available, and it is relatively easy for the English Department to retrieve and use a record bought by the Music Department or for the P.E. Department to use a loop film bought by the Science Department. There are no valuable resources hidden away in the store cupboards of individual departments, under-used because of lack of knowledge of their existence.

The system also has the potential to offer pupils nonbook items in their learning. Slides, filmstrips, loop films, tapes, and records are just as available for pupils to use as they are for staff.

Once they have been trained in the use of the centre, and we do this in one area of the curriculum devoted to Interdisciplinary Enquiry (I.D.E.) in the first year, pupils find the punch-card system at least as helpful as Dewey and are able to select nonbook items, and make use of slide and filmstrip viewers and tape recorders available in the centre.

It is also possible for staff to draw cameras and tape recorders from the resource centre stock and for staff or pupils to use these in the recording of information they wish to present.

A number of departments have now begun to establish satellite resource centres. They vary in purpose, but all have some close connection with the main resource centre; some will have their own retrieval system linked to that in the centre, and the worthwhile books available in the department will all have at least one duplicate copy in the centre. This is essential particularly for those departments which have stopped buying whole sets of textbooks and are now relying almost entirely on a wide range of single or multiple copies of reference books.

At this stage the centre contains far more book items and printed items than audio and visual aids, mainly because the range of audio and visual aids commercially available is still quite small, such items are expensive, and they are not as easy or cheap for teachers to create for themselves as are book and printed items. We are conscious of the fact that we have revealed the potential but have not yet achieved the fulfilment of that potential.

Although the centre can no longer cope with the growing demand to use it, it will be extended by an additional 3,000 square feet in our next extensions.

We have no full-time librarian but, determined to keep it open as much as possible, we have timetabled the teacher-librarian to be in there, sometimes as a member of a team—the Interdisciplinary Enquiry team, for instance—for a major portion of the week, and other members of staff cover the rest of the week.

To encourage staff to supplement the commercial material available, relating it to their own and their pupils' needs, or indeed to create items of their own where they see the need, we have provided as much support for our teachers as possible. In addition to the audiovisual ancillary, who does all reprographic work and gives much technical help, we have appointed a full-time teachers' secretary to cope with typing where staff require it.

Our teachers are more able to devote themselves to the professionally creative work of planning and thinking out material, while the burden of completing the finished item is carried for them by ancillary staff. In addition much of the storage and retrieval system is organised and kept up to date for us by a group of volunteer parents whose help is invaluable.

Teachers need time to do all their thinking, planning, reappraisal, and creative work. We provide it where we can, including timetabled planning time for our teaching teams and an additional teacher so that one may be deployed where possible to prepare materials for a future topic or theme to be covered. In teaching there is never enough time, for which reason we fall far short of being as professionally adequate and effective as we have proved we can be. For our own and our pupils' sakes we must press for the time we need rather than lament the lack of time and accept as inevitable the deficiencies consequent upon it.

Financing the Developments

The development of a centre requires a degree of redeployment of finances within the school. The initial equipment is relatively inexpensive, costing between £750 and £1,000. The cost of larger numbers of reference books, slides, filmstrips, records, and tapes and the financing of home-produced materials must be set against a smaller outlay in the purchase of sets of textbooks and the more effective sharing of materials and equipment that takes place. What wastage there is in teachers creating their own materials and making mistakes in the process is entirely compensated for by the insight they gain into material production; and their increasing ability to discriminate between high and low quality commercial items is in itself an investment.

Centralised storing means that individual departments may lose a modicum of control over the expenditure of their capitation accounts. Each of our departments is allocated a capitation amount, approximately £30 of which is invested in the resource centre to be spent in consultation with the teacher-librarian. Such investments do more than all previous forms of persuasion in ensuring that departments take an active interest in what is happening in the library (resource centre); they have a vested interest in doing so.

It is also essential that the production department of the resource centre has an amount of working capital of its own. The production of materials by teachers from any department consumes much teacher time and energy. If it consumes the department's capitation also, it is likely that much less will be attempted. Departments have so many calls on what money they have that it might prove difficult to justify expenditure, which could include some wastage through learning, on material production. The school should bear this expenditure centrally so that departments are not only insured against any great loss of capitation in the learning process, but are also likely to gain financially to the extent that they involve their teachers in item production.

Helping Teachers to Work Effectively

Although teachers are carrying an increasingly greater burden of responsibility in helping to prepare mature young people for the proliferating complexities of life now and in the future, society has only recently become conscious of the need to give them direct and practical support. It is not even sure how to do it, any more than many teachers are sure how it should be done. They ignore their own precepts, perhaps less so now in emphasising the need for regular retraining for others without recognising the almost continuous and urgent need for themselves, but certainly in advocating understanding by doing for their pupils without realising that they too gain little from new theories in method without being able to explore them in practice, and learn in the process even by making their own mistakes.

Our centre is an agency for curriculum innovation and teacher development. One of its main functions is that of giving in-service training on the shop floor. We release members of staff from timetable for a week to follow a course in the resource centre, during which they explore the potential the centre has to offer, talk to other teachers about what they have achieved, and begin to make their own materials. Our director of resources is directly involved in this, in talking to all members of staff during the year about how the centre can serve their needs in relation to the curriculum and in offering help and advice where he can. He is a staff tutor in a fuller sense of the word than even the James Report envisaged.

One of the problems of Schools Council projects is that they pioneer approaches, but find difficulty in disseminating anything other than the material they have produced. One of the problems of local in-service training is that it introduces teachers to the enthusiasm and good ideas of other colleagues, but leaves them returning to schools where the introduction of those ideas is fraught with difficulties. One of the problems of teacher centres is that a teacher cannot pick up and continue his work there at any time during the day. The inconvenience alone is sufficient to discourage all but the more dedicated of teachers, and much of the training they offer is of a more elementary nature that should be available in the teachers' own schools. The fruitful collaboration at a more sophicated level in the development of area courses, that centres are ideally placed to support, is something they rarely manage to achieve.

The major problem with all educational thinking and innovation that goes on outside the school is how it can break the barrier and become part of the educational experience of the teachers who need it. We may go a long way towards solving that problem when the resource centre, as an organic part of any school, whose function includes extending the professional skills of teachers at shop-floor level, creates the dynamic for professional enrichment within the school itself. The teachers, concerned about real issues, will be responsible, as our own staff have been, for the success of such a provision. Indeed the more we can offer them professional conditions of a tangible nature, the more the vast majority will prove how professionally effective they are capable of being.

TEACHER CENTRES—SOME SUGGESTIONS FOR A STRATEGY
D.N. Hubbard and J. Salt

The empirical tradition in English education has long been a subject of comment. Nor is its importance purely historical. Even in present-day circumstances one would wish to see problems identified, new agencies brought into being to deal with them, and subsequent reevaluation of the nature and purpose of such agencies in the light of experience.

The real danger in this approach, however, lies in the fact that in the urge to solve obviously immediate and pressing problems we sometimes begin on too narrow a front. And having begun on this narrow front it is not always easy to broaden the functions of the agencies which have been created. Indeed, the very words chosen originally to describe them can act as curious constraints on their subsequent development.

Now all this, we would suggest, applies very directly to the teacher centres which are becoming an increasingly important feature of the educational scene. Clearly there is a need for teachers constantly to review their methods and approaches—in this we have probably a good deal to learn from aspects of North American experience—and clearly there is a need for institutions in which this work can be undertaken. But in an age when the importance of consciously integrating the efforts of so many agencies in the education of the individual is increasingly recognised, possibly we should look for the appearance of institutions whose structure and outlook reflect the acceptance of this wider view.

This is, however, by no means an attempt to devalue the potential importance of these centres in a distinctive field of in-service education, although even there we are likely to find a need for a radical look at what are likely to be essential prerequisities for success. For instance, it would seem to us quite essential that a centre should be able to draw on the resources of a relatively wide area. There are, in fact, real dangers in adopting an essentially parochial approach to provision, although, in the short term, such an approach might have elements of attractiveness. How often indeed one feels that what was originally a very good idea in practical teaching has lost much because it has been over-exposed in too limited an area. And in such circumstances, the need to develop effective systems of communication *between* centres is of overriding importance.

Similarly, in discussing centres in relation to their more obvious role as agencies for in-service training, we would suggest that the need to secure a high degree of positive involvement on the part of their users must come high on any conceivable list of priorities. Partly, of course, this relates to the system of government of centres, which in itself is of considerable importance, but it is doubtful whether constitutional devices can ever really get to the heart of the type of problem posed here. What is perhaps of greater importance is that the centres should be placed where the individual teacher's practical ideas are not only discussed and the results of them displayed in lively form, but also in a real sense stored. In other words, what we would wish to see is a long-term commitment to these institutions as *teaching resources centres*—using the word "resources" not only in the sense of books and the *material* of educational technology, but also in the sense of work schemes, projects, photographed material, and so on.

A number of subsidiary factors would also appear to deserve comment here. There is, for example, an increasing emphasis in our schools on environmental work. Yet knowledge of an area and of its potentialities for exploitation in an educational sense is not always acquired quickly or easily by the individual teacher, particularly if he is new to an area—and this is an age when teachers, like other professional groups, have become increasingly mobile as an element in the nation's work force. Clearly the existence of efficiently catalogued and economically stored local educational archives could be a factor of significance in the future. In this way, too, some provision could be made for the special needs of the probationer teachers, a group for whom the centres have, or should have, a peculiar responsibility.

Also related to the question of teacher involvement is the question of the importance of those evolving institutions as social centres. Here, of course, social psychology has some fairly clear-cut points to make. In particular its adherents would stress the importance of the development of "psyche" groups—groups which hold together principally because their members have come to enjoy each others' company, quite apart from the existence of mere practical and utilitarian motives. And, obviously, where a centre does not officially promote social activities it should at least provide through its facilities and organisational attitudes the environment in which essentially supportive "internal systems" can develop. Once again, we would stress the potentialities of a centre particularly to meeting the needs (and not always the narrowly professional needs) of the newcomer to an area and the probationer teacher.

So far this discussion has been confined largely to the question of making the centres effective in relation to what might well be considered aspects of the more traditional role of the teacher. However, we have at least touched on momentarily that contemporary thinking on education which draws attention to the position of the teacher not as the sole organiser and arbiter of the learning process but rather as one element in the provision, partly formal, partly informal, of the wider educational experience. And if indeed in the light of *Plowden* it is impossible to think of the teacher as an isolate in relation to home and family, and the school as a closed system in relation to the community, on what grounds can we hold to the idea of a *teacher* centre rather than a *teaching* centre, or, better still, an *educational* centre?

What we feel most strongly here is that the centres could provide a valuable neutral ground on which teachers and parents could come together. All-too-often, indeed, the dialogue between the two, when carried on within the school environment, is of an impossibly stilted nature: it is not easy for a parent to establish a role which in so many ways seems to conflict with the pattern of his own earlier educational experiences. Nor does the alternative suggestion, that the teacher himself should inject himself, as it were, into the home of the child, offer a more radically hopeful solution to this important problem. A more broadly based educational centre, however, might well offer additional and possibly more advantageous avenues of approach.

Is it, in fact, over-idealistic to suggest that centres should open their doors to elements in the community other than teachers? Perhaps, but there are at least some developments in the educational world which suggest that this is not entirely a pipe dream. For example, there is the experience of the highly successful exhibition of children's art which drew wide audiences and was *not* held in schools. Of even more potential significance, however, is the successful scheme, run by at least one university extramural department, in which parents and tutor (again not in a school) came together to discuss practical aspects of child psychology. A more ambitious extension of this idea within educational centres might well come to embrace contributions from Health and Welfare Services. Moreover, the growing practice whereby Members of Parliament in their constituencies and councillors in their wards hold "surgeries" at regular times might well find a counterpart in the organisation of some aspects of the wider activities of centres.

In sum we would suggest that the widening role of the teacher ought to have profound consequences for the organisation and orientation of all the key elements in the infrastructure which is currently developing to increase professional efficiency. Possibly current ideas on teacher centres often represent an unconscious adherence to a more traditional view of the profession, its nature and responsibilities. There is still time, however, to take a wider view.

Chapter IX

Linking the Teacher Center to Teacher Training Institutions

Introduction

> There can be, potentially, a very close and powerful link between
> the teachers' center and other agencies and sources of expertise, in-
> service training, and curriculum development, but this relationship
> is not formally defined, and must remain dependent on local
> circumstances.[1]

One of the best known American teacher center models that attempts to link schools and universities together is the Maryland Teacher Education Center. One of its spokesmen, James Collins, now Dean of the School of Education at Syracuse University, has pointed out shortcomings as he sees them of the British model:

> The noticeable strengths of the Teachers' Centre (British Model) revolve around
> the fact that it places responsibility for improved teacher performance and the
> assessment of teachers' needs with the teachers themselves who are most closely
> associated with learners. Furthermore, the attendance to local needs as assessed
> by the teachers would appear to build in a continuing, updating factor which
> should result in meaningful, developmental, renewal experiences for teachers.
>
> However, even with the allowance for cultural differences between Britain and
> the United States, one might question the wisdom of what appears to be a "closed
> shop." It involves teachers only.
>
> One might ask if the British Teachers' Centre model isn't too pragmatically
> oriented, and if it doesn't depend too much upon provincial "in-house" talent
> and ideas.
>
> The most important question is always, "will it work in the United States?"
> And if so, in what contexts will it work effectively?[2]

Dean Collins goes on to say that Maryland was "convinced that the essence of true cooperation is joint decision-making with the resultant concepts of joint responsibility and joint accountability . . ."[3] He describes the board of a teacher education center as composed of representatives of the teachers, administrators, colleges or universities, teachers' associations, state department of education staff, and local community. He believes "the strengths of this plan lie in its attempt to form a parity relationship, thereby sharing the responsibility and decision-making power for improved teacher effectiveness and learner performance with all elements of the educational system."[4] The most notable difficulty of the plan he describes as

> initially establishing a working partnership among the groups involved. This does not come easily or quickly, but once developed tends to be highly productive, and provides for open challenge of ideas and techniques with the result that the best tend to come forward and remain. Any program or innovation which emerges from the policy-solving, program-development processes, conceived and carried out by the Center staff, has a far greater acceptance and chance for success than one imposed from outside.[5]

The problem here is that the teachers have no traditional power-base for curriculum matters in this country; all the other elements of the "partnership" do. In such a situation the usual domination of teachers is likely.

Contrasted to this model is the linkage effected by at least one educational authority (district) in England through the "curriculum development assistant," as described in this section. Chosen to be a link between the schools and the university from the teaching staff of the schools, the curriculum assistant was to work alongside the teachers in an effort "to meet some of those needs which, for practical reasons, they cannot meet themselves." The assistant was to "be acceptable both to the teachers and to a university school of education, and be able to offer positive help and guidance without usurping the initiative of the schools." Neither was he to assume control of any of the existing teacher centers. With this linkage and the strong power base for the teachers of centers of their own, this authority believes it has achieved significant partnership with local teacher education institutions. Fibkin here describes a similar arrangement at Stony Brook, involving the faculty of a junior high school and the university.

Certainly the problem of partnership in England has not yet been solved. The James Report, published in the spring of 1972, attempts, controversially, to resolve some of the problem. For its proposed third cycle of training for serving teachers (the first two cycles are concerned with the preservice and probationary years of training) it recommends "professional centres" mostly based at existing colleges of education but in some cases "developed from existing teachers' centres or placed in schools or F.E. (further education) colleges." This chapter includes pertinent paragraphs of the Report which involve teacher centers. In the third cycle a teacher would be given leave with pay for one term each seven years in order to pursue further training. The training would not be compulsory. The Report further states that local educational authority advisers would be an important link between the schools and the professional training centers, as they are "in close touch with schools. . . . aware of their day to day problems and able to assess needs as they arise and to make or suggest immediate arrangements to meet them." A similar role has been suggested by the more recently published White Paper, "Education: A Framework for Expansion." This proposes that one staff member of each school, designated as a "school-based tutor" (the James Report had discussed "professional tutors"), would be most active in coordinating institutional in-service training for the school. In small schools this role would be filled by the head teacher; in larger schools, by several senior staff members. Thus each school would officially be linked with higher education institutions.[6]

Teacher centers have cherished their autonomy in England to the extent that, as Alex Evans points out in these pages, "for the most part the Colleges have not been invited to join the teachers in the centers. . . ." With the James' proposals in the air the teacher centers are now concerned that the James professional centers may be a new threat to their autonomy. As Thornbury states:

> Centres have not had a captive audience—and teachers tend to vote with their feet. But how long will the teachers' centre tradition last in an era of compulsion by stealth, when teachers become "entitled" to curriculum materials? Will teachers in the schools and the teachers' centres be able to resist growing pressures from a variety of sources towards the centralised direction of curriculum? In my view, teacher control and public interest will provide the best safeguards against centralism.[7]

The future is cloudy for independent teacher centers of this country. Teachers need the expertise of those in universities and colleges and elsewhere. Yet they should be free to request it. Paul Pilcher's bold solution is included in the last chapter of this book:

> If, for example, the USOE followed simple logic and granted funds to groups of classroom teachers for the purpose of establishing self-renewal and in-service centers, the rules of the game would change dramatically. Teachers would then be free to hire (and fire) outside personnel on the basis that they (the teachers) wanted. In the Alice-in-Wonderland world of government, however, precisely the opposite is happening.

In the United States teachers (as well as many school districts) will pay for in-service courses if academic credit is given. Worth exploring is the idea of field-based, experiential courses given by university or college staff in teacher centers for credit. This approach to in-service could be relatively easily arranged by teacher center committees, and teachers themselves could insist that these courses meet their needs. With care and planning governing committees of teacher centers can insure the programs do not become "circular and impotent once the excitement of sharing ideas has run out."[8]

Notes

1. G.A.V. Morgan, "Teachers' Centers," *The Urban Review*, July 1974, p. 193.

2. James Collins, "Teacher Centers and Teacher Renewal," a paper prepared for the National Association of State Boards of Education, March 1972, p. 7.

3. *Ibid.*, p. 10.

4. *Ibid.*, p. 13.

5. *Ibid.*, p. 13.

6. See Harold Knowlson, "The School-based Tutor," *Trends in Education*, July 1973, p. 8.

7. R.E. Thornbury (ed.) *Teachers' Centres* (London: Darton, Longman & Todd, 1973; New York: Agathon Press, 1974), p. 141.

8. E. Brooks Smith in Leonard Kaplan, "Survival Talk for Educators—on Teacher Centers," *Journal of Teacher Education*, Spring 1974, p. 50.

A CENTER IN MARYLAND
Leon Boucher

Here the development of teacher centers resulted from an experimental cooperative venture in which the University, the State Education Department, and a County School Board were involved. Now there are 50 elementary and secondary schools in seven counties and in Washington, D. C., all associated over centers with five teacher education colleges, and the University of Maryland itself assigns about half its student teachers to centers.

A center is essentially a school, or a cluster of schools, headed by a coordinator who is appointed and paid equally by the college and the school system in question. He is responsible both for students in initial training who are assigned to the center and at the same time for the in-service experience of the staff of the schools forming the center. In satisfying these dual needs, he is able to draw on the resources available from both his employers. In effect, there is a tendency for the school staff to assume an increasing responsibility for the preservice training, aided by college staff where appropriate; and for college staff increasingly to act as "resource personnel" for in-service work. To emphasize this change of roles, however, is to miss one of the most significant features of this concept. The idea that preservice and in-service training are separate and distinct is giving way to the idea that all persons involved are "students of teaching," in which a given individual, whether a student at college, a teacher in the school, or a college lecturer might find himself at one or the other end of a continuum in various aspects of teaching. The center idea implies sets of students working with sets of teachers working with sets of lecturers all at different levels of experience, helping one another to learn more about teaching. While one of the partners may be teaching the children, the others are learning from each other.

The preservice student thus receives a variety of experiences. Some of these derive from intensive work with one or a few of the teachers in the school, others derive from extensive contact with a wide range of school activities and theoretical studies which can be based on and related to practical situations within the center. Study of the effects of this approach suggest that students who have been assigned to centers, when compared with those who have followed a more traditional program, participate more widely in the total school program, use a greater variety of instructional techniques, and become less close-minded, less apathetic, and less resistant to change. The in-service programs vary, naturally enough, from center to center. In some cases, there is little more than a facilitation of access to courses at the college, which are made available free of charge in return for the teachers' contributions to the preservice work. In other cases, however, the teachers receive guidance in techniques of supervision—for example, in the use of interaction analysis, of simulation games, and of micro-teaching, the technique by which a particular instructional skill is practiced on a small group of one to five learners, is video-taped, analyzed, and then retaught to another group until the skill is mastered; or they may take "mini-courses," small packaged programs applied to specific teaching behaviors.

Clearly, in these centers the school is really involved with the college in the teacher-education process. It would, however, be wrong to suggest that any one center is a "model" for all; they vary in terms of the situations and personnel involved. There are, too, many problems which are unresolved, a fact which Dr. Collins of the University of Maryland and his colleagues were at pains to emphasize at a "clinic" held in Washington in April 1970 and attended by persons involved in problems of student teaching from all over the United States and Canada. One major set of problems concerns role relationships—some teachers do not wish to be involved, some head teachers see a threat to their control over what is going on in "their" schools and do not readily accept the presence of the coordinator who has a responsibility, emphasized by the dual nature of his appointment, to persons "outside" the school.

A second set of problems concerns the degree of influence and responsibility to be accepted by the organizations involved. In a material sense, a center requires space and materials to operate effectively, and it has not always been easy to agree on the extent to which the college, the individual center, the school district or the state should provide these facilities. Nor has it been easy to decide who should determine the policy and practice of a center, and indeed this problem is as yet entirely unresolved. Apart from the schools and colleges themselves, the student-teachers have a voice which may well be heard; the local communities may also wish to be heard, especially where they are deeply involved in "their" schools; and the professional associations are obliged to think very clearly what is meant by greater participation in the training of new entrants to the profession by teachers serving in the schools.

A third set of problems concerns the extent to which it is practical and desirable to extend the center concept. In a situation where there can be a degree of selectivity of schools, teachers, classes involved in in-service training, it is possible to create a center which can provide suitable facilities, but all concerned in Maryland admit that some schools, some teachers, some classes cannot provide these facilities. Furthermore, while the authorities concerned have welcomed centers as a practical expression of true partnership, it is also true that authorities maintaining the schools on which centers have been based tend to see the centers as an invaluable source of recruitment and as "models" for the kinds of teachers they desire; teacher colleges, on the other hand, as institutions of higher education, must necessarily have a wider perspective, a more "universalistic" view of the role of the teacher, which may conflict with that exemplified in the center.

It is no easy task to create a center which embraces a variety of social environments, a variety of organizational patterns, a number of independent but interrelated institutions, and an even larger number of individuals, each with his own perceptions and expectations. The difficulties, however, should not detract from the idea behind the teacher education center concept. It merits a great deal of attention by those who are searching for ways to achieve closer relationships between schools and colleges, to integrate theory and practice, to replace the separation of pre- and in-service training by the notion of continuous training implied by the phrase "students of teaching."

TOWARD A PARTNERSHIP IN TEACHER EDUCATION
The Maryland State Department of Education

The Problems and Challenges
of a Teacher Education Center

The program of the teacher education center has progressed satisfactorily toward the solution of many of the problems identified earlier in this report. However, a program as ambitious as this can create problems and intensify old difficulties. In this section a number of problems encountered in teacher education center programs are identified. Also, in some cases, an attempt is made to indicate the relationships of the State Department of Education and the colleges and universities in the alleviation of these difficulties.

Human Relations. Most of the developers of the teacher education center concept agree that the single most difficult problem area in the program is in the field of human relations. The success or failure of the program often is determined by the ability of the participants, especially the coordinator, to work effectively with people. In view of the fact that so many roles are changed in the teacher education center, human relations are, at least in the beginning, often strained by the uncertainties of a new situation and the interrelationships of the participants.

It has become clear to those who have initiated teacher education centers that certain types of persons should not be given leadership roles in the development of the centers. Some people are so inflexible and insensitive to the needs of others that they further the human relations difficulties rather than lessen them. This lack of insight and understanding of the need to have flexible and adaptable people in leadership roles is not limited to one institution alone. Examples could be cited in which the various institutions participating in teacher education centers have contributed people who never should have been involved in the development of experimental programs. Flexible persons who can adjust easily are needed in the successful implementation of the teacher education center concept.

Communication. Closely related to the matter of human relations is communications. Human relations may be effective or poor depending upon the quality of interpersonal communications. In the Maryland M-STEP Center, in an effort to improve communication, a coordinating committee was developed to meet regularly at the center. Its major purpose was to identify the concerns of teachers as well as the resources that could be used to further the recognized objectives. The steering committee, involving the major institutions participating in the center, serves a useful purpose in communications.

In spite of the attempt to develop a steering committee that would make face-to-face communication and decision making possible, the original plan did not include provision for teachers to be represented on the steering committee. Teachers soon made this point known and arranged to have an elected representative attend the regular meetings of the committee.

Role Identification and Clarification. When an experimental program such as the development of the teacher education center is begun, roles, regardless of the thoroughness of the planning, are actually developed through practice and are somewhat unclear in the beginning of the program. Therefore, these roles must be clarified and tested in the real world of the school. Since the building principal was asked to give up his role as a director of the teacher education in his building, the nature of his participation was of some concern. Likewise, the teacher education center coordinator was serving in a position that was newly created, and precise role identification needed to be developed. Although the program has had considerable experience in this matter of role identification, the concept is modified somewhat by the professionals in the school where it is implemented.

Qualifications. The matter of qualifications is closely related to role identification. A significant difference of opinion exists about the background of experience that should be expected of the person who is designated as the teacher education center coordinator. The University of Maryland has developed a preparation program designed to qualify personnel for this role. A new two-year graduate degree program should provide a corps of professionals who can serve in this capacity.

The Development of Expertise. Although a teacher education center may have a very effective in-service program designed to meet the needs of a specific group of teachers, a serious problem arises in the maintenance of a level of expertise within the faculty. This matter of continuous in-service development is of common concern to the colleges and universities involved in teacher education center programs for center faculty turnover is an annual fact of life.

Another aspect in the development of expertise relates to the need to provide college and university faculty members with experiences to update their understanding of newer approaches in education. For example, many faculty members have read about micro-teaching, but have had little real experience working with this kind of program. A serious problem arises as to how to provide these kinds of experiences for college and university personnel.

The Lack of Centers in Sparsely Populated Areas. The teacher education center movement in Maryland has been centered primarily in the metropolitan and suburban school systems that have considerable resources for this purpose. The children of the state in sparsely populated areas have the same need for competent teachers as the children in suburban and metropolitan areas. The state has to find ways to move this exciting and successful approach to teacher education into those areas of the state where it is now not possible because of the sparseness of population. One approach advanced by the Maryland State Department of Education is the development of regional teacher education centers. These centers would work with a number of colleges and universities that could send some students to the centers in the sparsely populated area.

Finance. A complicated, vexing problem which needs the attention of all levels of government and education is the financing of teacher education and teacher education centers. Directors of programs utilizing the teacher education center concept indicate a need for materials and equipment to carry out the various aspects of an effective center program. Also, the need for consultants is emphasized by those directors who are especially interested in improving the competence and service of both the center and the college and university faculties.

During the life of the Multi-State Teacher Education Project, the teacher education center program was funded by the Maryland State Department of Education, the University of Maryland and the Montgomery County Public School System. When the project ended, the university and the school system assumed joint financial responsibility for the program. When any of the participants are unable to assume this kind of financial support for teacher education, financial assistance should be provided from state or other sources.

Incentives and Rewards. The teacher education center faculty is expected to contribute a high level of skill and dedication and more time and energy than that expected of the regular classroom teacher. The education profession needs to give serious thought to the development of ways to recognize this service, competence, and responsibility. The possibilities for titles, degrees, awards, recognition, services, benefits, and salary adjustments have not been adequately explored in the teacher education center program.

TEACHERS, TRAINERS, AND DEVELOPMENT CENTRES
Alex Evans

As a member of the original "Lockwood" Working Party which laid the foundations for the Schools Council, and a member of the Council and some of its committees since its inception, I have rejoiced—and been rather staggered—at its rapid development. Through its investigations, its curriculum development projects, and its publications, it has succeeded in stimulating us all into a radical rethinking of what we do in the schools. No less important is the way in which it has sparked off a chain reaction of teacher centres throughout the country, not so much through its own direct organization but through—if one has to use the word—its inspiration. And in all of them teachers study curriculum development and new approaches to teaching through the child's own discovery.

Where do the colleges of education come in? The position on the surface is very encouraging. Some important Council projects have been based on colleges. Their staffs are being drawn increasingly into development projects and are to be found working with teachers in a number of centres. One is delighted to read in *Dialogue* (No. 5) that fourteen teacher centres and curriculum development committees have extended links with their neighbouring colleges, and that *Dialogue* would be interested to hear of additional arrangements of the same kind. One can add to this that the development work of the Council and the teacher centres is having a substantial impact on the colleges. Nuffield science and the "new" mathematics, for instance, involve both staff and students, and both look forward to teaching practices in those schools where they can advance their learning by actual teaching, where the new teaching methods are the same as those taught in the colleges.

All these are very encouraging signs, but the involvement of the colleges with the teacher centres has not by any means gone far enough. We can be pleased to read in *Dialogue* that some teacher centres have linked up with some colleges but the fact that this is *news* can disturb as well as please us. I for one would have liked to assume that they would have linked up with colleges from the start. I know, too, that at meetings of college lecturers there have been expressions of regret and, indeed, resentment that they have not been invited to join the teachers in the centres and that, although individual lecturers have been involved, there has been no planned attempt to involve the colleges as a whole.

An extremely interesting sign of this lack of coordination has been the criticism voiced recently by some teachers that the colleges, in their conservatism, are not bringing new ideas into the schools through the teachers they train and that new ideas are fermenting in the schools while the colleges remain wrapped in the old maismal mist. This is a curious *bouleversement* when one remembers that up to only a few years ago the colleges were accused by conservative teachers of being too progressive, of teaching new-fangled methods which their students would do well to forget when they had to face the realism of the actual classroom.

The present situation has been well summed up by Brian Cane in his recent *In-service Training* (NFER, 1969), an invaluable study of teachers' views and preferences. He recognizes that colleges have fitted into the local in-service pattern by offering accommodation for teacher centers and by organizing short courses for teachers. But he notes that lecturers have staffed in-service courses "but often informally—as an extra task over and above their normal duties." He adds: "the Colleges' contribution to in-service training has yet to be fully explored . . . that many of them could make a more significant contribution to local teacher training than they do at present."

But the omens are favourable. The fact that an increasing number of colleges are becoming involved in curriculum development and that college lecturers are increasingly involved in teacher centres itself creates an expansionary movement. The Council has now appointed an officer to liaise with the colleges. Hindsightedly one realizes that such a person has been needed for several years. The Department of Education and Science is proposing to finance an expansion of curriculum development and in-service training through the colleges and the area training organizations.

There is a growing realization that, more than ever before, teachers constantly need to be updated in the knowledge from which they teach, the methods through which they teach it. They need to reexamine the curriculum and the concepts on which it is based in a world which is subject to continuous and rapid changes, a world in which we must always be looking forward and not backward in a vain hope of a return to a never-recurring "normal." This is recognized not only by inspectors, advisers, and trainers but by the teachers themselves. We do not possess at present facilities to satisfy this need or exploit fully those facilities which we do possess—the colleges of education.

There are over 160 colleges of education, not only concentrated in the denser areas of population but also in smaller towns with a rural environment. No teacher centre need be out of touch, for the colleges now have experience in the establishing of outposts. They possess facilities such as audiovisual aids, CCTV, workshops, studios, laboratories, and lecture and seminar rooms. They are staffed by experienced teachers, the majority of whom have been recruited from the schools over the last five years. Their supervision of students on teaching practices takes them into many schools through the whole age-range. Nor would it be a one-way process. The school and college teachers would teach and learn from each other. Theory would be inseparable from practice for nothing sharpens a teacher's mind so much as practising in the school what he has been learning as a student. Thus the teacher will bring his up-to-date experience in the classroom situation right into the lecture room and laboratory of the college.

Those colleges which have been able to offer one-term or one-year full-time courses for teachers appreciate fully that the teachers contribute to the life and work of the college, particularly in their relationships with the younger students. To have the teachers of the surrounding schools, in which the students "do" their practice, working in the college and frequenting the common rooms and bars would be of enormous benefit to both. The teachers would find a stimulus in the freshness and adventurousness, the willingness "to have a go" of the younger students. Both would realize as the Report (soon to be published as Working Paper No. 33) on the Council's recent conference on Curriculum Innovation in the Secondary Schools maintains: "training—like curriculum development—can never be 'complete.' Continuous self-education needs a complementary flow of up-to-date information and advice."

All this might have seemed a pipe-dream only ten years ago. But there are beginnings, tentative and perhaps even haphazard, and the declared policy of the DES could result in a rapid development over the next five years. It would do more than anything to dissipate the impression of the separateness of training and teaching. The colleges would then be, in reality, teachers' colleges.

Readers Reply

From Cynthia France: Alex Evans speaks from experience and authority—I am one of his college lecturers "recruited from the schools over the last five years." Like him I find encouraging signs but so much remains to be done.

Why has there been a lack of cooperation between colleges, centres, and teachers? Is it that college lecturers have feared to intrude on local teachers in their own preserve and stood modestly on the sidelines waiting to be asked to play? If so, were they right in assuming a "we/they" attitude implicit in teachers from the start? Do teachers genuinely fear authoritarian domination by the local college or perhaps continue to regard college staff as ivory-towered idealists remote from the realities of the classroom? Do college facilities appear unfairly grandiose to hard-pressed teachers battling on in old, inadequate buildings? Do teachers believe, as I have heard it put, that lecturers have retired from the "coal face" to the "board-room" and no longer share their problems and frustrations? Or is it that the recent increase of pressures on college staff, resulting from B.Ed. courses and post-graduate training has left them too busy to support their teacher centre as much as they would wish.

Whatever the cause, all are agreed that greater cooperation is essential, although whose responsibility it is to provide the initiative is far from clear. Should the lead come from the Colleges, the ATO's, DES, or LEA's (Area Training Organizations, Department of Education and Science, local Education Authorities)? An integration of advisory services is needed—not possible grounds for conflict.

I should like to see in *Dialogue* a fuller analysis of the links forged by teacher centres with their colleges, stating the difficulties involved, the price paid in solving them in time, money, and status. If there is a genuine partnership between LEA, teacher centre, and college, how is this implemented in the organization of the centre? How readily are the specialist services of the college staff utilized?

Were all three partners mutually sympathetic from the first or, if prejudice had to be dispelled, how was this achieved?

Much depends upon the siting of the centre. If it is close to the college or even part of the campus, frequent and close contact between school and college staff is relatively easy; if it is at a distance, college lecturers need to be committed to regular courses and working parties rather than offered occasional invitations. If all new lecturers were to visit their local teacher centre—if they were encouraged to involve themselves more actively—it would lessen their feelings of initial isolation from teachers in the schools. If a member of the college staff were to undertake liaison work with the teacher centre and Schools Council, it would be easier to keep abreast of curriculum development work both locally and nationally. If students were invited to the centre for joint discussions with teachers and college staff, this would ensure that they entered the profession already aware of the vital role which the centre can play.

What of contacts between colleges and the Schools Council itself? Now that the Schools Council has a field officer whose particular concern is with the colleges we can look forward to personal contact, but this must necessarily be infrequent. What more can be done? Schools Council Wallsheets seem to be more in evidence in teacher centres than in colleges, and although the big materials like *Scope* and *Breakthrough to Literacy* are well displayed in college libraries and education departments, I wonder if the individual subject departments are always sufficiently aware of the work which is going on in their field. We need more particularized information. We would like to know what colleges are involved in what projects and at what stages? If one's own college is not participating, one needs to know where to make contact with those which are. If Schools Council subject information reached heads of subject departments, it would percolate via them to the method lecturers and through them to the students and the schools. This itself might help to dispel the criticism referred to by Alex Evans—which I regard as ill-judged and ill-informed—that exciting new development work is going on in the schools, and we in the colleges are the conservatives, leading from the rear.

Obviously, as Brian Cane says, colleges could and should make a much more significant contribution to local teacher training. They are in contact with research through their local school of education at the university. Not to use their resources fully as an integral part of in-service training and curriculum development work in teacher centres is a crime and a waste.

From Ewart Taylor: Alex Evans is rightly encouraged by the burgeoning of teacher centres throughout the country. Regrettably, he is also right to point to the fact that there has been no planned involvement of the colleges of education as a whole in this development. There is plenty of room for argument about the reasons for this.

Who should be showing the initiatives, anyway? Are the ATO's appropriate vehicles of policy-making and planning in this field? At the moment opportunities abound for treading on professional toes as all the parties to in-service training go their several ways. Surely, then, it is time for the administrative map to be drawn so that some semblance of coherent planning might emerge. In such an exercise one might expect the colleges to be given a clearly defined role such as Alex Evans hopes for. Simultaneously they might also be afforded the staffing resources to meet such a role.

Might it not also be argued that the colleges of education have failed in the last ten years to demonstrate to the schools that they are front-runners in curriculum development and that their preoccupation with matters of expansion and the four-year course have given the impression of neglect of an area of work which the schools rightly regard as central? However valid the argument, those who advance it must take into account the substantial amount of in-service work undertaken by college staff who, whatever the difficulties, see such a commitment as vital.

Such arguments aside, the commitment of colleges to a sustained programme of work in teacher centres would bring obvious benefits to all. Where colleges have already managed to develop such a relationship, the by-products have been immense in terms of a growing mutual respect between teachers, college staff and students. Fresh ideas for strengthening that relationship are being promoted. The work of LEA advisers, teacher centre wardens, college lecturers, and teachers overlap enough to make possible the creation of posts which embrace more than one professional base. Moreover, not only do students in initial training gain from an introduction to the work of the centres but, during the probationary year, the centres provide a very suitable meeting ground for teachers, college staff, and students to hold regular nonevaluative seminars especially concerned with the problems of the first year of teaching.

Alex Evans has submitted his comments at an interesting juncture. Following the launching of the B.Ed. degree, it would seem opportune and proper for a shift of emphasis to be encouraged. The colleges must consider a future in which many students may have no commitment to teaching. Far from discouraging colleges from heightening their commitment to curriculum studies, such a future provides an opportunity for recruiting to teaching able students who are attracted by the relevance and excitement of shaping, in the regular company of teachers, lecturing staff, advisers, and children, the content and methodology of an education more stimulating than their own.

THE WORK OF THE CURRICULUM DEVELOPMENT ASSISTANT IN ONE COUNTY

The British Schools Council (*Foundation Stones—1966-1968*)

The appointment of the curriculum development assistant created a new post which was in several ways unique. He was seconded from a teaching post in the county, initially for a period of two years. It was considered important that he "should be acceptable both to the teachers and to a university school of education, and be able to offer positive help and guidance without usurping the initiative of the schools." (From the terms of appointment.)

The school of education had agreed to cooperate in a concerted project of curriculum development in the humanities, and the assistant was expected to play a fundamental part in this work and to act as the link between the schools and the university. In other words, it was envisaged that he would encourage local groups and individual schools in the county to undertake work of an experimental nature in the humanities, and make available to them the research techniques and expertise of the school of education. Through the coordination of such empirical studies it was hoped that a scheme would eventually emerge that most teachers would be willing to use and adapt to their local circumstances.

It should be stressed that the assistant has never been primarily responsible for the activities of any one particular committee or of any one of the teacher centres. These have always remained teacher controlled. Nor, indeed, can he be equated with a local inspector or adviser although he has a desk in the education offices and must, of course, supplement certain aspects of their work. Essentially he is a teacher, working alongside and cooperating with other teachers in an effort to meet some of those needs which, for practical reasons, they cannot meet themselves.

And their needs are diverse, as might be expected in such a large geographical area which embraces an immense variety of social and economic factors. On the one hand there are the groups that meet in school time and conduct their experiments in the classroom. They ask for the provision of a cooperative headmaster and school where they can carry these out, special equipment, an abundance of duplicated materials, and often secretarial assistance. On the other hand, there are those groups that are much more concerned with the broader aspects of curriculum development and require information about

247

up-to-date research; exhibitions of books, materials, and new teaching aids; lectures; and conferences. The curriculum development assistant is expected to work with teachers in the classroom, to discuss, to talk, to provide the means of communication; he must visit schools and colleges of education, and, when the opportunity arises, do his own reading and research.

As the work has developed, the development groups are more and more viewing the problem of the last year at school in its proper educational context: in terms of a continuing education which starts in the primary schools and affects all age and ability ranges. As a result, the work of this assistant has tended to grow from the major concern with the less able adolescent to a concern with the needs of pupils in the earlier years of the secondary school, and even in the primary school. It has also been generally agreed that there is a danger of creating an irrevocable dichotomy between the kind of education offered to one set of pupils and the kind of education offered to another. Some schools are now experimenting with mixed ability groups, particularly in the humanities.

Nor has it in practice been possible, or even desirable, to confine this work rigidly to the humanities. Some groups have been much more concerned with the wider implications of curriculum development, and have been much occupied with identifying general educational objectives and the needs of pupils at different age levels, particularly those being transferred from primary to secondary education. Others are making enquiries into peripheral subjects like personality development and school counseling. In one way and another, they have all sought assistance of some kind.

There have been problems. Some teachers feel that they should not be expected to attend meetings after school to pursue educational research for which they are neither adequately trained nor equipped. Headmasters point out the problem of releasing members of staff during school hours, and sometimes release only those who can most easily be spared. Some groups meet once a month or less and much of the time is spent in reorientation and in regaining a consensus of thought. Progress is often so slow that some teachers become frustrated because they can see no immediate advantages in the work. There have been the inevitable dropouts after the first flush of enthusiasm has paled into the realisation that there was no ready-made panacea and that most of the thinking was required to be done by the teachers. Groups have needed reassurance that they can make a positive contribution towards reshaping the curriculum. They have needed to produce tangible results to convince their more sceptical colleagues; and they have needed to show that what they have done is relevant to their own school situation.

In the kind of grass roots development which is considered desirable these are the kinds of problems that confront the curriculum development assistant and it is possibly here that he can make his most valuable contribution. Firstly, he must be aware of, and sympathetic towards, the difficulties of individual schools, so as to ensure that his relationship with them inspires confidence. Secondly, whilst not imposing a programme of work on the groups, he must try to ensure that they have something worthwhile to bite on. Thirdly, he must provide an effective means of communication, so that the results of their work can be seen and critically appraised by a large number of their colleagues.

The growth of the work makes it evident that there are some teachers who find curriculum development work more challenging and more rewarding than do others. It is to these teachers, who will have selected themselves, that the assistant looks for the power to steadily increase the momentum of the work. Their effort will be mainly responsible for getting the movement to change the curriculum started, but the assistant concludes that there is still much to be accomplished before it passes beyond the stage of beginnings.

PASSAGES FROM THE JAMES REPORT
The Department of Education and Science

Institutional Requirements and Implications

Implications for the schools. **2.21.** Inservice training should begin in the schools. It is here that learning and teaching take place, curricula and techniques are developed, and needs and deficiencies revealed. Every school should regard the continued training of its teachers as an essential part of its task, for which all members of staff share responsibility. An active school is constantly reviewing and reassessing its effectiveness and is ready to consider new methods, new forms of organisation, and new ways of dealing with the problems that arise. It will set aside time to explore these questions, as far as it can within its own resources, by arranging for discussion, study, seminars with visiting tutors, and visits to other institutions. It will also give time and attention to the introduction of new members of staff, not only those in their first year of teaching but all those who are new to the school. Heads of schools, heads of departments and other senior teachers should be especially concerned to assess the needs both of their schools and of teachers on their staff and to encourage teachers to take the opportunities offered outside the school for inservice education and training, whether these involve part-time day release, attendance at full-time courses or participation in vacation, weekend, or evening activities.

2.22. It would be unrealistic to expect hard-pressed schools to take on additional responsibilities without an increase in teaching staff. Nevertheless, this degree of involvement in the purposes and practices of the third cycle is a responsibility which the schools will not wish to evade. It is fortunate, therefore, that there is now a prospect of a steady increase in the supply of teachers. A high priority should be given to improving staffing ratios so that schools are able to play their full part in the third cycle and thus help to raise the status and standards of the teaching profession as a whole. As soon as better staffing and the expansion of full-time courses allow, all teachers should be entitled to release with pay for a minimum of one school term or the equivalent (a period of, say, 12 weeks) in a specified number of years. The immediate aim should be to secure teachers' entitlement to a minimum of one term or the equivalent in every seven years, but this should be regarded as only an interim target. As soon as possible, the level of entitlement should be raised to one term in five years. It would be undesirable, at least initially, to make in-service education and training compulsory. It would also be undesirable to offer direct financial incentives to take training courses, except insofar as these courses led to qualifications recognized by the Burnham Committee as justifying salary additions. It is to be hoped that teachers would soon come to regard continued education and training as a normal and welcome feature of their professional careers. Meanwhile, an entitlement to in-service training on the scale suggested should be included in every teacher's contract of service.

2.23. The secondment of all teachers for one term in seven years, if evenly spread, would nominally represent the release of 5 percent of the teaching staff at any one time. The reality, however, would be very different, since the teaching force always includes a substantial number of teachers who will not remain in service long enough to be concerned with opportunities for further training, and many teachers approaching the end of their careers may not choose to take training courses. Although all teachers should be strongly encouraged to take up their entitlement, there is no doubt that if the training were voluntary some teachers would choose not to do so. In practice, it is unlikely that the number of teachers released at any one time would exceed about 3 percent of the teaching force. Nevertheless, this would amount to a formidable burden and would create problems of organisation, particularly for small primary schools and for specialist subjects. In some cases the employment of more part-time teachers or the temporary full-time employment of existing part-time teachers (often acceptable to married women) might ease the problems. In others it might be necessary to increase the number and types of permanent relief staff or to make inter-school arrangements. Whatever the difficulties, they should be faced. The substantial improvement in staffing ratios now in prospect should help a great deal but, whatever improvements were made, a systematic programme for the third cycle, on the lines suggested here, would undoubtedly require the rearrangement of timetables and the redistribution of responsibilities in ways that would often be difficult and inconvenient.

2.24. There is no general agreement on the most appropriate length for full-time courses in the third cycle. Nor can there be, in view of the widely differing needs to be covered. At present such courses normally last either one term or one year, although there have been experiments involving six-week or half-term courses with a number of schools releasing staff on a Box and Cox arrangement. Precise patterns should not be prescribed, but it is important to emphasise that a teacher's entitlement to in-service training should be satisfied only by release for substantial courses, each of which should last at least four weeks full-time or the equivalent in a coherent and continuous part-time course. Courses acceptable for this purpose would be those designated by the new regional bodies proposed later in this Report. Any evening, weekend, or vacation courses or other short-term activities which might, or might not, involve release from school should be in addition to the basic entitlement. Many teachers already give up their own time to attend courses designed to improve their professional competence. There is no doubt that they would continue to be willing to do so. The development of longer and full-time courses should not be bought at the expense of those valuable short-term activities, which should themselves be expanded considerably. Indeed, it might be necessary to devote to them alone resources equivalent to the total now expended on third cycle courses of all kinds.

2.25. Every school should have on its staff a "professional tutor" to co-ordinate second and third cycle work affecting the school and to be the link between the school and other agencies engaged in that work. Whether the professional tutor were the head or deputy head, as might be the case in a small school, or a designated member of the staff in a larger school, it would be important for all teachers designated as professional tutors to be among the first to be admitted to third cycle courses, so that they could be trained for their new tasks. Among the responsibilities of the professional tutor would be that of compiling and maintaining a training programme for the staff of the school, which would take account both of the curricular needs of the school and of the professional needs of the teachers.

Professional Centres. 2.29. The provision and management of a programme of third cycle activities on the scale proposed here, together with the training to be given to "licensed teachers" in the second, largely school-based, year of the second cycle, as described earlier, would depend upon the existence of a countrywide network of centres, for which the title "professional centres" is suggested. Existing professional institutions (colleges and departments of education) would normally include the functions of professional centres among their other functions—that is, in addition to their responsibilities for the first year of the second cycle and for first cycle work—but there would also need to be other centres as described below. The existing professional institutions, in assuming the functions of professional centres, would be even more widely involved than at present in a range of in-service work. They would be the main providers of full-time substantial courses, including those leading to recognised professional awards. They would become centres for expertise in learning and teaching and for curriculum development, would act as channels for interpreting the results of educational research, and, in some cases, would conduct research themselves. They would make use of the part-time services of experienced teachers and LEA advisers. Their close contact with serving teachers in the schools, and especially with licensed teachers, would be of great benefit in helping them to evaluate and modify their own training procedures.

2.30. For the proper development of the third cycle, and to ensure that licensed teachers in the second year of their second cycle training were given the help they needed, it would be essential for all schools and F.E.* colleges to have easy access to at least one professional centre. For this reason, there should be, in addition to the centres in existing professional institutions, other more widely dispersed centres. These would be maintained by LEA's, and in many cases developed from existing teacher centres or placed in schools or F. E. colleges. The various forms of in-service training for F. E. teachers would make it particularly important to establish professional centres in polytechnics and other selected F. E. establishments, as well as in the present college of education (technical), but these centres should also be open to teachers from the schools. The institutions in question would often be able to run educational, as distinct from professional, courses which teachers from the schools would choose to follow as part of their third cycle activity. Even more important, there would be opportunities to offer professional courses which were suitable both for some F. E. teachers and some teachers from secondary schools; courses of this kind would not only encourage a welcome exchange of experience but would also be relevant to new and developing patterns of education for adolescents.

2.31. The number, distribution, and size of professional centres (other than those based on professional institutions) would depend on local circumstances. Although there can be no hard-and-fast rules it is important that each centre should serve a sufficient number of teaching staff in schools and F. E. colleges to be economically and professionally viable, without becoming so large that teachers in the institutions with which it was associated could not develop a sense of personal engagement in its work. The extent of a local professional centre's responsibilities must obviously determine its need for accommodation. It should have its own basic premises and equipment and

*Further education.

would need to have access to a workshop, tutorial rooms and common rooms as well as to books, materials, and equipment. For many purposes, however, it could share supplementary and specialist resources with other professional centres or with other institutions, and make use of facilities, such as laboratories and gymnasia, in schools with which it was associated. Only rarely, at least during the early years, should it be necessary to envisage establishing new purpose-built professional centres.

2.32. All professional centres would have a general training role in relation to the schools with which they were linked. While it would plainly be very important that they should be consistent in achieving high standards, professional centres would vary in their emphases and specialisms. The regional organisations would recognize and approve professional centres for specific purposes, and it would be an important part of their coordinating and rationalising function to do so. All professional centres, wherever based, would need approval for general purposes but the length of their list of "special approvals" would depend upon their size, their areas of excellence, and the resources at their disposal. In a densely populated area in which there were several centres it would be sensible to encourage some centres to specialise in particular subjects, in addition to their general role, while other centres specialised in others. Rationalisation could go further than this: it would be open to the proposed regional agencies and their coordinating national body to designate regional, multiregional, or national centres for particular purposes. For example, a large institution with exceptional resources in science and languages might serve the immediate area for general purposes but be designated as a centre for science and languages for the region or a group of regions, and as a language centre for the whole country. Lists of all approved professional centres, and the purposes for which each was recognised, would be published and kept up to date by the regional bodies.

2.33. To obtain recognition, professional centres would have to achieve standards laid down by the regional bodies, in terms of staffing, facilities, and other resources. Unless a centre satisfied the professional criteria defined by its regional body, it would not be able to function as a professional centre. Local professional centres would have close links with professional institutions accessible to them and would look to them for support and access to library and other facilities. They would have management committees, representative of the teachers in the schools, and F. E. establishments in their locality, as well as of any training institutions with which they were associated, their providing LEA's and their regional bodies. Each would have a full-time warden, of at least senior lecturer status, who would be selected by the centre's management committee, approved by the regional body, and paid by the LEA. He would have an independent role and his chief responsibility would be to draw on all available sources to meet the training requirements of the teachers served by his centre. He would be supported by some full-time staff and by a panel of part-time tutors, drawn from experienced teachers in schools and F. E. colleges as well as from college and university lecturers and LEA advisers. The supporting staff would also be approved by the regional body. The warden should himself have time for study, reflection, and "training" for his task. There should be opportunities, for him and his full-time colleagues, to spend some time teaching in schools nearby. Teachers in the schools, in return, should be enabled to contribute to the work of the professional centre.

2.34. Professional centres, whether based on professional institutions or elsewhere, would become a forum for the exchange of ideas, information, and experience between new and experienced teachers, teacher-trainers, and LEA advisers. They would cover most of the day-to-day training requirements of the schools they served, and many of them would house, or arrange, more substantial courses. The third cycle courses and other activities run by these centres would be mainly for home-based students. It should be possible to cater for most of the needs by providing locally-based courses, although for some purposes (for example, courses for teachers living in thinly populated areas and special courses at regional or national centres) residential facilities would be required. They would not, however, be needed on a large scale and the prospective reduction in the number of initial training places required should make it possible to provide them without undue difficulty.

Other resources and facilities. 2.35. The system outlined here would work in conjunction with other resources and facilities. Access to resource centres and library services, for example, would be important and the value of these services to practising teachers would be enhanced if there were established links between them and the centres to which teachers went for third cycle activities. The important place of LEA advisers in the new system has already been mentioned. They are in close touch with schools, will be aware of their day-to-day problems and able to assess needs as they arise and to make or suggest immediate arrangements to meet them. The extent to which LEA's are able to employ advisers is bound to vary, but after the forthcoming reorganisation of local government all LEA's should be able to employ a sufficient number of advisory staff. Advisers should work closely with professional centres of all kinds and should be able to enlist their help and advice, as well as themselves offering part-time help as tutors, examiners, or members of committees.

2.36. The services of specialists from university and polytechnic subject departments would be enlisted in the provision of courses of subject refreshment for specialist teachers in schools and F. E. establishments. The Open University could also be a powerful influence in the third cycle, by developing specialist materials and in-service courses—for example, in the teaching of reading. The programme of third cycle opportunities would not be confined to courses and activities specifically designed for teachers, but would include courses offered by F. E. establishments of all kinds, university extramural departments, and other adult education bodies, as well as the Open University's degree courses.

Conclusion

2.38. To implement the proposals made here for the third cycle would be a major new departure, of profound importance to the future of education in this country. It would involve bringing into partnership diverse agencies— schools, universities, polytechnics, colleges of education, advisory services, teacher centres, resource centres, and further education institutions. The establishment of such a planned partnership would be more productive of quality and probably more cost effective than any other measure proposed in this report or in the evidence submitted to the Inquiry. Of all our recommendations, this deserves the highest priority.

THE WHYS AND HOWS OF TEACHERS' CENTERS
William Fibkins

One of the real hopes of the teachers' center movement is the potential it has for directly involving teachers in their own training and renewal programs. The movement to establish teachers' centers—physical facilities within a school where teachers can meet on a voluntary basis to share ideas related to their professional and personal lives—clearly is one of the first efforts in this country to encourage teachers to develop, through participation, a community of learning and sharing within the schools. The purpose of this article is to provide a "how-to-do-it" guide for school and university personnel interested in developing teachers' centers, and to suggest a new position in the school: facilitator for staff development.

The Bay Shore-Stonybrook Teachers' Center emerged from a district-supported in-service workshop we called "The Teacher as a Learning Activator." It was offered at Bay Shore Junior High School in the spring of 1972. I conducted the workshop, with the help of school psychologist John Hessel, as an intensive experience over a three-week period. We emphasized the identification of staff needs, resources available within the staff, and strategies that might be utilized to improve the educational climate in our building and classrooms. At the conclusion of the workshop the entire group wanted to continue this sharing/assistance process *during the school day* at a comfortable place in the school. A core group of about 40 teachers formed to consider a plan of action. Personnel at the Teacher Center Project at Stonybrook University expressed an interest in helping to develop our teachers' center. Strong support came from the building and district administrators in the form of an endorsement of the teachers' center concept, provision of a room to house center activities, encouragement to the university to send two university staff members to our building twice a week as teachers' center facilitators, and support of my interest in coordinating the activities between the various groups involved (e.g., core group teachers, university personnel, building administration, those teachers not involved at that time, and the nonprofessional staff).

In the initial planning stage, we believed the center should be available to all staff members, but with no pressure to participate. Staff would be involved because they wished to be. The center would begin with a core of teachers who had come forward for a variety of reasons; they would reach others. The teachers would decide if they wanted formal or informal in-service training courses or workshops, curriculum investigations limited to specific "weak" areas, exposure to different teaching modes, etc., and then proceed to coordinate a program that satisfied their goals. It was thought that personnel from the university would be helpful in offering resources in almost any discipline, but ultimately teachers from the junior high school would develop and run workshops for each other and share their own expertise. In fact, the main focus of the center was to encourage the use of our own resources to help each other: teachers teaching other teachers. It was also though that my role as a counselor and my training in participant observation would be useful in helping teachers to become involved in this process.

In the fall the core group of interested teachers, two staff members from the university, and I began to talk informally with other faculty members about the center concept and the notion of identifying staff needs and a professional development curriculum for the junior high school. The initial response was positive, although I observed that the notion of staff members offering training for other staff members during the school day was at first difficult for many teachers to accept. Some teachers also noted initial concern about the role of the university and the possibility of a hidden agenda on the part of the district administration. Others were concerned about my role in the project. I had only been in the building one year—what was I really about?

By the end of September, we had informally contacted every faculty member, emphasizing that this was an experimental idea and that, hopefully, they would be interested in participating in center programs at the level where they felt most comfortable. We pointed out that there was no preplanned program; it was a voluntary endeavor and there was no clear program definition at this point. Our main approach would be to provide informal training for each other in the easiest, most attractive way, and to learn by doing rather than the lecture method. At the same time the building and district administration kept a low profile but provided maximum support for the project. Our initial efforts, then, were of a grass-roots nature—reaching out to as many people on the professional staff as possible, and asking them to participate. Attention was also given to the nonprofessional staff so that they were aware of the development of the center and hopefully would participate as well. In fact, the notion of encouraging the nonprofessional staff to participate emerged as a top priority after we received a positive response, particularly from the personnel who served as cafeteria aides and in clerical roles.

By October we had interested approximately 60 teachers (out of a staff of 120) in participating in center activities. With this core group we developed an experimental series of daytime workshops to be held during October and November. The workshops were 1) Utilizing Audiovisual Aids in the Classroom, 2) Utilizing Small Group Procedures in the Classroom, 3) Ecology for Classroom Teachers, 4) Utilizing Behavior Modification Techniques in the Classroom, and 5) Utilizing Individual Instruction in the Classroom. Each was offered by a team of staff people during their preparatory and/or lunch periods. Fortunately, the center room we used was adjacent to the teachers' dining area. Workshops lasted a minimum of three days, with new material presented each day. Teacher and administrator attendance was encouraged by word of mouth and through announcements prepared by the initial group. Announcements were placed in lavatories, teacher rooms, even on windshields. Students were enlisted to hand out notices before and after school. It was our feeling that teachers, being busy people, like to be asked and reminded.

The initial workshops were well received, with over 50 teachers and administrators participating in each workshop. Once this series ended, the core group met again and planned another grass-roots approach to the faculty in order to identify training needs and resources that might be offered at the center. It was thought that this process would best be carried on face to face, rather than by formal questionnaires. Upon the completion of this "new sounding," a new set of workshops was developed for December and January, featuring trips to other teachers' centers in New York City and Scarsdale, slides of faculty members' trips to Africa and Russia, and workshops related to achievement motivation (an all-day Saturday workshop), small-group procedures, music in the classroom, student/teacher communication, using novels as a motivating tool, and the movie *Future Shock,* to name a few of the offerings. As was the case in our first series, the workshops were usually offered over a three-day period during the teachers' prep and lunch periods.

At the conclusion of this series, we observed that interest in the center was increasing among faculty members who had not theretofore participated. We observed that teachers were beginning to see how a center might operate and how they might participate. The level of trust concerning the role of the administration, the university, and my role rose considerably. We even found ourselves faced with a rather fortunate problem. Some staff members indicated that they could not get in to see and participate in the workshops because of other commitments. Could we present them at other periods besides lunch? The idea was good, but how could we free presenters for a full day or a number of days? After we brought the problem before the building and district administration we were permitted to use substitutes to free those teachers who were offering workshops. This time could be used to prepare as well as to present workshops, an option well received by many faculty members.

During the remainder of the year we ran two additional workshop series (March-April, May-June) and concluded the center activities with an end-of-the-year brainstorming and planning session and buffet luncheon. The workshops in this period covered such diverse areas as presentations by student teachers, films by Carl Rogers, Spanish-speaking instruction, the inquiry method of teaching, the use of television in teaching/learning, drugs and students, Earth Week, first aid, teacher/parent interaction, human relations, the use of learning materials. There were more systematic workshops related to achievement motivation, individualization, small-group procedures, reading in the content area, and contract learning. In retrospect, we had more activities and interaction procedures available from our own resources than we were able to utilize.

In the fall of the 1973 school year we began with a series of brainstorming meetings with the staff, in order to identify professional development needs and possible workshops. The ideas that emerged were translated into a fall calendar that included over 40 workshops. Topics ranged from visual literacy, opera without pain, and group counseling, to feminism and the school curriculum. It appears that short-term workshops that respond to the here-and-now needs of the staff constitute the most useful training model for us. It also appears that, as building staff assume more initiative in setting up training programs, the role of the university facilitators also undergoes change. It may be that once a center is under way and a local center facilitator is employed, university facilitators may be used as resources only when needed. They then can be free to begin assisting other districts in establishing teachers' centers.

Although our program began in September, 1972, with little definition, in a relatively short time we involved over three-quarters of the professional staff and many support people in center activities that emphasized an atmosphere of sharing and help among the entire staff. We had begun the process of assessing our own needs, identifying our own resources, and stressing that the "teaching" going on at the center was a helping, not a command, relationship. New uses of space, time, and resources were developing, both at the center and in many classrooms. We had also, again in a short period, found a way for teachers, university personnel, and administrators to work cooperatively on a project that was beneficial to all concerned. I might add that this cooperative process did not "just happen." The core group of teachers, administration, and university personnel continually worked on sustaining an open atmosphere.

In summary, then, the following perspectives may be useful to others who are considering development of a teachers' center:

—In the beginning stages of center development teachers do not perceive themselves as having resources to offer to their fellow teachers.

—Those teachers who do identify themselves as having resources to share appear to serve as catalysts in helping other teachers to offer workshops and training.

—Administrative support appears to be critical to the successful development of a teachers' center. Materials, released time, space, and—most important—conceptual understanding of the teachers' center notion all require strong support from building and district administrators.

—The involvement of support staff in workshops appears to alter in a positive direction the working relationship in the school.

—It appears that teachers who serve as workshop presenters generally increase their own self-esteem and degree of involvement in the school.

—It appears that personnel trained in participant observation, organizational development theory, and communication skills, and having *time* to become involved with teachers, may be in the best position to help teachers identify resources and determine how these resources can be used in teachers' center and other staff development programs.

It is this last perspective, the development of a new position called the *facilitator for staff development,* that I wish to consider in closing.

It is my opinion that a new role, facilitator for staff development, is needed in the schools to help teachers and support staff personnel to utilize their own power, resources, and creative strategies in planning renewal and retraining systems. More specifically, personnel trained in participant observation, organizational development theory, child development, human relation and communication skills, and curriculum strategies might be utilized in schools to:

—Act as facilitators for teachers' centers.

—Assist teachers in planning renewal programs.

—Assist teachers in implementing and assessing renewal programs.

—Assist others in the school to assess the training needs of professional staff members, support staff, and administrators, and the resources available within the environment (e.g., school, district, community, university, etc.).

—Assist others in school in utilizing these resources in new and creative ways, particularly in reference to time, place and atmosphere.

—Assist others in the school in researching new *voluntary* approaches to certification and use of nonprofessional staff as assistants in the classroom.

—Demonstrate teaching, communication, and organizational development skills for teachers, administrators, and support staff personnel at the teachers' center and in other appropriate settings.

—Assist boards of education, district administrators, and department heads in planning staff development strategies.

—Carry on research activities related to the educational process in the school.

—Carry on research activities related to the impact of the school environment on teacher motivation, morale, and career satisfaction.

These are only a few of the activities that a facilitator for staff development might carry on. His work area might be in a specific school or family of schools. His main function would be to assist personnel within the school to develop programs that meet the professional development needs of their staff. He would not have an office, but probably would work out of a teachers' center and spend most of his time in face-to-face interaction in the school environment (e.g., classroom, teachers' center, hallways, custodians' rooms, and the community). He would be a specialist in the helping process. In carrying out this role, his major objective would be to share his knowledge with all of the people in the school community, while trying to avoid the know-it-all label. He would be trained in a variety of intervention strategies and be capable of facilitating renewal programs at the level of the staff desires.

I suggest that we need to develop a variety of teachers' centers with different models of participation and program development. We must, as Ivan Illich suggests in *Deschooling Society,* provide teacher access to "learning webs" designed to facilitate inquiry, expression, association, and skill development. Clearly, the pilot projects being considered in New York (see the Master Plan for Higher Education) and other states, e.g., Vermont and Florida, offer possibilities for further research concerning teachers' centers and the staff support systems required at these centers. My hope is that these programs will maintain their voluntary aspect and that teachers, administrators, and interested university personnel will be involved at all levels in the planning and development stage.

I would caution that programs be kept small and that we attempt to avoid large regional centers that may take on the characteristics of our present colleges of education. Teacher education seems to be moving toward school-based training and renewal programs. Perhaps the model presented here, which emphasizes a cooperative arrangement between teachers, administrators, and interested university personnel, can be applied in developing pilot training programs. The resources are at hand. We need only new organizational patterns that make it attractive for us to share resources.

Chapter X

Can Teacher Centers Work Here?
Introduction

Eric Midwinter remarked at a Plowden Conference at Cambridge University two years ago that "we are educating children to be their grandfathers." Much the same thing was said by Alfred North Whitehead four decades ago in *The Adventure of Ideas:*

> Our sociological theories, our political philosophy, our practical maxims of business, our political economy, and our doctrines of education are derived from an unbroken tradition of great thinkers and of practical examples from the age of Plato . . . to the end of the last century. The whole of this tradition is warped by the vicious assumption that each generation will substantially live amid the conditions governing the lives of its fathers and will transmit those conditions to mould with equal force the lives of its children. *We are living in the first period of human history for which this assumption is false.*[1]

And Jean Piaget has stated the same idea positively:

> The principal goal of education is to create men who are capable of doing new things, not simply of repeating what other generations have done—men who are creative, inventive, and discoverers. The second goal of education is to form minds which can be critical, can verify, and not accept everything they are offered. . . . So we need pupils who are active, who learn early to find out by themselves, partly by their own spontaneous activity and partly through material we set up for them; who learn early to tell what is verifiable and what is simply the first idea to come to them.[2]

Can teacher centers work here? I think they cannot unless their clear-sighted goal is to help teachers think for themselves as the teachers will then help children to think.

Then we must ask, are teachers actually to be allowed to think, to challenge, to question? Are children? Suppose teachers are encouraged to manage their own re-education. Owen, in a penetrating article in Chapter VI reports that in England this degree of autonomy has led to "a wallowing about." Undoubtedly. The process of development is long and cannot be artifically shortened. What teachers may want from a center at its beginning may be very different from what they request several years later:

> The first stage is that of catering for rudimentary needs ("tips for teachers")
> and attempting inappropriate in-service techniques (copying existing provisions).
> Then the Centre begins to develop an identity and its role becomes clearer.
> Teachers become more actively involved as they learn to dispense with authori-
> tarian leadership. As the surface needs of teachers become gratified, they become
> more aware of deeper needs—the need to examine critically what and why they
> are teaching. From this stage, I would prophesy that they will go on to want to
> examine critically the curriculum as a whole, from that point to a critical look
> at the education system.

The warden whom Owen quotes above suggests that teacher centers have a duty to make themselves interesting to the apathetic teacher; the centers "must not expect an automatic loyalty."

The fact is that renewal centers as envisioned by the Office of Education and described in this chapter by their leading proponents may not allow for this growth pattern or even see it as desirable. The old pattern and one that the Office of Education appears to be following, is that teachers are told what to do: consider the fact of state departments of education being funded by the Office of Education to set up teacher centers throughout a state. Alfred Bender, speaking of the megalithic Texas centers, remarks, "their size will make them as useful to classroom teachers as are the pyramids to Egyptians." He sees these vast bureaucratic networks *established for* teachers as "magnifi-cent memorials to the authoritarian and paternalistic patterns of the past"—"one more innovation which prevents change."[3] Whether or not this govern-mental policy continues, the federal scene may be too chaotic and ephem-eral for many teacher groups to cope with. What is needed is, as Crosby as-serts here, "a mechanism for bringing the extensive and rich resources of the education world to bear directly upon the most immediate needs of teachers and students." This mechanism may need to be provided by American teachers themselves as the Japanese teachers have done for years with their "study circles."

Grass roots teacher centers are entirely feasible. For those teachers who want to set up teacher centers themselves, there are several very clear mes-sages in this book:

(1) A group of teachers who want to learn together can start a teacher cen-ter. They can begin by inviting every teacher in a district, or "catchment area" of 400 to 800 teachers, including both elementary and secondary faculties.

(2) The group of teachers should decide on a governing board with a wide range of teacher opinion from among the group.

(3) The governing board should meet with administrators and boards of education requesting modest funding and a place to meet. These groups should be invited to have representation on the governing board.

(4) The teacher group decides on the in-service program it wants and elects a paid part-time director of the center. The group decides whether or not to assess itself dues. Each of these matters can come under review at the end of the first year and each year thereafter.

(5) Further development of a teacher center depends on beginnings, but a thriving center will establish liaison with the community and with a local college or university. This liaison should include representation of the governing board.

(6) The most successful centers will draw from their own local strengths of people, environment, heritage.

(7) The concept of "teachers teaching teachers" is critical to the success of a teacher center. Funding from national, state, or foundation sources is not essential. The control of the center must be kept in the hands of *teachers*.

Notes

1. Quoted in Neil Postman and Charles Weingartner, *Teaching As a Subversive Activity* (New York: Dell, 1969), p. 11.

2. Richard E. Ripple and Verne N. Rockcastle (eds.), *Piaget Rediscovered: A Report of the Conference on Cognitive Studies and Curriculum Development, March, 1964* (Ithaca, N.Y.: School of Education, Cornell University), p. 5.

3. Albert E. Bender, "Teachers' Centers in England and Wales," *Intellect*, March 1974, p. 389.

A U.S. PLAN FOR EDUCATION RENEWAL
Sidney P. Marland, Jr.

"American education is in urgent need of reform," President Nixon declared in 1970. His charge has been echoed by virtually all responsible educational leaders, teacher organizations, and local school board members.

To meet the President's challenge, the United States Office of Education has developed an education renewal strategy designed to help American schools reform themselves.

By concentrating selected Federal funds on the nation's neediest school districts, the plan will provide parents, teachers, and school administrators with an opportunity to develop and carry out renewal programs tailor-made to meet specific local pupil achievement problems.

Renewal, as we are developing the theme in the Office of Education, implies change from within, change involving every aspect of the schooling process, change regarded not as a short-term luxury or fad but rather as a continuous process, change geared to meeting local problems as discerned by local teachers and other citizens.

Renewal Sites

The renewal program will begin on a pilot basis in some school systems in fiscal year 1973—which corresponds to the 1972-73 school year. Eventually the plan calls for the establishment of some 1,000 "renewal sites" encompassing about 10,000 schools serving an estimated 5.5 million children from kindergarten through high school.

These sites, each of which will be funded for five years, will serve as demonstration models for encouraging change in schools throughout the region.

The program envisions the establishment of a State Renewal Center in each state, to coordinate the several renewal sites in the state, the creation at each renewal site of a "teacher center" on the British model, and the use of "education extension agents" not unlike agricultural extension agents to stimulate the use of new materials and techniques.

The Office of Education administers two kinds of Federal support programs—formula grant and discretionary. More than 85 percent of all Federal education funds are earmarked for formula grant programs. That is, each state receives a proportionate share of the program appropriation based on the number of children between certain ages or the number of children from low-income families or some such criteria.

The remaining funds are termed "discretionary." They are awarded on a project-by-project basis at the discretion of the commissioner within limits established by the Congress.

These are research and development funds, teacher-training and retraining funds, and funds for meeting specific problems such as bilingual education, dropout prevention, drug abuse education, and environmental education.

The essence of the education renewal strategy is best stated in two words—coordination and concentration.

Instead of awarding hundreds of separate grants for several different discretionary programs, many of them to the same school system, the Office of Education will concentrate in a single grant to each renewal site a package of programs to be administered locally in a coordinated fashion.

Eligibility requirements for such coordinated grants will, of course, be consistent with the legislative requirements of each of the separate programs included in the package, and appropriate accounting procedures will insure that local school districts receiving renewal grants satisfy the purposes for which Congress appropriated the funds.

In effect, the Office of Education intends to provide a more efficient and effective means of delivering discretionary grant program services to local school districts, thus enhancing the legislative intent of a variety of programs.

What is even more important, the local school district with the will and wisdom to renew itself will have concentrated funds to effect comprehensive change, rather than continue to tinker with bits and pieces of innovation. This packaging process is similar to the education revenue-sharing bill President Nixon has proposed as a means for the more efficient and effective delivery of formula grant funds to the states.

Each local renewal site, selected with the active participation of the chief state school officer, will consist of an average of ten schools, elementary and secondary, serving approximately 5,000 pupils, kindergarten through high school. All renewal sites will be in areas of concentration of disadvantaged children, two-thirds of them urban and the remainder in rural locations.

Function of States

Each state education agency will receive funds to establish a State Renewal

Center, and state education officials will share the leadership responsibility with the Office of Education, not only in selecting sites but also in facilitating the spread of new practices and techniques from the demonstration sites to the state school system at large.

The initiative for participating in the renewal program will rest primarily at the local level. Local school officials in each prospective site will be asked to get together with teachers, students, parents, and community residents to develop a local needs assessment.

It will be the Office of Education's responsibility to match local needs to available programs and funds.

The Office of Education will be responsible for preparing the Federal program package, which may result in a single renewal grant award under a variety of programs authorizations. The average annual grant award for each renewal site is expected to be about $750,000.

The linchpin of each renewal site will be a teacher center where teachers and other educational personnel from renewal site schools will be able to come together to discuss problems in an atmosphere free of competition or compulsion, receive assistance and advice, improve their competencies, and exchange experiences.

No matter how good an innovation may be, no matter how promising a technique, unless the teacher truly accepts it, believes deeply in it, and possesses it as his own, no change will occur. Once the classroom door closes, the teacher is in charge.

As a further means of stimulating the dissemination of new materials practices, the Office of Education intends to establish an adaption of the agricultural extension agent model.

This will create a new career in American education—the education extension agent. Just as agricultural extension agents carry to the farmers information on government-financed agricultural research and development, education extension agents will provide a link between teachers and other practitioners and those who are developing new educational materials and techniques.

TEACHER POWER AND LOCAL-TO-LOCAL DELIVERY
Allen Schmeider

Noninvolvement Means Nonimprovement

From the day that Sputnik made Khrushchev the most influential U. S. Commissioner of Education, this nation has tried a zillion ways to meet the googolplex of problems facing its mammoth educational enterprise. Unfortunately, as we have been widely and richly reminded by a plethora of publications on the subject, most attempts to improve the system significantly have failed. While reasons abound for the uneven yield of the innovative sixties in meeting our most critical school problems, one shortcoming seems to stand out: the relatively low level of involvement of the two groups that know most about how schools work—teachers and students. Although both groups are extremely important, this particular statement will focus on the teachers.

The classroom teacher is probably the most underutilized resource for change and improvement in American education. Most of the challenges and needs of formal education in this country are in the schools or come to rest in the schools; yet, most efforts to improve them usually start elsewhere. Those programs that have been developed within the schools have usually been relatively isolated from the mainstream, confined to a single classroom within a school system, making them just about as esoteric as those demonstration or innovative programs conducted somewhere on the outside. Throughout recent years, literally thousands of teachers ventured beyond the system to attend summer institutes and year-round fellowship programs—sometimes exciting and well-planned experiences—but because teachers were not generally involved in their development, these programs also proved to be relatively unrelated to the most crucial classroom problems of the teachers in attendance.

Programs intended to help classroom teachers must involve classroom teachers in their design. They have the most real experience with what it takes to excite children and to raise learning levels to new highs. They are the agents and implementers of any educational enterprise, the ones who know first whether something will or will not work. Our experiences in the sixties should have taught us the importance of beginning in the classroom where the action is, of working outward to draw to the teacher the resources needed to

271

do the job. The outside-to-inside approacn too often results in the creation of innumerable solutions in search of problems, of programs neither well related to nor understood by the teachers and students whom they were designed to serve.

Reports and Recognition

It is significant and encouraging that many of the recent high-level reports on education have highlighted both the great potential of the teacher in the improvement of educational systems and the increasing importance of the schools as centers of staff and curriculum development. After several years of extensive study, for example, Charles Silberman, in a report to the Carnegie Foundation, concluded that teachers were light years ahead of theorists and researchers. Edward Pomeroy, Executive Director of the American Association of Colleges for Teacher Education, when discussing the 1970's,[1] called for closer cooperation between the university and the schools and discussed the need to move teacher training into the more relevant setting of the schools. Recommendations of the recently released James Report[2] in Britain advocate a greater involvement of teachers in the whole educational process, ranging from full participation in preservice training programs to a greatly increased share of educational research. William L. Smith, Head of the Office of Education's National Center for the Improvement of Educational Systems, has repeatedly underlined the importance of the single school, including all its staff—paraprofessionals, teachers, and administrators—as the minimal, and possibly most significant, unit of educational change. Don Davies, Deputy Commissioner for Renewal, who considers the individual teacher to be the most important force for meaningful curriculum reform, has continually searched for new ways to involve teachers in the planning of Office of Education programs.

But these are only promising signs, not nationally accepted directions. Teacher power is still a long way from effective release and exploitation. Its promise will be fulfilled when classroom teachers become full partners in the development, implementation, and evaluation of all educational programs that relate to the teaching-learning process, including those of teacher training and educational research and development.

Local-to-Local Delivery

Any involvement of teachers in attempts to improve American education must place a high priority on overcoming the isolation and loneliness of teaching. It is probable that every classroom teacher does something better than every other classroom teacher; yet we are unable to take advantage of these successes because teachers simply do not have many opportunities to share ideas, problems, and solutions with one another. It is possible, therefore, that the greatest advances in education in the present decade could be gained through the finding of more effective means of linking the creativity, strength, and excitement of every classroom to every other classroom.

Just as the 1960's was generally a decade of innovation, it may be that the 1970's should be a decade of dissemination. To this end, there is already an increasing emphasis on developing better delivery systems for materials and approaches to be transferred from national, regional, and state levels into the classroom. There is still, however, very little effort directed at local-to-local transfer of proven products and processes. The problem of adapting the successful practices of others is made doubly difficult by the fact that little attention has been given to the problem during these recent years of widespread curriculum reform. It is an amazing paradox that millions of dollars have been spent on producing curriculum packages, with hardly a cent going toward the installation of the resulting new programs and materials. Consequently, problems of adaptation, especially for local-to-local transfer of products, will have to be explored from somewhere near ground zero.

The task of developing effective systems of local-to-local delivery of products and processes, validated in different ways for different purposes, will have to be vigorously pursued. More and better methods are needed for communicating successes from one teacher to another in the same school and throughout the local system. We need facilities where teachers can find the stimulation to develop conceptual packages that they might not otherwise have developed; where they can refine products that have proved successful for them over the years to the point where they can be used by other teachers; where those who are interested in the proven products of other teachers can learn about them, talk about them, test them, and finally, adapt them to their own classrooms. We need feedback systems of all kinds to relate the local-to-local process systematically to important questions of educational program developments—for example, how should the best of local practices be incorporated into pre- and in-service staff development programs?

Other Critical Needs

No matter how widespread or varied opportunities for teacher involvement may become, two needs seem to be outstanding: (1) large-scale, intensive training programs for teacher leaders focusing on the character, perspective, and problems of the current educational managers, teacher trainers, researchers, and curriculum developers; and (2) most importantly, more released time during the regular working day to enable teachers to participate actively in these new directions. The situation is best summarized in the report of a national cross-section of classroom teachers, who met at Harper's Ferry, West Virginia, under the auspices of Task Force '72:

> Teachers . . . are most desirous of change, of leadership, of new and better ways to serve the children they teach. . . . It is not change which disturbs them. It is expectations unfulfilled; it is being asked to deliver excellence in education without adequate training . . . support . . . time and money . . . and opportunities for personal growth and development. . . . One must be reminded that teachers conscientiously doing their job are so deep in their work that they . . . don't really have the energy to respond to the challenge of change. Thus to pick a handful of teachers up and show them that change may . . . be possible, to involve them in planning change . . . is to offer them a heady brew which must not later be allowed to go sour in their mouths.

The decade of the 1970's in American education will certainly be a time of googolplexity, interinstitutional cooperation, and accountability. But most of all, it will be an era of the teacher and the student.

Notes

1. Edward C. Pomeroy, *Beyond the Upheaval.* Good Lecture Series (Washington, D.C.: American Association of Colleges for Teacher Education, 1972).

2. Department of Education and Science, *Teacher Education and Training* (London: Her Majesty's Stationery Office, 1972).

AN INTERVIEW WITH DON DAVIES
from *Audiovisual Instruction*

The National Center for Educational Technology is a bureau-level activity under the Deputy Commissioner for Development, Dr. Don Davies. In this interview, Dr. Davies gives us an overview of the volume and complexity of problems he faces in trying to manage the Office of Education's renewal effort.

AVI: Dr. Davies, you were one of the chief architects of the idea of developing renewal sites—an idea which ran up against congressional opposition. Can you tell us what the renewal sites were supposed to be?

DAVIES: The renewal sites were collections of schools in school districts, something between five and 20 school buildings, elementary and secondary, serving substantial numbers of work units which would band together to plan a five-year reform program, starting with assessment of the needs of the community and the kids; then planning their own priorities, deciding what they were going to try to do differently and better. And then they were to get help from us in a packaged way from a variety of authorizations. That way, the program would have been carried out with a heavy concentration of funds in those places, with requirements for evaluation and requirements for an advisory council—a group that would be composed of parents, students, teachers, higher education, administrators, and so forth. That feature was one of the essential things; it was supposed to be a community-parents-student-teacher-based thing. It had no requirements as far as what the nature of the program was to be. It required a process of planning and involvement. The nature of the program was to be locally determined.

It was—and is—a great idea. It would have provided a response to what the real needs of those places are—which is very difficult to do with a collection of 25 or 30 separate discretionary programs, each in its own little bag.

AVI: What money was to go for the renewal sites?

DAVIES: Some EPDA money, some of the dropout money, and some of the Title III money in 1973 was to go for renewal sites. But it's not now, of course, because there will be no renewal sites.

AVI: What's happening with Project TREND (Targeting Resources on the

Educational Needs of the Disadvantaged)? When the renewal site idea was still alive, we heard that the Project TREND sites would be the first renewal sites. Are they still operating?

DAVIES: They were going to be considered for being renewal sites and some of them probably would have been—not automatically, because they were in various stages of readiness for such things. They're continuing about 10 or 11 of them.

AVI: Is there new legislation being planned?

DAVIES: We're in the process of talking about and trying to develop ideas and plans for possible legislation. It will be a little while before we even know whether we can come up with something that's worth trying to do, and then it will require having to go through the usual legislative process. I'm hopeful that we will be able to come up with something.

AVI: Would this be something introduced early in the next Congress?

DAVIES: Well, I think it will take a while to develop. I don't know exactly what the timing will be.

AVI: Could you tell us the subject of this possible legislation?

DAVIES: Well, sure, it's to provide legislative authorization for the *kind* of thing we were talking about in the renewal sites. But we've got to see if we can put together some way of getting at that. It has to be worthwhile in the sense of making sense, of being something different and better than existing legislation. We don't want just another bill. We have too many bills, too many programs now. Another categorical program called "renewal sites" is not needed.

Support for Training Programs

AVI: Will the Administration put in a request for funds for EPDA?

DAVIES: Yes, there'll be funds; there are funds in the 1973 budget. And there'll be funds in the 1974 budget; I don't know how much.

I would say that one of the big problems on that score—as well as all things that have to do with training, personnel development of any kind—is that there is a great deal of skepticism in Washington and in other places on the part of decision-makers about whether or not teacher training or staff development efforts are in fact worthwhile. People who are interested in teacher, administrator, and specialist training and development need to recognize that outside of our own fraternities there are very large numbers of people who don't believe in staff development at all. Those are the people who need to be convinced by the results—and they haven't been.

AVI: Are *you* convinced?

DAVIES: No, I am not convinced that many of the things that we do under the label of training and staff development are worth doing at all.

I *am* convinced that it's possible for adults to learn and that there are effective ways of helping people develop new skills and new attitudes. I don't see nearly enough of the things we do know about what's effective being applied. I still see massive use of very ineffective approaches to education.

AVI: If you could draw up a new piece of legislation, how would you write a bill that might make professional education more effective?

DAVIES: Well, I don't think we do need new legislation. We do have the Educational Professions Development Act, which is a very good piece of legislation. It's quite broad and flexible. . . .

AVI: But it's not being used . . . ?

DAVIES: Well, it's being used, but it's only a very small contribution to the support of some demonstration kinds of efforts that are related to the training of personnel. It was never designed to be any more than that and never can be. Most of the money that supports these activities is state and private institution money, not federal money. The federal money has always been small and it isn't the solution to that problem at all.

AVI: Where does the solution lie?

DAVIES: Well, it lies with the institutions that prepare teachers and the school systems and universities that hire those teachers, supervisors.

AVI: Then what's the problem? What's keeping them from being more effective?

DAVIES: It's complicated. There's no single villain in all of this, as is true of almost anything else. Historically, school systems haven't paid very much attention to or spent very much time or money or effort on in-service training or staff development. And much of what they've done over the years has been ineffective. Historically, in higher education, teacher education and other training of education personnel has been a very low priority, low status effort. Schools of education do not enjoy high status or prestige, so they haven't attracted generally the money or the talent. Now that can't be corrected by a federal effort. The federal effort can be useful in establishing models, demonstrations. That's exactly what we've tried to do over the last five years with the Educational Professions Development Act—along several important lines which suggest very specifically what's wrong with past practice. And the things that we and they have tried to do specifically are, first, to try to get the training close to the job, meaning out of the college classroom and into the school where the problems are. Second, to try to bring new kinds of people into the education business with a more diverse, richer bank of talent,

including minority people, poor people, and people from other kinds of backgrounds (liberal arts graduates, *etc.*), to diversify the education professions.
And third, to apply more effective training techniques when working with
education personnel, using things like micro-teaching and other applications
of technology, using all the kinds of things that we know about how adults
learn and don't learn. We want to replace the usual approach, which is to have
someone come into a classroom and lecture about all the groovy things that
teachers are to do. The clients—the students—have been saying forever: Why
don't these people who are training us practice what they teach?

AVI: Isn't there an old saying, teachers teach as they are taught, not as they
are taught to teach?

DAVIES: Well sure. I can remember enduring endless lectures about how as
teachers we ought to use audiovisual materials in our classrooms. Lectures,
endless lectures, about how teachers ought to have a close, warm relationship
with their students. Seven hundred people in the class; you could see the professor a week from Wednesday at 2:30 in his office.

So what we've tried to do is demonstrate a different way, to provide some
money for schools and colleges to make teacher education more effective.
And we've given much more money and responsibility to the schools themselves, trying to support the idea that you need a school, community, and
college partnership, not a unilateral role for the college. We've given money
either directly to the school systems or in such a way that cooperation and
partnership is required.

I'm talking about what used to be the Bureau of Educational Personnel
Development which I was the head of for 3½ years, which Bill Smith is now
the head of. But it's now called the National Center for the Improvement of
Educational Systems, because it includes not just teacher training money but
also the dropout prevention program and 15 percent of Title III.

Education Extension Agents

AVI: What about the idea of education extension agents?

DAVIES: That's in the National Center for Educational Communications,
and its program and money are now at NIE. And that's a question here at
DCD, because the extension agent program will be carried on under NIE. It
will be modified by that agency when its director and board establish a policy
and take a look at that and all the other programs that NIE has inherited
from the Office of Education. I couldn't predict what the modifications will
be, but they will appropriately make modifications.

AVI: Does that mean the program is sitting dormant for a while?

DAVIES: No, planning for it is underway. As early as 1971 we had three state pilot extension agent programs going. Those are continuing. Lee Burchinal, Associate Commissioner for Educational Communications, and his staff are continuing to do the planning for it with whatever modifications are made by the new set-up.

AVI: How are they doing? And which states?

DAVIES: Very well, as far as I can tell. The states are South Carolina, Utah, and Oregon.

AVI: Is this one person, or a little corps of people who are supposed to spread the word, so-to-speak, around the state?

DAVIES: In the three pilots, and I assume in extensions of the idea in 1973, there will be more than one person working in a state. Maybe four to ten in each state, something like that. In most cases they are actually physically located out away from the state department of education, although they are state department of education employees. They work very close to one or more school districts, directly with principals and teachers. They work very much like Agriculture's county agents work. They're a combination of consultants, sources of information, trainers, helpers. It's a very simple idea.

AVI: Yes, it is. Of course the Association's concern is the future of technology in education. How can we get those agents to spread ideas about the potential of instructional technology? It's so hard to filter information through to the school districts.

DAVIES: Well, that seems to be the idea behind the extension agent. Their responsibility is to know what *is* available—ideas, terms, products, things, and ways of working with kids in school. If they don't know that, then the whole thing breaks down.

AVI: How would the education agents disseminate information?

DAVIES: Well, using the Agriculture model, of an agricultural extension system, NCEC plans to provide for the same thing—an educational extension system, which means a place, or several places, where the ideas, the materials, are brought together. So the extension agent has a sort of home base, much as the agricultural agent has the agricultural extension station. This would include ERIC and all kinds of other materials brought together.

AVI: Where would the place be? In Washington?

DAVIES: Oh no, it would be decentralized. Maybe in a state capital, or in several places in large states.

AVI: That sounds like something for the future. It sounds like something that would actually work.

DAVIES: Yes, there'll be some reality to that, this year. There are those three states and there'll be some others. One of the things NIE will want to do is test out or research in a more formal way different ways of operating an extension agent program to see what works best.

The Development Bag

AVI: What exactly does the Office of Development encompass?

DAVIES: Well, there are five operating units. One is the National Center for the Improvement of Education Systems, which includes the dropout prevention program. Another is the National Center for Educational Technology. A third is the National Center for Educational Statistics. All the data collection activities of the office, including the national assessment, are now centralized there. The fourth is the Environmental Education Office, and the Fifth is Drug Education, Health and Nutrition—which has two separate legislative authorizations.

AVI: Why were Environmental Education and Nutrition and Drug Abuse placed in Development? It sounds like they are a little out of place.

DAVIES: No, not really. In the reorganization that was proposed as a part of the large educational renewal effort, the plan was to put a number of discretionary project grant programs together, so the planning for them and their administration could be coordinated. Those are discretionary programs, that's why they're here. Of course, there are others in other places. The bilingual program is back in elementary and secondary education by congressional desire.

AVI: What is done within the Office for Development that relates to instructional technology, other than what is done by the National Center for Educational Technology?

DAVIES: In my office we help NCET—Bob Filep and his staff—by providing a planning office and some administrative personnel, but basically, Bob Filep is the person in the office responsible for the educational technology area; what's being done in this deputyship for technology is his responsibility. Now, there are lots of other things being done for educational technology in other parts of the Office and DCD. Bob has the responsibility, to the extent that it's possible, to provide service and stimulation for these other activities, to know what they're doing, to provide coordination.

One of the things that we hope to do is to add staff to the National Center for Educational Technology this year, so that they will have more people who can provide technical assistance and help and ideas to other people in the

Office of Education. If they're going to carry out their role of coordination and stimulation and assistance over the whole range of technology, they have got to have people who have talent and skills in all kinds of things, because the interest in technology is all over the place.

Instructional Technology—Still a Toddler

AVI: About three years ago you spoke to the AECT convention in Detroit. You advised the audience to concentrate on applying technology to instruction rather than thinking of it as an information retrieval system. Do you think there have been strides in that direction?

DAVIES: Strides? The wrong word, I think. We tend to *creep* rather than to stride in educational change, and just in about almost anything you can name. Maybe you'll have to be satisfied with creeping. I'm not satisfied with it, but that seems to be where we are. I really don't know how much progress has been made. It's been very slow. My greatest concern about technology in education is that it has yet to be fully integrated into instructional systems. It's still by and large, in most schools and in most colleges, an add-on—both in terms of what it costs and in terms of what it does. We went in, we were big, at one point, on talking about technology as "enrichment." You did everything that you were already doing with all the same staff and then you added something on—a television program, movies or something, and that was educational technology. It always *costs* more.

That is a disastrous approach, because it makes technology vulnerable in a fiscal sense in that add-ons are very easy to cut out. And second, it doesn't get integrated in any way that affects the mainstream of the instructional program.

This, of course, is one of the things that Bob Filep, with the strongest kind of interest from (Commissioner) Marland and from me, is working on—ways to get at this productivity question. We hope to be able to demonstrate, on a limited basis, ways of using technology to make the educational system— schools—more productive and at the same time more responsive to the kids. Productivity I'm not interested in if its only a cost-effectiveness thing. Productivity, if it means richer, more humane services to kids, is really the ballgame as far as I'm concerned. And we've only begun to think about it. By and large, most of us in education, the educational leadership, have really been afraid to take on that productivity question because, for one reason, it sounds inhumane. When you're talking about productivity you're worried about dollars and cents; that's *not* what you should be worried about. You should be worried about individualizing and humanizing the school experience for children. We're also worried about all of the political considerations of the productivity question. But you can't do that. You just have to get at the problem.

Implications of Revenue Sharing

AVI: But it's very hard to get any kind of change into the education establishment. For instance, take revenue sharing. Now that there's a general revenue sharing bill, many people concerned with changing things in education are worried that there will be a special revenue sharing bill with funds for education without any kind of statement of how the money should be spent. Even with categorical programs, it is difficult to make technology effective in the schools. With pressure for salaries, for construction, isn't it likely that the money will go for more of the same—rather than into instructional technology?

DAVIES: Those things aren't in competition at all. They're two different things, two federal roles. One is general support and, I hope, an increasing level of general support for the schools systems; and the other is support for reform and change. Both roles are important. One is relatively small in dollars, will always be a relatively small percentage of the total, but still important. And I would always argue that that second role ought to be continued. There is no plan not to continue it. As a matter of fact, the creation of NIE is a major new addition to that side of the federal role in education. It was created specifically with that intent—to provide a focus for reforming a system through research and development. And NIE inevitably is going to have a major interest in, involvement in, and contribution to educational technology. So it's not time for the educational technology people to start thinking they're out of business because of revenue sharing.

And we have a National Center for Educational Technology, a budget request, money for demonstrations for the first time ever.

AVI: That's true, that's a new thing, that title, isn't it?

DAVIES: Oh, the title isn't new, but the program is new. This is the first time we've had a line item in the budget for technology demonstration. We never had that before. What we've done before has been under cooperative research, "Sesame Street," and odds and ends. I think we're in much better shape on that score than we've been before. No question about it. We've got major plans for major demonstrations—the Rocky Mountain satellite project, bilingual television, continuation of "Sesame Street," and so on.

A Role for Education Groups

AVI: What can we do as an association in Washington to contribute to the planning of programs and feeding in information?

DAVIES: Well, there are a lot of things associations can do. Communication with their constituency obviously is the thing that associations do best. They have a constituency—their members, affiliated organizations—that they communicate with through their various networks of communication. That's something the Office of Education doesn't have, and nobody else does. That's a very valuable kind of thing—communicating facts, ideas, concepts.

AVI: Is there a way associations could work on planning for projects, ideas for a demonstration project, something like that?

DAVIES: Well, sure. We try a whole lot of ways to do that as a matter of fact. The leadership training institutes (LTI) that we initiated were designed specifically to provide a continuing mechanism for exchange of ideas among a whole range of people, not just associations as associations (although we typically include association people), but representatives of both active members and staff people. The LTI idea is continuing in one version or another and I've always felt that it's a very effective approach. It provides our program with access to a lot of talent from the field and with resource people who can provide technical assistance which so often helps the projects beyond what we could ever do with limited numbers of staff.

AVI: Is there anything else associations could do? Not just AECT, but any association with concerns in this area.

DAVIES: The hardest thing to do is get at the substantive ideas. I think the associations—all of them, I think—tend to focus on the political funding, the legislative activities, those sorts of things which *are* part of their responsibility, while the people here are focusing on their bureaucratic responsibilities—administering programs and getting out grants. The substance tends to fall between the cracks.

And another thing, I think you can be very helpful on this whole very complicated, messy question of productivity. It's going to be full of problems. Nobody knows exactly what anyone is doing about it. There are lots of interesting ideas around, and Bob Filep has brought in some good people to talk to and consult with. He's in the process of preparing to have demonstration projects developed. There's the place that your membership could contribute. There will be a lot of people who are very concerned, negatively concerned, about that whole development, and we need as much positive interest as possible.

TEACHER CENTERS: CAN THEY WORK HERE?
Paul S. Pilcher

This year for the first time I have been an educational consultant. For me this has been a totally new role to play, and I started out full of enthusiasm, eager to share the new ideas and experiences I had gained in study and in visiting a wide variety of schools. Six months later, however, I find myself filled with a vaguely disquieting sense of frustration over my lack of effectiveness, and more generally over the viability of outside consultants in promoting lasting change in schools.

In recent discussions I have been surprised to find a large number of university people who feel similarly about consultant roles; I have even talked to one highly successful (in monetary terms) professor who has foregone consulting altogether so that he could "live with his conscience." In many cases, consulting seems little more than a cruel hoax perpetrated upon teachers, children, and parents by the educational establishment: raising their hopes, taking their money at $100 per day or better, and after 3 or 6 or 12 months departing for the friendly confines of academia, leaving schools and teachers largely unchanged. The very idea of "instant experts" being able to "fix it" in a few hours a week seems a purely American fantasy. It seems particularly absurd to those of us who believe that the most crucial changes must come in the attitudes of teachers toward children and that meaningful methodological changes will be the result primarily of teachers working positively and openly with children over a long period of time.

In this context of disillusionment with present in-service experiences, I began to read and hear about teacher centers. The idea was exciting, not just because it was different, but because it seemed to be based on some basic truths:

(1) Fundamental educational reform will come only through those charged with the basic educational responsibility, to wit, the teachers.

(2) Teachers are unlikely to change their ways simply because imperious theoretical reformers tell them to shape up.

(3) Teachers will take reform seriously only when they are responsible for defining their own educational problems, delineating their own needs, and receiving help on their own terms and turf.[1]

As Stephen Bailey described it in the *Kappan,* the model of the British teacher center seemed almost too good to be true:

> Teacher centers are just what the term implies: local physical facilities and self-improvement programs organized and run by the teachers themselves for purposes of upgrading educational performance. Their primary function is to make possible a review of existing curricula and other educational practices by groups of teachers and to encourage teacher attempts to bring about changes.

At last it seemed we had hit upon a viable in-service model which could meet the very real desires of classroom teachers for assistance and improvement without necessarily subjecting them to the hastily formed judgments and prescriptions of outside experts who came, looked, told, and left. Assistance from universities and other sources of expertise would come only if and when teachers wanted and requested it. As a corollary, teachers would hopefully feel free to use only that advice and assistance with which they felt comfortable and which fit their specific situation.

As a model, the teacher center seems to answer most of the doubts and problems I believe surround present in-service programs. Teacher growth would be self-initiated, insofar as possible self-directed, and it would be continuous. The question then becomes one of translating the idea into reality in American public schools. This process is where I believe we are on the verge of making some potentially disastrous mistakes.

The Bandwagon Effect

Just because we speak the same language, Americans seem prone to the misconception that British institutions will work here. This has been true of the British infant school reforms, at times with tragic consequences. It seems no less true of teacher centers. Amidst all the ballyhoo and enthusiasm over the idea of American teacher centers, it is important to take a hard look at some of the issues posed by their creation. The issues involved are not merely ones of "improved education" (whatever that means), although the debate may be carried on in those terms. To the extent that teacher centers make a statement about who controls what goes on in schools, the issues are political. To the extent that establishing teacher centers involves a redistribution of that power, the issues become those of political change and of strategies for achieving that change.

One of the most important features of British teacher centers is their home-grown, indigenous nature, arising from the needs and interests of specific districts. National coordination and planning has tended to be supplementary and largely after the fact. Teacher centers are thus the product of and compatible with the particular set of power relationships extant in British state schools. How do such power relationships differ from those found in American public schools? What are the consequent implications for American teacher centers? These questions have gone largely unexamined in the current rush to jump on the teacher center bandwagon.

In place of such an examination, one finds a disquieting naive acceptance of the idea by many American educators. On the campuses of such leading innovators as the Harvard and University of Massachusetts Schools of Education, there is a sudden rush to form groups to plan and implement teacher centers. Fifteen thousand-dollar planning grants for 20 teacher center sites have suddenly materialized from the U. S. Office of Education. Three state departments of education have received federal funding of $250,000 each to set up teacher centers. Houston, Texas, projects are receiving USOE funds in the million-dollar category for teacher training programs, including teacher centers. Amazingly, within six to eight months of the appearance of Bailey's article, some 75-100 teacher centers were reportedly *in operation* in the United States. Such breathless and unquestioning action seems wasteful and moreover dangerous to the survival of the teacher center concept, for reformers in such a hurry obviously cannot take time to consider the thorny and multifaceted problems of power redistribution implied by the British model. The prospects for American teacher centers having a significant impact on American schools will remain gloomy, however, unless we can deal satisfactorily with such questions of power.

At least three sets of power relationships seem to be involved in the establishment of teacher centers: (1) the relationship of teachers with university and other outside, "R & D-type" experts; (2) the relationship of teachers with the school administrators; and (3) the relationship of teachers with the local community.

Teachers and Outside Experts

The American public school teacher has for years been the "nigger" of the system. Nowhere is this more obvious than in his relationship with university and other outside experts. Deferentially, he scrapes and bows, listening politely and following obediently the dictates of the obviously superior minds of the outsiders. Just as predictably, when the outside expert leaves, the teacher typically reverts to his old ways. If necessary, he may continue to follow the form of the expert's prescription without its underlying rationale. Indeed, American teachers have proven quite ingenious at sabotaging the carefully laid plans of the most eminent university minds. (Remember the teacher-proof curriculum?) One would think the outsiders would have caught on by now. Instead, like the plantation owners of the previous century, the R & D people return to their "big houses" to sit and scratch their heads in wonderment: "Why the hell haven't these workers in the field improved when, after all, we've shown them how to do it!" Disgusted heads shake amidst comments about the general incompetence and intransigence of American teachers.

Admittedly, this generalized picture of total failure is an exaggeration for many cases. What is vitally important and no exaggeration, however, is the master/servant, superior/subordinate role relationships of curriculum developers, consultants, *et al.* to the classroom teacher.

The set of relationships between British universities, curriculum theorists and developers, and classroom teachers stands in stark contrast. British teachers seem to look upon these outside agencies as resources or, in certain instances, as partners. The key word is *partner;* teacher and curriculum developer are equals, professional colleagues engaged in different aspects of the same enterprise. As far as particular children are concerned, the classroom teacher is regarded as the "expert." Decisions as to what is appropriate for a class of children rest with the teacher and the principal.

If all this seems so eminently logical and obvious as to be hardly worth comment, we should note that this is *not* the usual pattern in American public schools. I have found myself in the position of being expected to know more about a classroom from a couple of one-hour consultation visits than the teacher who has been working full-time for several months. On one occasion I was asked to prescribe curriculum remedies before I had even visited the class! Such unfortunate examples are more frequent than we might like to believe. On the other hand, in England there have been reports of university professors going to teachers for advice and actually visiting classrooms to learn from the practitioners. In the schools of education which dominate our educational hierarchy such a thought is barely conceivable.

This whole set of relationships might be somewhat irrelevant if universities and consultant agencies were not directly involved in the creation and running of teacher centers. If, for example, the USOE followed simple logic and granted funds to groups of classroom teachers for the purpose of establishing self-renewal and in-service centers, the rules of the game would change dra-

matically. Teachers would then be free to hire (and fire) outside personnel on
the basis that they (the teachers) wanted. In the Alice-in-Wonderland world of
government, however, precisely the opposite is happening. One looks at the
list of participants in a government-sponsored teacher center conference and
there is an overwhelming preponderance of university and "curriculum expert" personnel. The few representatives of school districts turn out to be
primarily curriculum supervisors, resource people, and so on. One searches in
vain for a few genuine classroom teachers.

The funding process to date has followed a similar pattern. The primary
agents for setting up teacher centers are—who else—university groups and educational laboratories or consulting agencies. To be sure, a major part of their
mandate is to facilitate the wishes and desires of teachers. Predictably, teachers
are skeptical about this idea, and rightly so. They perceive that the real power
relationship remains unchanged; in the final analysis it is the outsiders who retain control over money and policy. In an effort to overcome this suspicion,
some "facilitators" have even gone so far as to say the university has no vested
interest in the project and that teachers are free to make *all* the decisions.
Here again we run into a stumbling block. If someone has power and tells me
he is giving it to me because he has no vested interest, I am forced to one of
two likely conclusions: (1) he is lying and will only refrain from interfering
as long as I do what he wants me to or (2) he is telling the truth; he really
doesn't have a "vested interest," which is to say he has no real interest at all,
which in turn says he has no real commitment to the project's eventual success. In either case, I doubt if I would be anxious to jump headlong into the
project. Even if a particular group of facilitators were both sincere and committed to the project, it seems unlikely that teachers can depend on the universities' altruistic motives to sustain that commitment if and when personnel
change and the going gets rough.

The USOE has predetermined that outside experts will maintain the power
not only by conferencing and funding patterns, but also by the set of criteria
it has erected for teacher center formation and evaluation. Accountability is
Washington's latest discovery. As a result, the USOE has insisted upon a set
of academically rigorous performance criteria for teacher centers, necessitat-
ing a certain amount of research expertise not possessed by most teachers.
Classroom teachers are thus effectively barred from meaningful participation
in a variety of ways. One might well ask what happened to the original idea
of a local site set up by teachers to meet their particular needs as working
professionals.

Clearly what is happening is that, wittingly or not, the USOE is allowing a basically sound idea to be co-opted by the educational establishment of university professors, educational consultants, and curriculum developers, who are at least several steps removed from the classroom. This group has proven notably unsuccessful in effecting change in American public schools despite the millions of dollars spent yearly for their services. While such a development is hardly surprising in view of the enormous power and influence of these groups, it is still disheartening.

The Teacher and Political Pitfalls

Even if a group of teachers and outside consultants were somehow able to overcome the difficulties inherent in their relationship, there are other related pitfalls that stand in the way of teacher centers. These have to do primarily with the intertwining relationships of the local community and school administration with classroom teachers.

There is no history of professional autonomy for teachers in the United States. Our schools have been publicly created, publicly owned, and publicly directed. Since the days of the one-room frontier schoolhouse, Americans seem to have operated on the assumption that since they created the school and hired the teachers, they had the right to determine what went on in the classroom. This led to a system of local financing and control of schools, which in theory makes education responsive to the public's will.

What has happened, however, is that since schooling is universal, local financing and control have put schools in the impossible position of trying to please everyone. Schools have become highly susceptible to the pressure tactics of organized special interests.

One consequence of this search for consensus has been the tendency to reduce the content of public education to the society's lowest common denominator, with the resulting brand of curricular pablum that avoids anything human, emotional, controversial, or in fact even interesting. Another consequence has been to blunt the initiative of the classroom teacher. American teachers are understandably reluctant to strike out into uncharted waters when they are well aware that any "mistake" which antagonizes parents may cost them their job. Even in cases where job security is protected by tenure the teacher is not freed from the fear of community reaction. He is aware of the curriculum innovations that have been banned and the budget fights that have been lost over the issues of teacher "permissiveness," social radicalism, and other unpopular-sounding causes.

If the teacher is not fully aware of the political dangers involved in moving in innovative directions, the school administrators are. Like any established institution which must fight political battles for public money, the school system takes steps to ensure its own survival. This requires a supervisory and evaluative bureaucracy to see to it that the rank and file (that is, the teachers) do nothing to jeopardize the system's political advantage. Thus we see the creation of the generally oppressive system of monitoring and checking teacher behavior to make sure that teachers do not stray from the prescribed curriculum; that they do not, in short, rock the political boat.

Such generalizations do not, of course, apply with equal force to all school districts. What does seem to be almost universally true, however, is the rigidly hierarchial superior/subordinate, master/slave relationship between administrator and teacher. This encourages, even demands, a role of passive obedience from the teacher and, incidentally, drives many of the best people out of public school teaching. In such a context, it is hard to imagine a teacher center flourishing—at least not without some major political battles being fought and won.

British education has followed a different path. Two interrelated elements seem to be of primary importance: traditional attitudes toward education and teachers and the source of financing for the schools.

Chief education officers in Britain do not have to wage a constant battle over tax support for schools based on local issues. Funding for local schools comes from the national government; this process serves to insulate schools from local power struggles and free education officials to attend to the task of education for children. A concomitant result is that positions in British schools tend to be created primarily for educational, not political reasons. Thus the head teacher really teaches, the chief education officer really is an official who deals primarily with children and learning, and so forth. The British apparently see no need for as rigid a hierarchy of supervisors, checkers, and evaluators as Americans do.

Such relationships can be traced to an attitude of trust which seems to pervade British education. Local education authorities seem reticent to interfere in the internal affairs of a school. They seem to feel that these are best left to the professional educators on the scene. Similarly, many British head teachers, involved as they are in the daily business of actually working with children, grant far greater autonomy to classroom teachers than would be deemed "wise" in most American schools. British parents, too, seem far more reticent to criticize school officials, on the premise that they know what they're doing, although there is some evidence that this may be changing.

The cause-and-effect relationship of these various factors is open to inter pretation. What seems indisputable, however, is the net effect. British teachers are often given great latitude in determining what they will teach and how they will teach it. The result is a teaching profession more in control of classroom practices and more likely to strike out in new directions than its American counterpart.

Evolutionary Promise

Clearly we are operating in a significantly different political context from Britain when we speak of reform in American public schools. Even from this brief analysis, certain implications for American teacher centers seem obvious. To establish effective teacher centers will require either the abdication of power by those who now hold it or a process of political in-fighting and compromise by those who don't. If the first alternative seems highly unlikely, then we who would have teacher centers must prepare ourselves for the second. This may well necessitate a "go-slow" policy of small changes over a period of years. Certainly it will require more careful examination of the power relationships involved than has been made to date. American educators will probably also have to involve the community on an equal basis in the planning and implementation of teacher center projects.

The picture is not entirely bleak. There will doubtless be districts where teachers and outside personnel will find a way to work together congenially and will find support from an understanding administration and an enlightened citizenry. Such will be the exception rather than the rule, however. A more likely prognosis is that most teacher centers will die on the vine. Many of those that do survive will doubtless be stunted by the domination of school administrators, university consultants, or both.

We should not let this happen, because the teacher center idea is still a basically sound one. If put into practice in this country, it would mark an important step in the evolution of public education toward a more enlightened and more rational system of schooling. Good ideas in education are rare, and it would be a shame to let this one go down without a real chance. That, however, is precisely what will happen unless we take note of the political dimensions of educational change and act accordingly.

Notes

1. Stephen K. Bailey, "Teachers' Centers: A British First," *Phi Delta Kappan,* November 1971, pp. 146–149. (See Chapter III, this book.)

A TEACHER LOOKS AT TEACHING CENTERS AND EDUCATIONAL REFORM

J. Michael Crosby

While recently sitting in one of those "high level" meetings that we all attend from time to time, I recognized principals, supervisors, superintendents, deans, federal and state officials, and leading experts from my subject area. All nice people. And I had the good fortune to know most of them and respect them for their good works. As my mind wandered to the problems of my students and responsibilities of my teaching, I tried to bring all of these people and the institutions they represented into clearer focus. I could not think of one example of how any of them had helped me in any important problem confronting me during my seven years in the classroom. I have been restless in my profession ever since.

This revelation of my conference day-dream is in no way intended to impugn the value of what all of those many kinds of folks in education do— it is merely to emphasize that most teachers must do their day-to-day thing without any *direct help* from all those people whose jobs are designed to help. There is no existing mechanism for bringing the extensive and rich resources of the education world to bear directly upon the most immediate needs of teachers and students. The teaching center may be just the place to finally pull it off.

The Problem

Teachers once were "safe." We had clear-cut roles in definite subject areas, were the wise couriers of good information and the manifest providers of training in clearly identified "basic" skill areas. There were, of course, our "citizenship" responsibilities of passing on to innocent children the traditional norms inherent in our social fabric. Students had to be prepared for college and the world of work. Most, in Glasser's words, were very "goal oriented" and willing to accept whatever came along.[1] "Problem children" dropped out of school early or were steered into vocational programs—anything to get them out of the way so teachers could get to the important tasks at hand. We had a traditional role that could be easily played. We simply did to others as we had been done to in our own schooling.

That blissful era to which some may look back with nostalgia and regret is no longer with us. Instead of that earlier, comfortable role, we are asked to perform a myriad of tasks designed to prepare students for life in our contemporary world. We are asked to be modern miracle workers. We must understand and interpret a world that is in continuing revolution—and at a time, as Lord James points out in his signal study of the schools, when the increasing demands upon us combined with the isolation of the classroom from the real world are giving us less experience with what is really going on day-to-day than is commonly experienced by trash collectors and crossing guards.[2] We must find effective ways to mesh our 13,000 hours of good works with students during their K-12 stay in school with the vagaries of the 15,000 hours of public media to which they are also exposed.

We must develop a child's self-image. We must act as his parents in absentia and deal with his emotional problems, with drugs, with sex education, with moral upbringing, and with conscious and unconscious racism. We must develop his ability to think, using new curriculum materials that dazzle us with their novelty and complexity. We must individualize instruction in order to help each child "do his own thing" and develop to his full potential as a human being. And not only are we to accomplish all of these wonders with those "nice normal kids" our precedessors worked with (many of whom have now developed an identity crisis and an antagonistic, militant generation gap), but we are also expected to succeed fully with kids who bring to our classrooms some of the scars of poverty and deprivation marking our multiethnic, bilingual, ethnocentric society.

In sum, teachers and schools are being asked to do too much. And to further aggravate the situation, teachers are not well trained to do what it is they can and should be able to do. Preservice education is generally irrelevant to the real needs of teachers, and in-service programs are random, grossly underfinanced (according to a recent survey, less than 1 percent of the budget), and equally unrelated to the priority problems of teachers and students. The situation is best summarized in the report of a national cross-section of classroom teachers, who met at Harper's Ferry, West Virginia, under the auspices of Task Force '72:

> Teachers . . . are most desirous of change, of leadership, of new and better ways to serve the children they teach. . . . It is not change which disturbs them. It is expectations unfulfilled: it is being asked to deliver excellence in education without adequate training . . . support . . . time and money . . . and opportunities for personal growth and development. . . . One must be reminded that teachers conscientiously doing

their job are so deep in their work that they . . . don't really have the energy to respond to the challenge of change. Thus to pick a handful of teachers up and show them that change may . . . be possible, to involve them in planning change . . . is to offer them a heady brew which must not later be allowed to go sour in their mouths.[3]

There are obviously no simple solutions to such important and complex problems. And it is not the purpose of this paper to either suggest that the sky is falling or that there are easy answers at the ready. It is in fact the opinion of the author that, given some of the immense demands and constraints outlined earlier, the schools and teachers of this nation have succeeded mightily and should be showered with appropriate medals of distinguished service and accomplishment. But even a healthy and properly recognized finger in a sprouting dam does little to make things better. There is great need to do at least several things: (a) reexamine the role of the schools and determine what they can and cannot do; (b) greatly increase the resources available to the educational process; (c) make staff development programs much more relevant to the most pressing problems of schools; and (d) place the teacher and student "center stage" in the development, installation, and evaluation of educational programs. Because this article is directed at teaching centers, some elaboration on the most related points—the last two—is needed.

Making Staff Development Programs More Relevant

The teaching center holds considerable promise for breaking away from the traditional models of pre- and in-service teacher education, and it is hoped that many of the following recommendations about centering will not only offer some ideas for "building better centers" but include some constructive perspective for all educational personnel development programs:

1. Teaching centers should be developed as a local responsibility. Although it is desirable, and probably necessary, to have federal and state funding in early stages of development, center programs should follow local guidelines and be responsive to local needs.
2. To retain maximum flexibility and sensitivity to the needs of its constituency, the teaching center should not be the sole domain of any existing educational institution, university school district, or teacher organization. Educational institutions should play important parts in organizing and supporting teaching centers, but none should be in a position to impose its dogma.
3. Constituent teachers should have major influence in determining policy and

programs in the centers. Centers must reflect the needs of local teachers and students.

4. Teaching centers should be dedicated to the concerns that teachers, parents, administrators, and students have in common: the desire to understand the learning process and to know how to make meaningful interventions into that process at all levels. Only then can meaningful educational change take place.

5. The teaching center should be a place where practice and theory come together. Major emphasis should be placed on meeting the practical needs of teachers, and the best of related research and development products should be brought to bear on meeting those needs.

6. Centers should include both preservice and continuing education opportunities. The learning-teaching process is not confined to any age group or to holders of a particular degree.

7. The center should be a place for "action research," providing a setting where practitioners can become more involved in the study of the learning process.

8. The center should be diverse in scope in order to meet the needs of as many individuals as possible.

9. The center should be dedicated to the growth of those involved, not only as educators but as individuals.

In addition to these recommendations, there are several questions that center operators and builders might find helpful when sizing up their mission:

1. How will the teaching center be significantly different from the existing models of student teaching and in-service training?

2. Will the teaching center be an agent for educational change or a bastion of the status quo?

3. Will centers be designed to meet the most important needs of students and teachers?

4. Are there design possibilities which would guarantee openness and flexibility?

5. What kinds of delivery systems—local, state and national—can be developed to channel new ideas and methods into and out of centers?

6. Should the center have the power of certification so as to provide material as well as professional reward for those involved?

7. How can we best negotiate the diversity of opinion about the nature and purpose of teaching centers?

Of all the recommendations listed above, the ones that need most emphasis are those relating directly to kids. Although they are the target of almost everything we are about in the educational system, kids almost never enter any discussions of educational reform.

Kids: A Surprising New Element in Questions of Educational Reform

The one non-negotiable recommendation, then, is that, as much as possible, centers must develop programs that focus directly on the needs of kids and that those needs be largely determined by going directly to the students of the educational personnel being served by a particular center.

Most in-service training programs are designed to deal with staff needs which are often not consonant with the most pressing needs of students—both personal and academic. A recently released Report from the U. S. Office of Education summarized some of the early results of a study of 18,000 seniors (1972) from high schools across the nation.[4] It was very revealing to find that, although the majority of the students considered their schools to be good or excellent, about half felt that teachers had little interest in student needs. An examination of some of their most unmet academic needs showed a surprising degree of practical orientation—as well as deficiencies in areas that most adults would consider to be of high priority. (I make this point because many adults feel that students should not be significantly involved in decision making because their concerns are often esoteric to the main purposes of schooling.) Almost 90 percent agreed that the "school should have provided more help for students who were having trouble with subjects like math and reading," about one-half felt that more emphasis should have been placed on basic academic subjects, and nearly three-fourths wanted more practical work experience. Even in areas of pedagogy there seemed to be some important student messages, as three-fourths of the respondents reported that "individualized instruction" was relatively rare. These selected findings are used to emphasize the point that many important student needs are not being met and to provide some rough indicators of possible program priorities for teaching centers. It may be that rather than argue about whether or not centering should fly under the label of teacher center, teaching center, staff development center, etc.,[5] we should label them for what they really need to be— "student learning centers."

Two "Profession-Wide" Views of Teacher Centers

The following two extracts from a task force report provide a "profession-wide" teachers' view of teaching centers. Although both considered centering within a more narrow context than that generally presented in this thematic section of the *Journal,* the viewpoints and recommendations presented would probably not change much if they had been directed at the wider context. In both cases, the original statements are much longer than space would allow for inclusion here, so it was necessary to condense them. In doing so, priority was given to specific recommendations about the nature and purpose of centers. I strongly urge interested readers to secure both documents in their entirety, as they provide some rich insight not only into centering but also into other important aspects of educational reform.

Report of the National Teachers' Field Task Force on the Improvement and Reform of American Education[6]

The National Teachers' Task Force, a USOE-sponsored group which included a cross-section of American teachers, dealt with a wide variety of reform issues, one of which was teacher centers. The Task Force saw teacher centers as a "positive solution to some of the current problems associated with achieving educational accountability." Selected portions follow.

Maintaining Professional Competence

Most teachers who are teaching today will still be teaching ten years from now. What will they be teaching and how will they be teaching it? Staffing a school with well prepared and competent teachers is no guarantee that staff competency will continue.

. . . . To assign responsibility where it can be carried out effectively and to maintain a responsive system staffed with competent teachers, a new unit is proposed for all public schools—the teachers' center.

. . . . The function of a teachers' center is to maintain an effective educational program through continual teacher preparation in the knowledge, attitudes, and techniques of teaching. The teachers' center will provide opportunities for teachers to participate in a continuing effort to maintain and upgrade skills. Continual education and training are an obligation upon both the teaching profession and the school district, and it could serve as the pivotal component of an educational planning system.

The program within the teachers' center is a continuous process, cyclic in nature, the first step being to determine the needs of students and teachers. This assessment is both responsive—identifying current deficiencies, and creative—initiating new procedures and developing new materials. This needs identification is the basis for determining specific program goals. These goals are interpreted, by teachers, into specific program objectives. This allows teachers to design specific activities by which they demonstrate competence in the understanding and accomplishment of the objectives in their unique teaching situations. The final component of the cycle is evaluating the degree to which the objectives are attained and observing the effect of their attainment on reaching the predetermined goals . . . The teacher's role and responsibility in the teacher center is the same as it is with students; but the focus is on assisting and directing the learning of teachers, rather than students. . . .

The elements of a teachers' center program must be determined by those teachers whom the center serves. Such elements include, but are not limited to:

1. Better techniques and procedures for dealing with individual student problems in basic communication skills, particularly reading, oral, and writing skills. This involves identifying, developing, and using diagnostic materials and techniques. . . .

2. Developing activities through which students can discover how to wisely and creatively use their freedom for self-fulfillment and social improvement.

In addition to activities related to student-teacher relationships, the center serves as a base for cooperative endeavors between teachers and those involved in educational research. Such program elements could lead to:

1. Dealing in a positive way with the multicultural aspects of a class, as well as of the community at large. This aspect of a teachers' center program requires special attention where the learning-teaching process is affected by bilingual conditions.

2. Race relations programs in which understanding, not accommodation, is the goal.

3. Developing group practice techniques. This is a clinical approach to the development of teaching patterns that fully utilize the unique talents found in groups of teachers and permits a student to have interaction with more than one teacher.

4. Keeping an up-to-date record of what is working in the educational programs of other school districts, and providing a means for determining the appropriateness of their adoption. . . .

Placing program determination in the control of teachers is essential if the center is to respond to teacher-discerned needs. If program control is maintained within existing governance bodies, it is realistic to expect that system concerns will take precedence over identified educational needs—as is true in most district-controlled in-service programs.

The teacher center's primary funding should be public sources: local, state, and federal. Local funds currently used for in-service activities are appropriate; a portion of state funds used in research and similar programs should be allocated for teacher centers, but the primary source should be federal. This consists of a specific grant to each state to be distributed to districts establishing teacher centers. Teacher centers could also seek funding from other public and private agencies where locally determined programs make the use of such funds appropriate.

The obligation of each of these participating agencies, the school district and the professional organizations, should be agreed to and formalized in the master contract that defines working conditions and specific responsibilities for the profession and the local district.

Teacher Centers: Who's in Charge[7]

CHANGING AMERICAN EDUCATION

In-service training has a bad reputation among teachers. For nearly half a century American teachers have been required to attend courses throughout their working careers, very often because of the bureaucratic imperative that everyone be treated alike rather than because of a desire by teachers to improve their skills. Too many of these classes have been spiritless time-fillers. Instead of being an instrument for educational change and teacher renewal, in-service training as we have known it has tended to increase teacher resistance to new methods and concepts. Teacher bargaining agents now regularly include elimination of "Mickey Mouse" in-service courses as a standard working condition improvement demand. . . .

PARITY

From what we have said in previous sections of this paper, it should be clear that we do not believe "parity" in a governing or operating equality sense can have practical meaning in teacher center governance. Yet the stimulation which can come from the college intellectual community, minority groups, and the young is a valuable ingredient in educational reform which should not be neglected. Hence the need for a strong advisory board.

NON-TEACHING STAFF

If we abandon the parity principle in teacher center governance, how exclusive should the center be in its clientele? Should the teacher center be concerned only with the craft of teaching, or should it be concerned with over-all staff development? If other staff functions are to be served by the center, should not representatives of such groups be included on the governing board? And should not the name be changed to "staff center?"

First, we can be very positive about the need to exclude principals and other administrators from the scope of the "teacher center." Certainly administrators need retraining; their re-education may be crucial to the educational renewal effort, in fact. But unless administrators are carefully segregated in the functioning and governance of the center, their presence will inevitably defeat the purposes of the agency. They are too assertive, too used to exercising authority, and they have too much spare time to carry out their purposes to be assimilated easily. The best idea is to exclude administrators, leaving their retraining to other agencies.

How about other non-teaching educational personnel? In school systems—or fractions of school systems designated as renewal sites—which are into (*sic*) differentiated staffing, the center should serve all non-supervisory personnel who are directly involved in the instructional/learning process. In such a case, however, not every rank or functional group need have representation on the governing board. Representation of "paraprofessionals" in addition to teachers should suffice. The same could be said for more traditional set-ups using only teachers and teacher aides in the classroom.

So far as guidance counselors, social workers, psychologists, curriculum coordinators, community coordinators, nurses, et al., are concerned, it would be better to set up school-by-school arrangements for their participation in policy-making and technique development, rather than set such groups up as special interests in the governmental structure.

FINANCIAL ARRANGEMENTS

It doesn't seem to us that it would be possible to operate much of a teacher center for under $250,000 a year. It would be quite easy to spend many times this amount considering what has been happening to local school budgets. It would be impossible to generate such funds from local sources alone. Therefore, it is essential that there be an open-ended commitment from the federal government as well as state and local sources.

Control of the expenditure of funds should be in the hands of the board of directors of the non-profit corporation. Its annual budget, however, would require approval by the contributing governments. There is nothing unusual in such an arrangement. Almost all big city budgets must run this sort of gauntlet.

A DECENTRALIZED BUREAUCRATIC MODEL

It would be possible, of course, to conduct continuing teacher development through an agency of a local education authority. An administrator would be appointed (and paid) by a school board, presumably subsidized by USOE. The director would be responsible for developing plans for a continuing teacher education project, and, after approval by the superintendent of schools and perhaps the school board, would be given the authority to implement the plans.

The decentralized bureaucratic model has some advantages. Once the structure of the project was established and personnel placed on the payroll, there would be a tendency (not necessarily overwhelming) for the local board of education to continue financial support even if the federal government were to withdraw from the field. Furthermore, the program of the training agency could be tailored to local needs. The curse of authoritarianism could be somewhat counteracted by a teacher advisory committee. Finally, local school districts do have a wide range of resources, and these could be utilized more easily by an agency which was a part of the system than they could be utilized by an autonomous agency.

But, the force inherent in an official board of education agency would erect a barrier which even the most benign director would have difficulty overcoming. An official board of education agency would take the responsibility for technical improvement out of the hands of teachers. Once again, teachers would be responding to administrators rather than engaging in the problem-solving process through their own initiative and energy.

AN AUTONOMOUS MODEL

It would be possible to establish an autonomous, self-governing teacher center through the common device of the non-profit corporation. A charter or constitution could be drawn up in cooperation with teacher representatives, and the center would be officially incorporated under the laws of the state. A board of directors would then be chosen and the board of directors would in turn choose an executive director and other staff members as needed.

Note: The term "teacher representatives" above refers to representatives *selected by* teachers. Where there is a bargaining agent, this means that the representatives should be chosen by the bargaining agent. Where there is no bargaining agent, the representatives should be chosen jointly by the significant teacher organizations in the center's service area. If more than one school district is to be served, the bargaining agent for each district should select an appropriate number of members of the board.

Under the non-profit corporation form of governance, it would not be wrong to have all the members of the board of directors chosen in the way described above. If this were the case, there should be an advisory council to guide the teacher-controlled board of directors. The advisory council would include university, community, and administration representatives.

It would be possible to include university, community, and administrative representatives on the board of directors itself, of course, but in that case teachers should be in the voting majority.

Summary: On the Promise of Parity

My major disagreement with the two reports quoted at length here relates to the whole question of participation—to that exciting and widely misunderstood concept of parity. I applaud the contributors to the Task Force reports for their strong position in favor of more appropriate teacher participation in all phases of center development—and fully concur that highest priority must be given to teacher and student needs. But just as all other major reform efforts involving only a segment of the educational mix of "movers and shakers" failed to make a difference, so too will teacher centers that are "of, by, and for" teachers. Just as teachers are able to determine finally whether or not a new mousetrap works once they take it behind the privacy of their classroom walls, so too can other major participants in the dynamic educational system gum up the works if they are not involved in the centering process.

It is the double promise of teaching centers that excites me and many of my fellow teachers:

1. The center is designed to be at the heart of staff development and to give first priority to the immediate needs of teachers; and
2. It facilitates real interaction between teachers and all the other major constituencies in the educational spectrum.

Notes

1. Glasser, William. *The Identity Society* (New York: Harper & Row, 1972).

2. Lord James of Rusholme. *Teacher Education and Training* (London: Her Majesty's Stationery Office, 1972).

3. *Harper's Ferry Report of Teachers Task Force on Educational Reform.* Task Force '72 (Washington, D.C.: U.S. Office of Education, 1972).

4. *National Longitudinal Study of the High School Class of 1972.* Preliminary Report (Washington, D.C.: U.S. Department of Health, Education, and Welfare, 1973).

5. See Schmeider, Allen A. and Sam J. Yarger, "Teacher/Teaching Centering in America," *Journal of Teacher Education*, Spring 1974, pp. 5–12.

6. *Inside Out.* Report on the Teachers' Field Task Force on the Improvement and Reform of American Education (Washington, D.C.: U.S. Office of Education, 1974).

7. Selden, David (AFT) and Dave Darland (NEA). *Teacher Centers: Who's in Charge.* Prepared for the Leadership Training Institute in Teaching of the U.S. Office of Education. Available as part of the Teachers Task Force Report, 1974.